THE LOVE *of* GOD

Library of Jewish Ideas
Cosponsored by the Tikvah Fund

TIK🎵AH

The series presents engaging and authoritative treatments of core Jewish concepts in a form appealing to general readers who are curious about Jewish treatments of key areas of human thought and experience.

THE LOVE *of* GOD

Divine Gift, Human Gratitude,

and Mutual Faithfulness in Judaism

JON D. LEVENSON

PRINCETON UNIVERSITY PRESS

Princeton and Oxford

Published by Princeton University Press, 41 William Street, Princeton,
New Jersey 08540
In the United Kingdom: Princeton University Press, 6 Oxford Street,
Woodstock, Oxfordshire OX20 1TW

press.princeton.edu

Jacket art: Modified detail of a mosaic in the Synagogue of Enschede.
Original photo courtesy of Kleuske / Wikimedia Commons

Library of Congress Cataloging-in-Publication Data

Levenson, Jon Douglas, author.
The love of God : divine gift, human gratitude,
and mutual faithfulness in Judaism / Jon D. Levenson.
pages cm. — (Library of Jewish ideas)
Includes bibliographical references and index.
ISBN 978-0-691-16429-8 (hardcover : alk. paper)
1. God (Judaism)—
Love. I. Title.
BM610.L45 2015
296.3'112—dc23
2015017872

British Library Cataloging-in-Publication Data is available

Publication of this book has been aided by the Tikvah Fund

This book has been composed in Minion Pro and Helvetica

Printed on acid-free paper. ∞

Printed in the United States of America

1 3 5 7 9 10 8 6 4 2

For Beverly,
Proverbs 18:22

He used to say: Beloved is humanity, for they were created in the image [of God]. Even greater is the love in that it is made known to them that they were created in the image [of God], as it is said, "For in the image of God He made humanity." (Gen 9:6)

Beloved are Israel, for they have been called the children of God. Even greater is the love in that it is made known to them that they have been called the children of God, as it is said, "You are the children of the LORD your God." (Deut 14:1)

Beloved are Israel, for a precious instrument has been given to them. Even greater is the love in that it is made known to them that the precious instrument through which the world was created has been given to them, as it is said, "For I have given you good instruction; / Do not forsake My Torah." (Prov 4:2)

Mishnah[1]

· ↜ Contents ↝ ·

Writing for both a scholarly and a general readership, I have transliterated the Hebrew more or less as it sounds in the contemporary spoken language. To avoid points that are of relevance almost exclusively to learned readers, I have omitted the diacritical marks that indicate vowel length and some other conventions of scientific transliteration.

For clarification, I simply note the following points:

Aleph appears as ' and *ayin* as '. Neither consonant is pronounced in the Ashkenazi tradition or by large numbers of speakers of Modern Hebrew, perhaps most.

The spirantized *bet* (known as *vet*) appears as *v*, as does *vav*.

Ḥet, which sounds like the *ch* in the German *Bach*, appears as *ḥ* (*h* with a subdot).

Ṭet, now pronounced like *t*, appears as *ṭ* (*t* with a subdot).

Kaf appears as *k*, unless it is spirantized (sounding, again, like the *ch* in *Bach*), in which case it is rendered as *kh*.

The spirantized *peh* is now pronounced like the English *ph*, and that is how it appears here.

The letter *ṣadi*, today usually pronounced like English *ts*, appears here as *ṣ* (an *s* with a subdot), except in the word *mitzvah*, which is given in its familiar English spelling.

Qof is rendered with a *q*.

Sin appears as *ś*, and *shin* as *š*.

In accordance with traditional Jewish practice, which forbids writing or pronouncing vowels in the tetragrammaton—the four-letter proper name of the God of Israel—I have used the conventional English euphemism "the Lord"; in quoting authors who have inserted the vowels, I have simply put the euphemism in brackets [the Lord].

Although love of God is a central focus of the foundational texts of Judaism, it is a subject that has received surprisingly little attention among contemporary scholars. In this volume, I have sought to remedy this omission by exploring the origins and ramifications of the idea in terms that can benefit the lay reader and the professional scholar alike. In the process, I have necessarily kept the technical details of history and textual interpretation to a bare minimum and focused instead on the larger outlines of theology and practice as they have developed over the millennia.

One consequence of the lack of sustained attention to our topic is the misperception that the love of God is essentially, or even exclusively, a sentiment and thus a purely private matter: either one loves God or one doesn't. Chapter 1 challenges this convenient misunderstanding directly. It traces the origin of the idea to ancient Near Eastern treaties (or, covenants), where love characterizes something very unsentimental—the proper stance of the lesser party toward the greater. At least as the language of such covenants is developed in the Hebrew Bible, those obligations are seen, however, as deriving from something very different from a sheer disparity of power; they are not only imposed but freely, in fact lovingly, accepted. The legal obligations thus derive from a phenomenon that is considerably warmer and more personal than "law" as that word is used today. They derive from a personal relationship, and they also encourage, deepen, and expand that relationship. And at the foundation of the personal relationship between the

God of Israel and the people Israel lie the undeserved gifts that the greater power has conferred upon them, especially emancipation from Egypt and the gift of the land of Canaan. In that sense, the observance of the laws is based in gratitude. It is an act of service toward Israel's unique and unparalleled benefactor, their God.

The love of God in the Hebrew Bible, then, is a matter of both action and affect, with each influencing the other. Efforts to separate action and affect, and conceptions of the self that disjoin the two, can lead only to a drastic misunderstanding.

The gratitude and the gifts that call it forth draw attention, in turn, to another meaning of the term "the love of God," namely, the love that God manifests toward his covenant partner, the people Israel. One of my key claims is that the two meanings of "the love of God"—the love God gives and the love he receives—cannot be disengaged. Although the God-Israel relationship in the classical Jewish sources is asymmetrical, as any relationship with God cannot but be, it is thoroughly mutual, as any relationship among personal beings inevitably is.

Chapter 2 probes the understanding of the love of God in classical Talmudic literature. For all its vaunted balance and precision, rabbinic religion brooks no compromise on the biblical obligation to love God. By this period in history, the commandment in the Torah to love God "with all your heart and with all your soul and with all your might" (Deut 6:5) has assumed utmost importance, and the rabbis draw out the behavioral implications they find in each of those three nouns. The middle term, "soul," evokes the possibility that, in a situation of lethal persecution, loving God may require even surrendering one's life.

As the rabbis saw it, the love of God is again anything but sentimental; to them it is not, as many today seem to think of it, a cheery feeling. On the contrary, it entails thanking God even in a situation of horrible suffering. In taking this position, the rabbis reaffirm and expand a key aspect of biblical covenant: it is the foundational moment of divine love and gift-giving, and not the horrors of the current moment, that discloses the true nature of the God-Israel relationship. Like all deep loves, the love of God harbors within it a dimension of self-sacrifice. When that dimension is ignored or explained away, the full radicalism of the commandment to love him cannot be grasped.

For many today, the paradigm of all loves is the erotic or the sexual. This has not always been the case, and in chapter 3 I argue that some serious misunderstandings can arise when contemporary conceptions of sexuality and marriage are assumed. But an erotic dimension does indeed arise in ancient Israel, specifically in the metaphor of Israel as God's wife and God as Israel's husband, which becomes prominent in prophetic literature and gathers force in rabbinic literature. The prophets, however, think of the relationship not as an idyllic romance but rather as a love story gone sour. The idyllic period lies only in the foundational past, before Israel played the prostitute or the adulteress, and in the days to come, when she will learn her lesson and her divine husband will redeem her and renew the broken marriage. Later, the rabbis develop the romance of God and Israel (by their time, already an ancient notion) through an interpretation of the Song of Songs, the greatest love poem of the Bible and perhaps of all literature. Against those who charge that the classical rabbinic interpretation smacks of the arbitrariness of allegory, I argue that, although it does not reflect the plain sense (within a certain definition of that immensely problematic term), it does arise organically out of the prophetic marriage metaphor and certain insufficiently noticed features of the poem itself.

In chapter 4, the focus shifts to the Middle Ages and, more specifically, to philosophers whose thinking reflects the Jewish-Muslim cultural symbiosis of medieval Spain.

In the *Duties of the Heart* of Baḥya ibn Paquda, for example, the love of God becomes the consummation of the spiritual life, the goal of the ascent of the soul toward God. Baḥya goes to great lengths to describe the characteristic attitudes and practices of those who successfully carry out the all-important commandment. The *Duties* is thus both a work of philosophy and a moving devotional manual, one that continues to be studied to this day.

For Moses Maimonides, the love of God is equally central, and, though this great Jewish philosopher is often taken as a cold, analytical rationalist, he describes the person who loves God in language that bespeaks intense passion and reflects the rabbinic reading of the Song of Songs. What one does not find in Maimonides, though, is an equivalent description of the other sense of the love of God, one that is, in fact, also abundant in the rabbinic interpretation of the same biblical book—namely, God's own love for the people Israel. The explanation lies in Maimonides's intense resistance to the application of human language to God, both the language of embodiment and, related to it, the language of feelings. To Maimonides, such usages fail miserably to reckon with the perfection of God; they imply a deficiency.

Later, however, in Christian Spain the philosophers Ḥasdai Crescas and his student Joseph Albo challenge this forcefully, arguing that the ability to love is a sign, not an impairment, of divine perfection. Albo goes so far as to recover the key biblical notion that God's love for the people Israel is based in passion and thus not rationally explicable.

Finally, chapter 5 takes the discussion into the twentieth century, focusing on two of its most important religious thinkers, Martin Buber and Franz Rosenzweig, and on the spirited argument between them about the status of Jewish law. As post-emancipation figures, they live, as we do, in a time when the social force of Jewish law has, for most Jews, quite disappeared, and a combination of modern science and historical discoveries has rendered immensely problematic the traditional claim that God speaks through the classical texts. In response, these two philosophers seek to renew the Jews' involvement in Torah. Although they differ on whether such involvement must include observance of the traditional commandments, they agree that, ideally, what lies behind any valid observance is the voice of a personal, loving God, and not simply a moral ideal, a natural process, a human need to identify ethnically, or any other modernistic substitute for the living and loving God of the ancient sources. That the notion of the God who loves and is to be loved could be reclaimed by modern sophisticates like Buber and Rosenzweig testifies, I believe, not only to the centrality of the love of God in the Jewish tradition but also to the inherent power of the idea.

Anyone familiar with Jewish religious literature can, of course, readily think of texts that I might have discussed but did not or of implications or complications with which I have not dealt. This is all the more the case with professional scholars of Judaica. An example that immediately comes to mind is the complicated erotic symbolism of Kabbalah (Jewish mysticism). But herein I have tried to write a book that is representative and illuminating rather than comprehensive and exhaustive. I have also tried to bring to life for the contemporary reader (and not only for the professional historian) what I perceive as the immense power in the classical Jewish idea of the love of God. Readers will determine for themselves whether I have succeeded.

· ✑ Acknowledgments ✑ ·

I am very much indebted to a number of scholars who have assisted me in different ways with this project. Some have generously commented on all or part of my manuscript at various stages of its composition, and others have responded with their impressive erudition to specific inquiries. I owe special thanks to Diana Lobel, Larry Lyke, Yehiel Poupko, Bernard Septimus, Suzanne Smith, Keith Stone, and Andrew Teeter. Needless to say, I alone am responsible for the errors that remain.

I also owe a large debt of thanks to my two editors. Neal Kozodoy, the editor of the Library of Jewish Ideas, was enormously helpful to me at every stage, and Fred Appel of Princeton University Press has shepherded the volume through the process with his characteristic efficiency and good humor. I must, finally, also thank two other individuals at Princeton University Press who have assisted me in the process of publication, Juliana Fidler and Leslie Grundfest, as well as my copy editor, Cathy Slovensky, whose impressive expertise has improved my manuscript markedly.

I did much of the research for this volume in 2011–12 during a leave from Harvard Divinity School, to which I am therefore grateful. I also very much appreciate the work of three student assistants who have proven invaluable to me in this project. The library work expertly performed by Michael Ennis and Justin Reed saved me much time and many errors. The same must be said of Maria Metzler, who also assisted with the proofreading and indexing.

Unless otherwise noted, all translations from the Hebrew Bible in this book are reprinted from *Tanakh: The Hebrew Scriptures* (Philadelphia: Jewish Publication Society of America, 1985), by permission of the University of Nebraska Press. The quotations from 2 Maccabees are taken from the New Revised Standard Version Bible (copyright © 1989 Division of Christian Education of the National Council of the Churches of Christ in the United States of America. Used by permission. All rights reserved).

Books of the Hebrew Bible

1–2 Chr	1–2 Chronicles
Dan	Daniel
Deut	Deuteronomy
Exod	Exodus
Ezek	Ezekiel
Gen	Genesis
Hab	Habakkuk
Hos	Hosea
Isa	Isaiah
Jer	Jeremiah
Josh	Joshua
Judg	Judges
1–2 Kgs	1–2 Kings
Lev	Leviticus
Mal	Malachi
Num	Numbers
Prov	Proverbs
Ps	Psalms
Qoh	Qohelet (or, Ecclesiastes)
1–2 Sam	1–2 Samuel
Song	Song of Songs

Rabbinic Literature

b.	*Bavli (Babylonian Talmud)*
m.	*Mishnah*

y.	*Yerušalmi (Jerusalem Talmud)*
Siphre Deut	*Siphre Deuteronomy*

Other Abbreviations

NJPS	New Jewish Publication Society Bible translation (*Tanakh: The Holy Scriptures*)
NRSV	New Revised Standard Version

THE LOVE *OF* GOD

ONE

A Covenantal Love

> With an everlasting love You have loved the
> House of Israel Your people.
> Torah and commandments, decrees and laws
> You have taught us.
> *Evening Prayer Service*

For many, one of the most familiar passages in the Bible is the first part of the three-paragraph affirmation known, after its first Hebrew word, as the Shema:[1]

[4]Hear, O Israel! The LORD is our God, the LORD alone. [5]You shall love the LORD your God with all your heart and with all your soul and with all your might. [6]Take to heart these instructions with which I charge you this day. [7]Impress them upon your children. Recite them when you stay at home and when you are away, when you lie down and when you get up. [8]Bind them as a sign on your hand and let them serve as a symbol on your forehead; [9]inscribe them on the doorposts of your house and on your gates. (Deut 6:4–9)[2]

In the traditional Jewish liturgy, the Shema is a critical component of the morning and evening service every day, without exception. Why was it considered so important?

Because, as the rabbis of the Talmudic period conceived it, reciting the Shema was an efficacious deed: it was the act of "accepting the yoke of the kingship of Heaven" (*m. Berakhot* 2:2). "Heaven" being a common rabbinic euphemism for "God," the Shema is thus thought to reenact the Jew's acclamation of God as the ultimate sovereign, and of human beings as subjects living in his realm and devoted to his service. In the words of one Talmudic authority, by reciting the Shema, one has "made him king above, below, and to all four corners of the universe" (*b. Berakhot* 13b).[3]

In rabbinic theology, of course, God is king whether one accepts his reign or not: among human beings, however, his kingship is fragile and easily defied. Unless the commitment to it is reaffirmed regularly, divine kingship fades and eventually vanishes from the mind. What is more, to the rabbis the reaffirmation must be verbal and not merely mental; it requires a ritual action and not merely a thought. So readily available is the sin of "casting off the yoke" (as they called it) that it must be parried continually, at least twice every day. Through the Shema, just as its first verse (Deut 6:4) implies, the people Israel (the Jews) heed the commandment to proclaim that the LORD, and he alone, is their God. "The LORD" is not quite a synonym for "God" in Biblical Hebrew. Rather, it is a rendering of the unpronounceable four-letter *proper name* of the God of Israel. He, and no other deity, is Israel's God.

But what are we to make of the next verse, "You shall love the LORD your God with all your heart and with all your soul and with all your might" (Deut 6:5)? One might think that it expresses only an option (though the ideal option), but not an obligation. For how can an emotion be commanded? How can we be required to generate a feeling within ourselves? And yet the rabbinic tradition regards this verse as a separate obligation, listing it as one of the 613 commandments it finds in the Torah. This, in turn,

raises the question of just how to fulfill this commandment. What must we do in order to love God?

Other questions, too, arise from this seemingly straight-
forward verse. What is the connection to the affirmation
that immediately precedes it? What, that is, links Israel's
acclamation of God's unique claim upon them to their obligation (not simply their aspiration) to love God? And
if, as the rabbis maintained, the Shema is about the kingship of the God of Israel, how is love linked to kingship?
Granted, one must serve and respect one's king, but must
one also *love* him?

LOVE AND SERVICE

Fortunately, the Bible presents several parallels to the wording found in Deuteronomy 6:4–5. Consider this one, from
King Solomon's speech on the dedication of the temple:

> O LORD God of Israel, in the heavens above and on the
> earth below there is no god like You, who keep Your gra-
> cious covenant with Your servants when they walk be-
> fore You in wholehearted devotion. (1 Kgs 8:23)

The first half of this verse, with its affirmation of the
uniqueness of the LORD, the God of Israel, immediately
recalls Deuteronomy 6:4 ("Hear, O Israel"). In this instance, Israel is not the addressee but the speaker, profess-
ing to the LORD just what the Shema, in fact, expects them
to believe. The second half of 1 Kings 8:23, however, speaks
of Israel as living in covenant with the LORD, whom they
serve "in wholehearted devotion," or, more literally, "with
all their heart" (*bekhol-libbam*). This last expression recalls
the commandment in Deuteronomy 6:5 to love the LORD
"with all your heart" (*bekhol levavekha*). It would seem,
then, that the two halves of 1 Kings 8:23 stand in a relation

similar to that of Deuteronomy 6:4 and 6:5. The outstanding difference, of course, is that the verse in 1 Kings says nothing about the love of God.

Or so it seems. For another passage, speaking in very similar language, mentions the love of God (that is, the love people have for God) explicitly:

> [9]Know, therefore, that only the LORD your God is God, the steadfast God who keeps His covenant faithfully to the thousandth generation of those who love Him and keep His commandments, [10]but who instantly requites with destruction those who reject Him—never slow with those who reject Him, but requiting them instantly. (Deut 7:9–10)

In these verses, too, we hear of the LORD's faithfulness in covenant, as in the verse from 1 Kings. What is different is this: whereas 1 Kings reads "[You] keep Your gracious covenant with Your servants (*'avadekha*)," Deuteronomy 7:9 speaks of his "keep[ing] His covenant faithfully to the thousandth generation of those who love Him (*'ohavav*) and keep His commandments." One text speaks of servants; the other, of lovers. "Those who love [the LORD]," it would seem, are synonymous with those who "keep His commandments," that is to say, with his "servants."

If we put all this together, we come up with an identification of the love of God with the performance of his commandments. Love, so understood, is not an emotion, not a feeling, but a cover term for acts of obedient service.[4] And if we apply this insight to the opening of the Shema, we can say that Deuteronomy 6:5, with its demand of undivided love, simply states the logical implication of the previous verse, with its reminder to Israel that the LORD alone is their God.

But there is something that this deceptively simple formulation does not explain. Why must the love be undivided? Surely, love, even understood as service, is eminently divisible. A father and a mother can love all their children, and the children, in turn, can love both parents, without having to choose. An employee can have two jobs, work at each, and serve each employer with equal devotion and no conflict. Love, in other words, is not a zero-sum proposition. Indeed, in the modern world, it is not easy to think of a relationship in which either love or service (for we moderns tend to separate them) is expected to be absolute and unqualified.

Perhaps the first candidate to come to mind is one that has, happily, vanished from modern societies—the relationship of slave to master. But even that relationship, most would say, is one of service only and not of love. For the institution of slavery hardly seems to reflect or promote love, either of the slave for the master or of the master for the slave. Whatever the personal relationship between the two individuals may happen to be, the institutional dynamics seem to us to sacrifice love to service. And yet the Bible can identify love and servitude and even use the same Hebrew word (ʿeved) to refer to the loving "servant" of God as well as to the miserable "slave." Could it be that in reality the love of the Lord demanded by the Shema amounts to nothing more than the degrading and dehumanizing service of a person in bondage? And if not, how shall we conceive an arrangement in which love and service work in tandem, not in opposition, and can even be synonymous?

But What Is a "Covenant"?

To address this question, we must now pay close attention to a key word in both Deuteronomy 7:9 and 1 Kings 8:23 that we have passed over, namely, "covenant" (Hebrew, *berit*).

In the Bible, for the most part, a covenant is a kind of treaty; it establishes or formalizes a relationship and spells out the obligations. A good case study is 1 Kings 5:15–26, which tells of a covenant between Solomon, king of Judah and Israel, and King Hiram of Tyre. The arrangement with the young Solomon continues one that his father David had maintained, "for Hiram had always been a friend of David" (v. 15). It is noteworthy that the word for "friend" here (*'ohev*) derives from the root used to translate the verb "you shall love" in the Shema. The point, though, is not that David and Hiram felt any special affection for each other but rather that the two rulers stood in a mutually beneficial and cooperative relationship.

At the end of this account of Solomon's covenant making, our text employs the term *šalom* to describe the relationship that Solomon, in turn, has established with Hiram through the covenant between the two of them. Although some translations render the word as "peace," a sense it often has, here the English term "friendship" is preferable. There is no reason to think the two kings would have been at war without the covenant, for there had been no hostilities beforehand. What the covenant does, rather, is to continue and renew a relationship of goodwill and mutual service: Hiram will provide the cypress and cedar logs for Solomon's projected temple, and Solomon will provide Hiram with wheat and oil on an annual basis (vv. 22–25).

If we extrapolate from this example to the "gracious covenant" that the LORD established with Israel (1 Kgs 8:23), we see that the operative framework assumes a kind of service that is far from slavery. It is, rather, a relationship of service founded not in conquest and subjugation but in good relations and mutual benefit. We can go further. Since covenant in the ancient Near East is usually a relationship between kings, Israel's status is best seen not as that of a slave but more like that of a regal figure. Indeed, when the LORD promises Israel at Sinai that if they keep the covenant, they "shall be to Me a kingdom of priests and a holy nation" (Exod 19:6), "kingdom" there may well refer not to the regime but to the people, understood collectively as a royal and sacral body.[5] All Israel can stand, in other words, in the position of a regal figure faithfully serving his own covenantal lord—a king, not a slave.

Because Deuteronomy is the biblical book of the love of God par excellence, much of our discussion in this chapter will focus on it and its resonances elsewhere in the Bible. It is also, not coincidentally, the book in which the first paragraph of the Shema appears. William L. Moran, who first explored the love of God in Deuteronomy in light of other ancient Near Eastern literature, lays out the behavioral implications:

> Love in Deuteronomy is a love that can be commanded.... Above all, it is a love which must be expressed in loyalty, in service, and in unqualified obedience to the demands of the Law. For to love God is, in answer to a unique claim (6:4), to be loyal to him (11:1, 22; 30:20), to walk in his ways (10:12; 11:22; 19:9; 30:16), to keep his commandments (10:12; 11:1, 22; 19:9), to do them (11:22; 19:9), to heed them or his voice (11:13; 30:16), to serve him (10:12; 11:1, 13). It is, in brief, a love defined by and pledged in the covenant—a covenantal love.[6]

This notion of a covenantal love accounts as well for that odd indivisibility of affections to which we drew attention: Why must Israel serve the LORD alone and with all their heart? To answer that key question, we must distinguish between two types of covenant.

In the case of Solomon and Hiram, the covenant is between equals—neither king is the other king's lord—and the language that Moran identifies in connection with the love of God in Deuteronomy, the language, that is, of loyalty, service, and obedience, is absent. But the ancient Near Eastern world offers us another type of covenant, a covenant in which one party—the more powerful—is the suzerain (to use the less than ideal terminology of European feudalism) and the other is his vassal. In a letter of one Mesopotamian king to another from the eighteenth century BCE, for example, the writer avows that he is the servant and "friend" of the recipient.[7] Here, too, the Akkadian word, like Hebrew *'ohev*, derives from a verb that means "to love," and here again, service and love, so understood, are not at odds but in deep harmony.

Closer to ancient Israel in time and space is an extraordinary set of letters to the king of Egypt sent by beleaguered rulers of Canaanite city-states early in the fourteenth century BCE. In one of these letters, Rib-Hadda, the king of Byblos (a site now on the Lebanese coast), pleading with his lord to send reinforcements, asks, "Who will love if I die?"[8] Interestingly, in another letter to the pharaoh, the same Canaanite king describes his own subjects as "those who love me."[9] Hoping the pharaoh can rescue him from the insurrection he faces, he pleads, "Half of [the city] loves the sons of ʿAbdi-Aširta [the ringleader of the rebellion], and half of it [loves] my lord."[10]

Here, too, the love in question, though it may possibly reflect the subjects' actual attitude, is a matter not of sentiment but of loyalty and readiness to serve. In the context of covenant, the alternative to love is not neutrality but rebellion. The divided heart of Rib-Hadda's city is a dagger aimed at the very existence of the covenantal relationship.

Still another example, this one from the seventh century BCE, is especially apposite, and for four reasons. The first is that it comes from the period in which much biblical literature was taking shape—from the century, in fact, in which most historians think Deuteronomy itself was composed. Another reason is that it is in the name of an Assyrian emperor, and the language of the Assyrian vassal treaties finds especially rich resonance in the Bible in general and Deuteronomy in particular. The third is that this particular text is itself a covenant. But the most potent reason is that the love of the suzerain here is not simply presupposed or alluded to, as in the previous examples we have examined, but instead, as in the Shema, it is commanded.

The emperor Esarhaddon, seeking to ensure that after his death his vassals remain loyal to his son and successor, Assurbanipal, phrases the key stipulation thus: "You will love as yourselves Assurbanipal."[11] The analogy to Deuteronomy 6:5 is patent. In this case, were the vassals to divide their love between Assurbanipal and other suzerains—other aspiring emperors seeking to build up alliances that could threaten and eventually subjugate Assyria—then the whole point of the arrangement would be defeated.

In a related text, we find an oath that Assurbanipal, facing a revolt by his own brother, imposes on his vassals and government officials: "the king of Assyria, our lord," they are to swear, "we will love."[12] Here, too, as in the case of the Canaanite king six centuries earlier, the failure to love the suzerain means the disintegration of the alliance. The covenant requires love, and the suzerainty covenant requires exclusive love. In a covenant text from the fourteenth century BCE, a Hittite emperor puts it forthrightly to his vassal: "Do not turn your eyes to anyone else! Your fathers presented tribute to Egypt; you [shall not do that!]."[13]

In the case of the Shema, the suzerain who demands undivided love is not a mortal emperor but the LORD, Israel's God, and the threat to the covenant comes not from aspiring rulers but from other gods and the very real temptation to worship them. Underlying these differences is a momentous shift from the world of diplomacy to that of theology. Now covenant is not only an instrument of statecraft between rulers but also the defining metaphor (or perhaps more than a metaphor) for the relationship of God and his people.

So far, we lack strong analogues for this shift from elsewhere in the ancient Near Eastern world.[14] Whether or not any come along, the shift itself is surely of the greatest importance for understanding the love of God in the Bible, as well as Jewish (and Christian) theology more generally, including political theology. That no human ruler can claim the same degree of allegiance that God claims; that God's kingship or suzerainty relativizes all human regimes; that all human political arrangements, even the most just and humane, fall short of the kingdom of God: these are ideas that have reverberated over the centuries and into our own time.

A Jealous God?

The exclusive or undivided love that the LORD demands of his people Israel is also, however, the source of what many today find to be one of the most problematic concepts in the Bible: the description of the LORD as "a jealous God" (Exod 20:5). Jealousy is such a base attribute that it is hard for many to respect a theological tradition that ascribes it to God, and we should therefore not be surprised to find that translators and commentators alike have long sought to deflect the criticism elicited by the Hebrew phrase *'el qanna'*. The NJPS *Tanakh*, for example, renders the expression as "an impassioned God," and a Talmudic authority from the early third century CE glosses the phrase to mean, "I am jealousy's God: I rule over jealousy, but jealousy does not rule over me" (*Mekhilta de-Rabbi Išmael, Baḥodeš* 6).

This rabbinic interpretation protects God's sovereignty: he is not the victim of his jealousy, as we mortals are of ours, but can, as it were, turn it on and off at will. But even this leaves open the question of why he would ever want to turn it on, and with such fearsome intensity. As a Hindu student once asked me, "Why is God so jealous?"

The answer is that God's jealousy is a response to baseless and fraudulent claims by others upon things that belong to him alone. It is analogous to the response of the victim of identity theft or adultery. (In chapter 3, we shall explore the marital metaphor for covenant in the Bible.) Were the victim to keep silent or to grant instantaneous forgiveness, the fraud and deceit would only grow, with devastating consequences for all involved. The jealousy of the injured spouse and the anger of the person whose identity has been stolen are measures of the damage done. In the thinking that underlies the Decalogue, the "other gods" (Exod 20:3) of whom the LORD is jealous are impostors or counterfeits.[15] They are not the true source of Israel's high status; it was not they who took the nation "out of the land of Egypt, the house of bondage" (Exod 20:2). To allow them the position rightly held by him alone is to debase the currency of his relationship with Israel. To allow other lords into the same relationship is to ensure that it will no longer be, in fact, the same relationship. Some things can, and should, be shared. Others simply cannot.

If we are to employ the term "monotheism," long used to describe Judaism, the only meaning the term can have within the specific context of covenant is in reference to this rigorous exclusivity of relationship. The key issue in covenantal theology is not the number of gods; texts can easily be found in the Hebrew Bible that mention other deities without implying their nonexistence. The issue is, as it were, political rather than philosophical. It has to do with loyalty and service, not with the nature of being.

To be sure, even within the Bible, there is plentiful evidence of another way of envisaging monotheism. This one speaks of the LORD's incomparability and of his unsurpassable power: the other deities, having been bested in combat, have proven not to be deities at all in the same sense as he.[16] Whereas the idiom of covenant speaks of the unique relationship of the LORD and the people Israel, the idiom of incomparability has a more universal focus, in fact, a cosmic one. "For the LORD is a great God," it hymns, "the great king of all divine beings" (Ps 95:3).

But we need not choose between the particularistic and the universal idioms of biblical monotheism. Indeed, sometimes they occur together:

> [5]Now then, if you will obey Me faithfully and keep My covenant, you shall be My treasured possession among all the peoples. Indeed, all the earth is Mine, [6]but you shall be to Me a kingdom of priests and a holy nation. (Exod 19:5–6)

It is precisely because all the earth and the peoples on it are the LORD's that his relationship with Israel appears special and unique. Were he but their tribal deity, powerless outside their borders, his singling them out to be his priestly kingdom and holy nation would be unremarkable. The universal scope of his realm makes his special covenantal relationship with Israel all the more significant.

God's jealousy does not, however, imply that Israelites are prohibited from loving anyone or anything else. In fact, this is very much not the case.

In the theology of the Jewish Bible, and in Jewish theology more generally, the love of God is not set at odds with all other loves—only, that is, with those that infringe upon Israel's relationship with him.[17] In the case of the Shema, the demand to love the LORD with all one's heart in no way implies that Israelites are not to love anyone else or that doing so is a tragic, unfulfilled act. Deuteronomy itself commands its hearers to "love the resident alien" (10:19),[18] as does Leviticus (19:34). And, as often noted, the outstanding Talmudic figure Rabbi Akiva, in a passage properly adduced as a parallel to passages in the Gospels about the love of the neighbor, identified "Love your fellow as yourself" (Lev 19:18) as the "great rule of the Torah."[19] In the cov-

> Hillel said: Be among the disciples of Aaron, loving peace and pursuing peace, loving humanity and bringing them near to the Torah.
>
> *Mishnah*[20]

enantal understanding of the love of God, nothing implies that the faithful and wholeheartedly devoted Israelite cannot love people or things, even passionately. The love at issue here is a quasi-political—or, to be more precise, a theopolitical—allegiance. It is a love that becomes real and attains social force in acts of service and homage.

Law and Covenant

And what are the acts through which the covenantal love of God is fulfilled in the Hebrew Bible?

Positively, the covenantal love of God means heeding the LORD's commandments and walking in his ways. Negatively, it means scrupulously avoiding actions that signal disloyalty: sacrificing to, or invoking the name of, another god, for example; imitating the modes of worship of the idolatrous Canaanites; or following a prophet or family member who urges the worship of another god.[21] These negative commandments, the behaviors that an Israelite lover of the LORD must avoid, are eminently familiar to scholars of ancient Near Eastern treaties, for they are logical implications of the objective that such arrangements seek to secure—namely, the complete fidelity of the vassal and his wholehearted reliability as an ally.

In the case of the positive commandments ("thou shalt"), the matter is more complicated—and more revealing. For the structure of the Torah itself makes the norms of biblical law into stipulations of covenant. Thus, between Exodus 19, in which the LORD offers Israel his covenant and they accept it ("All that the LORD has spoken we will do!" [v. 8]) and Exodus 24, in which the Sinai covenant is solemnly and ritually inaugurated, we find collections of *laws*. These not only include the Decalogue (Exod 20:2–14), which is given in direct address, as might befit an address from a suzerain to his vassal; they also include laws cast as cases ("When men quarrel and one strikes the other ...")

[Exod 21:18]) and dealing with a host of matters that are not addressed in ancient Near Eastern covenants—slavery with all its regulations, a goring ox, theft, kidnapping, the mistreatment of the poor and vulnerable, and much else.

Those legal norms, of course, are in many instances paralleled in other collections of law, especially those from Mesopotamia, sometimes strikingly so. What is not paralleled there (as far as we currently can know) is the placement of law within a covenantal framework.

The change is momentous. It means that the observance even of humdrum matters of law has become an expression of personal faithfulness and loyalty in covenant. Even when the commanding voice of the lord in covenant is not explicit in their grammatical structure, laws have become commandments. Israelites trying to heed those commandments and walk in God's ways face a far larger and more encompassing task than that facing a minor ancient Near Eastern king trying to maintain faithfulness to the emperor with whom he is in covenant and whom he is commanded to love.

Another way to say this, however, is that the Israelites' opportunities to demonstrate their love for the LORD are vastly more numerous, effectively encompassing the whole of their communal life. Good deeds become acts of personal fidelity, faithfulness to the personal God, and not simply the right things to do within some supposedly universal code of ethics (though they may be that as well). Conversely, bad deeds become acts of betrayal, akin (as we shall see in chapter 3) to adultery. They are not simply morally wrong in the abstract: they wrong the divine covenant partner.

What is more, some deeds are commanded or forbidden simply because such is the will of God and violating his will impairs the personal relationship between the parties in covenant; whether there is some moral logic behind his decree is, in this case, beside the point. Rabbinic tradition thus offers a startling interpretation of a common biblical word for "law" (*ḥoq* or *ḥuqqah*): the rabbis tend to see it as a decree for which rational explanations are not knowable. The authority of a *ḥoq* lies solely in the fact that the LORD is Israel's God, sovereign, and suzerain: "I, the LORD, have decreed it (*ḥaqaqtiv*) and you have no right to criticize it" (*b. Yoma* 67a). Observance of such a law is dramatic evidence of the people Israel's willing acceptance of their God's covenantal lordship. Their relationship enables them to trust him even when they cannot comprehend his decrees.

A revealing midrash on the words "I have set you apart from other peoples to be Mine" (Lev 20:26) points to a psychological implication of the covenantal ethic. It instructs Jews *not* to say that they are without any desire to practice what is prohibited to them, such as wearing garments of mixed linen and wool, eating pork, or engaging in forbidden sexual practices. Instead, they should say, "I do have the desire! But what can I do? My Father in Heaven has decreed it upon me" (*Siphra, Qedošim* 9:10). The key point, in other words, is not the preferences or values of the Jew but once again the will, however mysterious, of the covenantal lord. This is not to deny, of course, that some undergirding logic for the practices at issue may be found in a rationalist account of morality. Nor is it to deny that an explanation of seemingly bizarre practices can be readily located in the cultural code of the ancient society as an anthropologist might describe it. It is to say, however, that the Jew's observance of the norms does not *depend* on such moralistic or social-scientific logic, but rather on the readiness of the beloved to carry out the will of the sovereign. The religious meaning of the practice is not exhausted by the values implicit in it or the social or cultural situation that called it forth. Values can exist outside a covenantal framework. In the biblical thinking, mitzvot cannot. Even when historical change has caused the underlying

He said to them: By your lives! No corpse has the power to contaminate, and no water has the power to purify. Rather, this is a decree of the Holy One (blessed be He!).

Midrash[22]

explanation for a norm, a mitzvah, to be forgotten, the covenantal theology can keep the norm alive—and meaningful.

In this context, the term "law," often used as a synonym for Torah, can be dangerously misleading. In the modern Western world, law mostly defines a realm of freedom: my right to swing my arm ends at my neighbor's nose. To put it another way, we tend to prioritize rights over duties. We have some duties to the state (for example, paying taxes), but mostly our duties are derived from the guiding obligation not to infringe on the rights of others. In the Bible, by contrast, both positive and negative actions are *commanded*; "thou shalt" and "thou shalt not" are both in plentiful evidence. Simply staying out of the way of others, practicing an ethic of "live and let live," does not suffice. The king must be served; the lord in covenant must be loved. And that love must be enacted in deeds—not only good deeds in general (indispensable though they are) but the specific deeds that he commands.

The point is made pithily in a Talmudic saying: "Greater is he who has been commanded and does the deed than he who has not been commanded and does the deed" (*b. Bava Qamma* 38a). The same act, in other words, assumes greater importance—and accrues greater merit—when done in obedience to a divine directive and not simply in response to one's own inner promptings. A good deed is surely precious, but in the larger perspective it is not the same thing as a commandment (mitzvah), even when its content is the same. There is no substitute for the covenantal relationship between God and the people Israel; deeds performed outside that very special relationship are of a different, and lesser, character from those performed within it.

Love and Deeds

The notion of a love demonstrated through the observance of law, even law reconceived as personal commandment, will be disappointing to many today. For surely "love," whatever constraints it imposes on behavior, is primarily and most importantly a matter of the heart. The term describes feelings, it will be said, and not merely norms (however admirable) dutifully but impassively observed. In the context of ancient covenants, in which we have placed the demand for the wholehearted love of the LORD in the Shema, "love" would seem to be merely a metaphor, and a most inadequate one at that.

We shall soon consider the question of whether covenantal love entails only deeds and not emotions. But now it would be useful to ask whether the definition of love as a set of actions is really so unusual—or so deficient.

About thirty years ago, the sociologist Francesca M. Cancian argued that the familiar restriction of love to the realm of feelings is a gender-biased phenomenon and one that is characteristic of certain distinctly modern developments. With the emergence of the market economy, she wrote, "Work became identified with what men do for money while love became identified with women's activities at home. As a result, the conception of love shifted toward emphasizing tenderness, powerlessness, and the expression of emotion."[23] Thus, in contemporary America,

> We identify love with emotional expression and talking about feelings, aspects of love that women prefer and in which women tend to be more skilled than men. At the same time we often ignore the instrumental and physical

aspects of love that men prefer, such as providing help, sharing activities, and sex. This feminized perspective leads us to believe that women are much more capable of love than men and that the way to make relationships more loving is for men to become more like women.[24]

Alongside the gender bias, as Cancian saw it, there was also a difference in social class. "Among the general public, love is also defined primarily as expressing feelings and verbal disclosure, not as instrumental help," she wrote. "This is especially true among the more affluent; poorer people are more likely than they to see practical help and financial assistance as a sign of love."[25] In short, in Cancian's thinking, at least in America at the time she wrote (global generalizations are dangerous), there are distinct male and female perceptions and styles of love, and to a significant degree they correlate with the lower and upper social classes, respectively.

It bears noting that Cancian was speaking as a social scientist and mostly about gender relations in the United States. Exceptions to her generalizations surely existed then, and the question of the reliability of generalizations about gender over the course of history is, again, fraught with problems and controversy. Whatever weaknesses one may detect in her typology, however, it does offer a striking parallel to the question of love and law that we have been exploring.

If we try to map covenantal love as it appears in the Torah onto this rough grid, we would have to say that "love" is not at all an inappropriate or inadequate term for the phenomenon that we have been describing, but the love in question is more like the perception held (according to Cancian) by men and poorer people than like the characteristic perception held by women and the more affluent. In particular, Cancian's term "instrumental help" seems a very apt way of epitomizing the relationship of the suzerain and the vassal in covenant. At the core of that relationship stand the duties of the two parties, manifested principally in the material assistance they provide to each other. Strikingly, when Cancian writes of her subjects, "The men actually saw instrumental actions as affection,"[26] she could just as easily be characterizing the semantic question of how the Torah, and its ancient Near Eastern antecedents and parallels, could have described the performance of duties as love. The answer is that these sources held a concept of love that was more outward, action-oriented, and practical than the one that has come to dominate modern Western culture.

But, in truth, this sort of love is also not so unfamiliar, even in modern societies, as may at first seem the case. Our discussion has been focusing on romantic love, and it is in the context of romantic love that the factors of emotions and their expression come to the fore. In that context, a love focused on acts of service with little or no affective language would generally seem lacking (though, if Cancian is right, more so to women than to men and more so to the affluent than to the poor). But what if we were instead to speak of the love of parents and their children? In that case, it seems to me, we are more likely to speak of actions than affects. A mother and a father work extra hours to put their children through school, to pay for music lessons, or for orthodontia; parents of a rebellious and unruly adolescent quietly endure the provocations, responding as seems appropriate to the situation at hand but never simply walking away from their own child. For their part, children take on extra responsibilities around the house or a part-time job to help a disabled parent; adult children assume special burdens to assure that their aging parents are receiving good care and dwelling in appropriate quarters. In all these cases, is it not reasonable to infer a relationship of love from the practices themselves, even in the near or total absence of verbal expressions of affection or of kisses and hugs?

Lest this analogy to the relationship of the LORD and his people Israel seem far-fetched, it is worthy of note that the metaphor of father and son, unlike that of husband and wife amply attested in the prophets (as we shall see in chapter 3), is very much present in Deuteronomy, the book containing the Shema and its commandment to "love the LORD your God with all your heart" (6:5; 11:13).[27] Indeed, a good argument has been advanced that the very expression with which the Shema opens, "Hear, O Israel!" (Deut 6:4), reflects a setting of parental instruction, as in these verses from Proverbs:[28]

> My son, hear (*šemaʿ*) the discipline of your father
> And do not forsake the instruction of your mother.
> (Prov 1:8)[29]

> My son, listen to my wisdom;
> Incline your ear to my insight. (Prov 5:1)

> So now, sons, pay heed (*šimʿu*) to me,
> And do not swerve from the words of my mouth.
> (Prov 5:7)

> Now, sons, listen (*šimʿu*) to me;
> Pay attention to my words. (Prov 7:24)

> Listen (*šemaʿ*), my son, and get wisdom;
> Lead your mind in a (proper) path. (Prov 23:19)

None of these verses mentions the covenant of God and Israel. That subject is altogether absent from the book of Proverbs, whose focus is on universal norms and not on historical narrative. Yet Deuteronomy, too, employs the situation of a father disciplining his son in describing the relationship of the LORD and Israel in the difficult years of the wandering in the desert between the Exodus and

Moses's final address (which Deuteronomy purports to be) and in urging that the commandments be kept:

> [5]Bear in mind that the LORD your God disciplines you just as a man disciplines his son. [6]Therefore keep the commandments of the LORD your God: walk in His ways and revere Him. (Deut 8:5–6)

Here, we do not find the language of love, to be sure, but we do find a father's instruction connected with the covenantal norms. Should we assume that those norms have no connection, in turn, with love?[30] Would it not be more reasonable to assume that (like the covenantal norms) the LORD's discipline is itself an expression of love—not romantic but parental love? For the latter is the kind of love that in ancient Israelite culture, as in our own, is characterized more by the actions it prompts than by words or gestures. Like covenantal love, it is a love that entails service.

ACTION AND AFFECTION

I have been focusing on service as the key element in the biblical love of God for two reasons. The first is that the language of service is ubiquitous in connection with covenant, and covenant is exactly the context in which the love of God most often occurs in the Bible. The second is that the full strangeness of the biblical concept must be faced early on, lest one imagine that the love of God in the Bible (and in Judaism generally) is primarily a matter of emotion, a subjective phenomenon confined to the individual psyche. As we have just seen, in the modern West the assumption that love is a feeling is dominant. In my own teaching, I have found that when I ask my students (who are mostly in their twenties) what love is, they not only focus on feelings but also think only of romantic love. The love of parents for children, and vice versa, does not come to their minds so readily. Even the love of country very rarely occurs to them. The modern interpretation of love as essentially erotic has left them with scant resources with which to understand the love of vassals for their lords.

Now that we have set forth the nature of covenantal love—and its inextricable association with service to the suzerain through obedience to his stipulations—we must ask whether there is nonetheless an affective dimension lurking there as well. This is not to retract any of the points made above: I am not speaking of affect in place of service, or love in place of law. I am asking whether some element of feeling is also entailed in Israel's covenantal love of the LORD as portrayed in the Hebrew Bible.[31]

The nature of the evidence makes it difficult to give an answer. So thoroughly associated with norms of behavior is covenantal love that one might argue that they altogether exhaust its meaning in the covenantal context—in other words, that "love" in this context is a term of art for the proper behavior of a vassal, and nothing more. Such an argument is hard to refute, since it is easier to know what people say than what they feel, and in the case of the Bible, we have no way of finding out what feeling may lie behind the texts. Still, there are reasons to think that the equation of love with covenantal service alone is extreme.

One such reason has to do with the origins of covenant itself. We have been focusing on covenant as an instrument of diplomacy, and specifically as a binding agreement between an emperor and a lesser king. Especially in Deuteronomy but also throughout the Bible, the influence of these international treaties is strikingly present,[32] and, not surprisingly, the discovery and study of ancient Near Eastern treaties have proven enormously productive for our understanding of the biblical variant.

But covenant does not *originate* in international diplomacy. Instead, it borrows much of its character and force from something more primal: namely, from family relations. "In tribal societies," Frank Moore Cross writes, "there were legal mechanisms or devices—we might even say legal fictions—by which outsiders, non-kin, might be incorporated within the kinship group." He adds, "Oath and covenant, in which the deity is witness, guarantor, or participant, is also a widespread legal means by which the duties and privileges of kinship may be extended to another individual or group, including aliens."[33] So understood, covenant is like adoption or, for that matter, like conversion to Judaism: it makes the outsider a member of the family.

The resonances of this in the Bible are plentiful. When Ahaz, king of Judah in the eighth century BCE, accepts vassalage to the Assyrian emperor Tiglath-pileser III, he sends a message to the latter, saying, "I am your servant and your son; come and deliver me from the hands of the king of Aram and from the hands of the king of Israel, who are attacking me" (2 Kgs 16:7). Tiglath-pileser becomes the besieged king's father, and Ahaz accepts the obligations of service, as a dutiful son would rightly be expected to do.

Whether Ahaz felt any affection toward his new father is much to be doubted. It is far more likely that he was simply seeking relief from the two kings who were trying to topple him.[34] But the fact remains that his vassalage is cast as sonship. This point alone, to revert to those verses from Proverbs cited above, casts doubt on any hard division between a suzerain imposing his stipulations on his covenant partners and a father giving instruction to his son. The mixture of the two situations that we found in the language of the Shema is more natural than we may at first think.

Still closer to the point is the arrangement that Jonathan, the son of King Saul, makes with David, the man who will eventually succeed his father on the throne:

> [12]Then Jonathan said to David, "By the LORD, the God of Israel! I will sound out my father at this time tomorrow,

[or] on the third day; and if [his response] is favorable
for David, I will send a message to you at once and disclose it to you. ¹³But if my father intends to do you harm,
may the LORD do thus to Jonathan and more if I do [not]
disclose it to you and send you off to escape unharmed.
May the LORD be with you, as He used to be with my
father. ¹⁴Nor shall you fail to show me the LORD's faithfulness, while I am alive; nor, when I am dead, ¹⁵shall
you ever discontinue your faithfulness to my house—not
even after the LORD has wiped out every one of David's
enemies from the face of the earth. ¹⁶Thus has Jonathan
covenanted with the house of David; and may the LORD
requite the enemies of David!" (1 Sam 20:12–16)³⁵

Here, Jonathan undertakes to extend protection to David,
quite conceivably saving his friend's very life from Saul's
murderous rage.³⁶ More important for our purposes, this
act of generosity on Jonathan's part serves as the prologue
to a covenant that he makes not only with David but also
with David's lineage to come.³⁷ The stipulation of this covenant is that David and his descendants shall forever show
the same faithfulness to Jonathan's own descendants. The
term rendered as "faithfulness" in verse 15 (Hebrew, ḥesed)
is one that we have actually seen before. It appears as the
second noun in the phrase in 1 Kings 8:23, rendered above
as "gracious covenant" (ha-berit veha-ḥesed), and in Deuteronomy 7:9, where it describes the God "who keeps His
covenant faithfully." The idiom seems to be a hendiadys,
that is, the use of two words connected by "and" to convey
a single idea: the idea of "covenant"/ḥesed.

I have left ḥesed untranslated here because it lacks a
good English equivalent, and, depending on context, such
words as "love," "kindness," "generosity," and "lovingkindness" can all render it appropriately. (The last term seems
to have been coined in sixteenth-century England specifically for the purpose of translating ḥesed.)³⁸ The same term

appears in Jonathan's stipulation to David, "Nor shall you fail to show me the LORD's faithfulness" (1 Sam 20:14), of which the NJPS correctly notes that the reference is to "the faithfulness pledged in the covenant before the LORD." As often in the Bible, *ḥesed* and covenant implicate each other. Having done David an enormous favor, Jonathan seeks to perpetuate throughout the generations the relationship of kindness and mutual service that the two men have. The mechanism for this is a covenant solemnized in an oath in the presence of the LORD, who will presumably enforce it.

Now, it is possible that in so doing, Jonathan has no feelings for David at all. One could, I suppose, view the two as allies pursuing Machiavellian self-interest without any genuine friendship. (How Jonathan helps himself by saving David may be difficult to see at first, though if he thinks Saul will be among the enemies David destroys, one can understand why he would want to obligate David to spare both him and his descendants.) But the next verse casts strong doubt on such a Machiavellian reading:

> [17]Jonathan, out of his love for David (*be'ahavato 'oto*), adjured him again, for he loved him as himself (*'ahavat-naphšo 'ahevo*). [18]Jonathan said to him,… [23]"As for the promise we made to each other, may the LORD be [witness] between you and me forever." (1 Sam 20:17–18, 23)

The pronouns in verse 17 are, alas, ambiguous. Contrary to the translation above, the verse never names David, and this makes it unclear at the end just who is loving whom. In principle, one might therefore interpret the verse this way: "Jonathan, out of his (Jonathan's) love for him (David), adjured him (David) again, for he (David) loved him (Jonathan) as himself (David)." But, as one commentator has recently put it, "given the reciprocal nature of true love, the ambiguity does not matter."[39] The point that does matter is that love motivates the formation of the covenant between the two young men, and it is difficult to view "love" here as simply a technical term for covenantal service and nothing more.

If we extrapolate from the covenant of David and Jonathan to that of the LORD and Israel—recognizing, of course, the obvious differences—it would seem likely that the language of the love of God in Deuteronomy, too, has an affective dimension and should not be seen as only a technical term for obedience in covenant. At its foundation, to use a spatial metaphor, lies an emotional bond (about which more later); or, to put the issue in temporal terms, at its origin, predating the actual offer of covenant, there was a close personal relationship, a relationship of *hesed*. Obedience to the stipulations of covenant—which, as we have seen, came to encompass all of Torah law—is essential to the continuing relationship, but those norms are not the sum total of the bond between God and Israel, and drily and austerely observing them does not do justice to it. No choice between love and law need be made, for in this case love and law entail each other.

Once we recover the affective dimension that is essential to the observance of God's law in this thinking, we can better understand a feature prominent in Deuteronomy in general and in the Shema in particular: namely, the insistence on regular verbal repetition and the importance of visible reminders of God's commandments. Consider again these verses from the first paragraph of the Shema:

> ⁶Take to heart these instructions with which I charge you this day. ⁷Impress them upon your children. Recite them when you stay at home and when you are away, when you lie down and when you get up. ⁸Bind them as a sign on your hand and let them serve as a symbol on your forehead; ⁹inscribe them on the doorposts of your house and on your gates. (Deut 6:6–9)

The "instructions"—Hebrew, *devarim*, can just as easily be translated "words"—are not simply to be carried out;

robotic observance does not suffice. They must be taken to heart, impressed upon the next generation, routinely recited, and made visible, indeed conspicuous, to the eye. As one scholar puts it, "The love of [the LORD] is not a wordless ebullience, but rather a love capable of expression, a love in words that can be repeated, not in the manner of a prayer wheel but as the inner expression of a reciprocated love. Therefore the words, namely the following commandments and prohibitions, must be 'on your heart' (Deut 6:6)—on the place in human beings at which God primarily communicates."[40] To be sure, in ancient Israelite culture the heart was often the seat of thinking rather than feeling, but even if that is the case here, the point stands that these verses demand more than acts of outward obedience: they demand an internalization of God's words, a continual refortification of the will to obey or, if necessary, a reorientation of the wayward self around the God from whom it has strayed.

In its more pessimistic moments, biblical literature seems to doubt that human beings can bring about the necessary internalization or refortification on their own. To adapt a phrase of Kant's, the timber of humanity is just too crooked to straighten itself out.[41] To get Israel back into the mode of covenantal service therefore requires nothing less than God's own gracious intervention, an act of divine ḥesed that replaces their hardened disposition or, as some biblical texts put it, their "uncircumcised heart," with an orientation that facilitates the love of him.[42] In the days to come, one such text tells us, God will enable Israel to love him, as they should have been doing all along:

> [6]Then the LORD your God will open up your heart and the hearts of your offspring to love the LORD your God with all your heart and soul, in order that you may live. [7]The LORD your God will inflict all those curses upon the enemies and foes who persecuted you. [8]You, however,

will again heed the LORD and obey all His commandments that I enjoin upon you this day. (Deut 30:6–8)

This passage envisages a situation in which the people
Israel, exiled and downtrodden, return to God and begin
to obey his commandments anew.[43] Thus does their restoration get under way—with the pain of divine punishment
and the self-examination and moral
reform that it provokes. But the verses
quoted above tell us that this is just
the beginning of the new relationship.
The restoration is consummated only
when God enables Israel to love him
as the Shema requires, with all their
heart and soul. This process of hu-
manly initiated repentance (brought
about, though, by punishment for
breach of covenant) and divine intervention into the recesses of the human
heart reverses everything: now it is
Israel's oppressors who are punished,
and Israel who fully and wholeheartedly observe their liberator and suzerain's commandments.

> [26]And I will give you a
> new heart and put a
> new spirit into you: I
> will remove the heart
> of stone from your
> body and give you a
> heart of flesh; [27]and I
> will put My spirit into
> you. Thus I will cause
> you to follow My laws
> and faithfully to
> observe My rules.
> (Ezek 36:26–27)

As the chapter in Deuteronomy containing that vision
of Israel's future unfolds, it becomes clear that the vision
serves a present purpose as well: to induce them to observe God's Torah now, to do their part to make the escha-
tological vision a current reality. And here again, it is the
ready availability of the revelation, its presence in words
that can be recited and thus impressed upon the heart,
that is the key point:

> [11]Surely, this Instruction which I enjoin upon you this
> day is not too baffling for you, nor is it beyond reach. [12]It
> is not in the heavens, that you should say, "Who among
> us can go up to the heavens and get it for us and impart

it to us, that we may observe it?" [13]Neither is it beyond the sea, that you should say, "Who among us can cross to the other side of the sea and get it for us and impart it to us, that we may observe it?" [14]No, the word is very close to you, in your mouth and in your heart, to observe it. (Deut 30:11–14)[44]

God's instruction, his commandment (mitzvah), is not an object, but a *word*. It is something that can be heard, recited, and internalized, made one's own. It is not an occult teaching brought from another world by a mystical adept. It is nearby and ready to be practiced, if only the heart will be opened to love God and to do his will.

I have been arguing that the language of love in the covenantal context has resonances of both service and feeling. It is not, or not usually, a mere technical usage to indicate the service that the lesser partner in the covenant owes his superior, though that service is essential to the relationship and without it the love demanded by the covenant is absent. Rather, in part because covenant is based on a more primal type of relationship, one of kin, and draws on its idiom, the affective dimension of the language is no mere metaphor. One stream of biblical literature, the Deuteronomic (from which, it will be recalled, the first two paragraphs of the Shema are drawn),[45] places special emphasis upon the language of love and, not coincidentally, also upon the need for recitation and internalization of God's commandments. It would be extreme to imagine that such internalization would not involve the emotions, and centrally so.

Love and Fear

This usage of the love of God in the framework of covenant recalls another problematic term, "the fear of God." The two ideas appear together in one especially memorable passage:

¹²And now, O Israel, what does the LORD your God demand of you? Only this: to revere (*leyir'ah*) the LORD
your God, to walk only in His paths, to love Him, and to
serve the LORD your God with all your heart and soul,
¹³keeping the LORD's commandments and laws, which I
enjoin upon you today, for your good. (Deut 10:12–13)

How genuine can the love of God be, I have often been
asked, if it is in an admixture with fear? How can we love
someone of whom we are afraid? A quick review of the
usage of the root for fear (*yr'*) in the Bible would readily
show that it can indeed denote a "crippling terror," to use
Bill Arnold's term; but, like "love," the term actually exhibits a wide range of meanings. As Arnold puts it, "At one
end of the spectrum stands a 'pathological anxiety' in the
face of the threat, resulting in crippling inactivity. At the
other end of the spectrum stands a positive course of action, which when used to characterize one's relationship
with [the LORD]/God is a response of obedience or exclusive worship."[46] This is not to say (Arnold is quick to point
out) that the "positive course of action" is devoid of an affective component.[47] There surely is a tinge of fear in the
negative sense, even in the reverence, the awe, or the sense
of being overwhelmed that one has in the presence of a
superior. And if the description of God in the Bible is at all
accurate, there would be something gravely wrong with
someone in whom the thought of God and the sense of his
immediate presence did not evoke those very feelings.

Some will, to be sure, doubt that there can be love in
such circumstances, holding that love requires equality, so
that one can never love a social superior or inferior. This
very contemporary idea is not one that the Bible enter-
tains. If a disparity in power prevents love, then the love
of human beings for God—of the creatures for their creator, of the emancipated for their emancipator, of the ben-

eficiaries for their benefactor—would be impossible by definition. Indeed, one wonders how many of our own most powerful loves would still be judged possible if this contemporary restriction were wholly valid.

Although biblical literature does not place the love and the fear of God in tension, the Talmudic rabbis often do just that. They tend to think of the fear of God as the fear of *punishment* and thus something to be contrasted with the love of God. They could argue, for example, about whether it was love or fear that motivated Job's righteousness and his endurance of the horrific calamities that, with God's approval, befell him. Similarly, they could be troubled about the fact that the Bible describes the revered patriarch Abraham as one who fears God in the identical language with which it characterizes Job (for the rabbis, a more ambiguous figure). Though a variety of approaches to this tension appears in rabbinic literature, it is important not to forget that the tension itself is foreign to the biblical sources about which the rabbis are arguing.[48] In biblical thinking, the love of God and the fear of God can, and should, coexist.

In sum, in the covenantal context in the Bible, both "love" and "fear" represent specialized usages of affective language. This is especially true in Deuteronomy, the biblical book that pays the most attention to the love of God and to which we, in turn, have therefore paid the most attention; but it is not unique to Deuteronomy. There is no reason to think the affective dimension has disappeared in either case.

What is more, if we bear in mind the two-sidedness of covenantal love—the active and the affective dimensions as forming a unity—we can give a more adequate answer to one of the questions with which we began: How can an emotion be commanded? The easy answer, as we have already seen, is that in this context love refers not so much to an emotion as to a set of deeds, those by which a vassal enacts his acceptance of his lord's suzerainty and demonstrates his fidelity to him.

The more sophisticated answer is that the emotion, if that is what love should be called, actually can be generated, though not directly. It is generated through regular reflection on the story of the relationship of God and Israel (about which more soon) and continual recitation and ritualized remembering of the words of his revelation in the context of a social group explicitly committed to those activities. For, as is well known among social psychologists, behaviors can generate and define emotions, and behaviors—the good as well as the bad ones—are to a significant degree learned from the sociocultural unit in which we find ourselves. In the words of a famous study in the sociology of knowledge, "Subjective reality is thus always dependent upon specific plausibility structures, that is, the specific social base and social processes required for its maintenance."[49]

The movement, in other words, is not unidirectional, only from inner states of mind to outward actions; it takes place in the opposite direction as well, from actions performed and texts recited to feelings and motivations. The Deuteronomic practices on which we have been focusing are not merely expressive; they are also cognitive and formative. They play a key role in generating, labeling, refining, and directing the emotion, just as the emotion plays a key role in energizing and revitalizing the practices, making them, like the God who commands them, beloved in the eyes of the practitioners.

A contemporary biblical scholar cautions us to beware of the bias promoted by both modern romanticism and, more recently, existentialism, with their counsel to be "true to one's feelings" or "authentic," as if "proper behavior proceeds from a correctly identified emotional source."[50] I would add that we need to beware as well of shallow talk

about "empty rituals." To be sure, rituals can indeed become empty, performed habitually and thoughtlessly, without regard to their meaning and the ethic that is supposed
to be associated with them. The prophets of Israel were
unstinting in their condemnation of just that sort of pro
forma religion. But it is also important to remember that,
like other habitual behaviors, rituals are hardy—like habits,
difficult to break—and thus likely to survive the spiritual
dry periods when faith and feelings are just not there.

The ritual without the theological truth to which it bears
witness, the act without the affect, can come alive—the
empty ritual can be filled up—when the dry period passes.
Indeed, the very existence of the ritual can help the spiritual dryness pass from the scene. Conversely, when the
ritual is no longer observed, the likelihood declines that
the message with which it is associated will survive, and
the likelihood that old practice will come to be associated
with new meanings declines still further.

Like the tension between love and fear, this notion of
the importance of the practice even when performed
with less than ideal motivation is not one to which the
Bible attests. But here, too, things are different in rabbinic
literature:

> Rav Huna and Rabbi Jeremiah said in the name of Rabbi
> Ḥiyya bar Abba: It is written, "They abandoned Me [and
> they did not keep My Torah]" (Jer 16:11). If only they
> had kept My Torah! Would that they had abandoned Me
> and kept My Torah! For if "they had abandoned Me and
> kept My Torah," the starter dough that is in it would have
> brought them back to Me.
>
> Rav Huna said: Study Torah, even if not for its own
> sake. From the very fact that you are studying it (though
> not for its own sake) and because you are involving your-
> self with it, you will turn back and do it for its own sake.
> (*Pesiqta de Rav Kahana* 15:5)[51]

To modern scholars, the two statements in Jeremiah 16:11 are simply an example of the parallelism that characterizes most biblical poetry: they say essentially the same thing in different words. The ancient rabbis, though, did not understand parallelism (or they pretended not to understand it) and instead insisted that the two halves of a poetic verse must make separate points or together make a distinction that either one could not convey by itself. In the present case, this logic pushes the rabbis to wonder why the verse says that the ancestors of the people whom Jeremiah is chastising not only abandoned God but also failed to keep his Torah. Why does the prophet even bother to mention their nonobservance once he has already described their desertion of God himself—to whose service their observance is supposed to be directed?

The answer in the first paragraph quoted above is that if they had kept the Torah, the spiritual force within it would have acted upon them to restore them to God, in the manner of a leavening agent transforming the dough into which it is released. The empty ritual turns out not to be so empty after all: the practice can regenerate the presence.

The second paragraph makes almost the identical point, though without direct reference to God. Anyone who has been a member of a traditional Jewish congregation knows that Jews may engage in the study of Torah for reasons very far afield from the religious purposes that should ideally motivate it. (The truth is, human beings cannot be sure of their own motivation and rarely have only one motivation for what they do.) They may, for example, engage in it because doing so brings them prestige in their social circle or enables them to show off their intellectual talents, or simply because they derive some other pleasure from it that is unconnected to any larger religious purpose. Or they may study Torah in order to receive a reward, or to avert a punishment, from God. In other cases, they do so for no better reason than force of habit, since they have grown up as observant Jews and have never made the effort to bring their adult life into conformity with their convictions or lack thereof.

One might think therefore that such individuals would be better off, because more consistent, if they dropped their involvement in Torah. As the famous lines in a play by T. S. Eliot put it, "The last temptation is the greatest treason: / To do the right deed for the wrong reason."[52] But the dictum at the end of Rav Huna's comment takes the diametrically opposite position: studying Torah for a lesser motive can lead one to study it for the highest motive, as an end in itself, or, as the paragraph above it implies, as a way to prove faithful to God himself, the giver of the Torah. In that case, the last temptation or the greatest treason, rather than doing the right deed for the wrong reason, is to give up doing the right deed altogether and thus dramatically lessen one's chances of arriving at the highest motive for the behavior.

A seventeenth-century French moralist and wit famously observed, "Hypocrisy is the homage vice pays to virtue."[53] To adapt this to Rav Huna's comment (with allowances for the obvious differences), we might say that so long as Jews study Torah, they pay homage, however obliquely, to the higher reality to which it claims to point and from which it claims to derive. They keep the standard in place, even when they depart from it in practice. But the dictum at the end of Rav Huna's comment makes a bolder claim still: Torah has a power—"the starter dough that is in it"—that can transform those who study it, elevating the motivation to match the deed. Once again, the activity, in this case routinized study of sacred material, can generate or restore the motivation.[54] Behaviors, over time, become dispositions; observances become acts of devotion.

Finally, to return to our question of what it is that generates or at least encourages the love and fear of God, in addition to the dimension of practice with which we have been dealing, there is at least one more factor worthy of note. This is an interpretation of suffering that enables the sufferers to overcome their hardened disposition, to cut away the thickening around their heart—its foreskin, to revert to that biblical idiom—that impedes obedience and places ego where faithfulness should be.

In this case, we are speaking of a mental template in terms of which one makes sense of the hard knocks of life. To be sure, there is a danger here of blaming oneself for an undeserved fate. But deserved or not, suffering has a powerful capacity to turn the sufferers away from the illusions of self-sufficiency and invulnerability, both of which appeal very readily to the successful but both of which, in the traditional Jewish view, powerfully inhibit the love of God and the strength and healing that it brings. Sometimes suffering opens up the heart when nothing else can.

GOD FALLS IN LOVE

The reader may have noticed that in our discussion some key components that one would expect to find in the relationship of love between the LORD and Israel have gone missing. The most obvious is God's love for Israel; so far we have interpreted the phrase "love of God" only as an objective genitive (the love God receives) and not as a subjective genitive (the love God gives). If true love is reciprocal, though, we should expect to find both types of love represented.

In fact, we find that ancient Near Eastern treaties that are the antecedents of the biblical covenants sometimes speak not only of the vassal's love for the suzerain, which we have examined, but also of the suzerain's love for the vassal. We dealt earlier with letters that Canaanite kings in the fourteenth century BCE sent to their Egyptian overlord; in those same letters, we also find that the pharaoh was expected to love his allies, and not just the reverse. Time and again, Rib-Hadda, the hapless king of Byblos whom we have met, tells the pharaoh that if the latter "loves his loyal servant," he will come to his aid.[55] Another king, after acclaiming the pharaoh as "my father and my lord," closes his letter with this plaintive question: "But if the king, my lord, does not love me and rejects me, what then am I to say?"[56]

Of course, the love of the suzerain for his vassal king is not identical to the love of the vassal for his suzerain. How could it be? Where the servant owes his lord obedience, the lord owes his servant protection, succor, and, if called for, rescue from enemies. Nevertheless, the relationship is still explicitly one of love; though it is not marked by equality, it is still marked by profound reciprocity.

At times, God's love for Israel falls squarely into that category of the obligations of the lord to his servant, and nothing more. Speaking of the Moabites' having hired a famous diviner to curse Israel on their march toward the Promised Land, Deuteronomy reports this: "But the LORD your God refused to heed Balaam; instead, the LORD your God turned the curse into a blessing for you, for the LORD your God loves you" (Deut 23:6). This love is not so different from the one Rib-Hadda expects from the pharaoh, the sort of love that yields aid and deliverance for the endangered underling. As a psalmist, speaking in a more individual voice, puts it:

> I love the LORD
> for He hears my voice, my pleas;
> [2]for He turns His ear to me
> whenever I call.
> [3]The bonds of death encompassed me;
>> the torments of Sheol overtook me.
> I came upon trouble and sorrow
> [4] and I invoked the name of the LORD,
>> "O LORD, save my life!" (Ps 116:1–4)

In all these instances, both the call for help and the rescue itself follow from the standing relationship of the two figures, the lord and his vassal, the protector and his protégé, the patron and his client.

Which brings us to a second aspect of the love between God and Israel that the reader may have found missing; namely, the question of its inception: How did this curious relationship begin? What was there in the LORD that first attracted Israel to him and not to his rivals? And what was there in Israel that caused the LORD to enter into covenant, or into this sort of covenant, with that nation alone?

Here, the matter is more complicated. We do sometimes find the language of love, but with a difference:

> [6]For you are a people consecrated to the LORD your God: of all peoples on earth the LORD your God chose you to be His treasured people. [7]It is not because you are the most numerous of peoples that the LORD set His heart on you and chose you—indeed, you are the smallest of peoples; [8]but it was because the LORD loved you and kept the oath He made to your fathers that the LORD freed you with a mighty hand and rescued you from the house of bondage, from the power of Pharaoh king of Egypt. (Deut 7:6–8)[57]

Before we discuss this passage further, we must confront honestly the deep moral problem that it poses. For the passage immediately follows, and is related to, one of the most painful in the entire Bible: one of the several texts in which the LORD commands Israel to doom to utter destruction the Canaanites who preceded them in the land, lest these idolaters turn the Israelites away from the worship of him and toward worship of their own gods.[58] "You must doom them to destruction: grant them no terms and give them no quarter," the text demands (Deut 7:2).

There are various ways, some based in tradition, others in modern historical research, by which a measure of the outrage provoked by this text (and others like it) can be mitigated. In rabbinic literature, for example, we find the notion that Moses's successor Joshua offered the Canaan-ites three options: evacuation, peace with the Israelites (who would henceforth hold title to the land), or war.[59] In other words, there were "terms" after all. It should also be noted that the genocidal norms in question apply specifi-cally to the moment to which the text speaks, the moment in which Israel takes over the land, and only to certain na-tions, the seven Canaanite peoples who were to be dis-lodged from the land promised to the Israelite forefathers. Any effort to generalize it as a continuing practice, or even as a practice aimed at all non-Israelites in biblical times, cuts against the grain of the biblical text and rabbinic tra-dition (and law) alike. It would be a mistake to see the lit-eral sense of the text as teaching some timeless moral, or immoral, norm.

Just what message, then, *did* such texts hold for later hearers and readers? The mystery deepens if we remember that the notion of the genocide of the Canaanites is char-acteristically Deuteronomic, and that most historians of biblical literature date Deuteronomy to the late seventh century or so—in other words, many centuries after Israel had become dominant in Canaan.[60] Why so much animus and so much violence against peoples who had long before yielded to the Israelites?

In recent decades, scholars have made a good case that the target in the minds of the original (seventh-century BCE) authors and audiences of such texts was not the long-vanished foreign peoples at all; rather, it was the tenden-cies among the Israelites themselves to worship those other gods or, similarly, to worship the LORD himself in ways that the Deuteronomic authors find deviant and danger-ous, or to do so with less than wholehearted devotion.[61] This does not render the problematic texts morally inof-fensive; it is likely that they did inspire violence, though not genocide.[62] But if we bear in mind the probable audience and the larger theological point of these offending texts, we are less likely to fall into the hasty—and too convenient—moralism that dismisses them out of hand and distracts us from their ongoing theological message.

Deuteronomy 7:6–8, which we quoted above, gives the positive side of the same theology. Israel must rigorously and uncompromisingly differentiate itself from the other peoples and their gods because it is "consecrated to the LORD." The people Israel, in other words, are something special and unparalleled, like the God who made them "His treasured people" (v. 6).[63]

But why did he do so? Why did the singular God make Israel his singular people?

The answer that may come to mind first is that the Israelites must have been special in and of themselves, so that, in singling them out, God merely ratified an objective fact already in existence. If that is the case, the chosenness of Israel is really something independent of any free choice on God's part: it is an inherent attribute of the chosen themselves.

Could it be their enormous numbers? This, alas, is the kind of position that Deuteronomy 7:7 unequivocally *opposes*: "It is not because you are the most numerous of peoples that the LORD set His heart on you and chose you—indeed, you are the smallest of peoples."[64] Could it be some other attribute: their intelligence, perhaps, or their moral probity? On this point, we might do well instead to ponder the verb translated here as "set His heart on" (Hebrew, *ḥašaq*). In general, this rare verb and its associated noun (*ḥešeq*) mean something on the order of "take pleasure," "find delightful," "have a desire," as when the Bible tells us about "everything (*ḥešeq*) that Solomon set his heart (*ḥašaq*) on building" (1 Kgs 9:19). In two instances, though, the verb clearly has a sense that is more specifically erotic.

The first appears in Genesis 34, the story of the Hivite prince Shechem. This young man had raped Jacob's daughter Dinah but had also fallen in love (*vayye'ehav*, v. 3) with her, and now his father Hamor and he go to great lengths to persuade her family to allow him to marry her. Pleading Shechem's case, Hamor tells them, "My son Shechem longs for (*ḥašeqah naphšo*) your daughter. Please give her to him in marriage" (v. 8).

The second instance occurs closer to our Deuteronomic text about Israelite chosenness. It imposes limitations on what the victorious Israelite warrior can do with a woman he has captured:

> [10]When you take the field against your enemies, and the LORD your God delivers them into your power and you take some of them captive, [11]and you see among the captives a beautiful woman and you desire (*ḥašaqta*) her and would take her to wife, [12]you shall bring her into your house, and she shall trim her hair, pare her nails, [13]and discard her captive's garb. She shall spend a month's time in your house lamenting her father and mother; after that you may come to her and possess her, and she shall be your wife. [14]Then, should you no longer want her, you must release her outright. You must not sell her for money: since you had your will of her, you must not enslave her. (Deut 21:10–14)

Here, too, the sense of our verb is more specific and more erotic than is captured in a translation like "set your heart on" or even "desire." More accurate would be something on the order of "take a passion to."

Is that also the case with *ḥašaq* in Deuteronomy 7:7? If so, God's choice of the people Israel, his singling out them alone to be his "treasured people," is being ascribed to an affair of the heart, as it were, and not to any attribute or accomplishment that they had to their credit at the time. Similarly, the next verse tells us, he took them out of Egypt not (as many moderns erroneously believe) because he had a moral objection to slavery or anything of the kind but because he "loved" them and had solemnly sworn to their patriarchs that he would give the land of Canaan to their descendants.[65]

To be sure, in that latter verse the word for "love" (*'ahavat*) may have only its narrower, diplomatic sense: it may signify merely that the LORD fulfilled his covenantal obligation to rescue his vassal and imply nothing about his affect in so doing. But the cumulative evidence of *ḥašaq* in Deuteronomy 7:7 and *'ahavat* in verse 8 argues, in my judgment, for something more passionate. It suggests that because God fell in love with the Israelites (or with their ancestors, the patriarchs of Genesis), he entered into a covenant with them, the very covenant that brought about their liberation from Egypt and now demands a reciprocal faithfulness from the beneficiaries of the redemption.[66]

As we shall see at length in chapter 3, the metaphor of husband and wife appears several times in the prophets to denote the God-Israel relationship. Deuteronomy 7:6–8 shows us the background of that powerful metaphor in the institution of covenant. As different as the God of Israel is from the warrior of Deuteronomy 21:10–14, and all the more so, obviously, from Shechem in Genesis 34, he, too, sought to marry the one for whom he took a passion, as it were. And, as the texts would have it, he did just that.

This is a metaphor whose implications will reverberate throughout Jewish history.

Why Did God Choose the Jews?

The notion that the Jewish people had done nothing to merit God's choosing them is a problematic idea, and we should not be surprised to find that its resonance in ancient Judaism decreased over time. The dominant position in the Bible, it yielded to a different one in rabbinic literature.

In the biblical narrative, the earliest sign that God would form a special relationship with the people Israel occurs when, for the first time, he speaks to Abraham, the grandfather of Israel (or Jacob, to use his other name), promising him that he will be a great nation and a byword or source of blessing.[67] But why Abraham? Genesis reports absolutely nothing to suggest that the future patriarch already merited such a distinction more than did, say, his brother Nahor.

Genesis does not use the language of love to describe the relationship of God to Abraham or, for that matter, to the next two fathers of the Jewish people, Isaac and Jacob. Although it twice records God's making a covenant with Abraham,[68] the characteristically Deuteronomic covenantal language of love is not present, and we would be mistaken to assume that the choice, according to Genesis, stemmed from God's falling in love with the grandfather of the Jewish people. Still, on the plain sense of the text, God's singling out Abraham for the special relationship, not to mention for the gift of the land that is central to it, does come as a bolt out of the blue. No reason is given for it. It seems mysterious.

It can be argued that as the narrative unfolds, Abraham proves himself increasingly worthy of the promise God made to him at the outset. And already in Genesis itself, we find the promise to Abraham reformulated so that it is a consequence of a specific deed—his willingness to sacrifice his beloved son, Isaac, on whom the promise rests, and his preparations to do so: "Because you have done this and have not withheld your son, your favored one, I will bestow My blessing upon you" (Gen 22:16–17). The passage in which these words appear is not only the earliest interpretation of the Binding of Isaac, or Aqedah, as it is known in Judaism; it is also arguably the earliest effort to remove the offense of Abraham's—and thus the Jews'—being chosen and promised so much on the basis of the grace of God alone, with no merit of their own to justify it.[69]

That effort grew over time. In the Second Temple period, Jewish literature presented an Abraham who rediscovered God, reasoned his way to a belief in the creator and thus to the subordination of all things to him, and saw through idolatry and astrology, along with the materialist and determinist assumptions they reflect—and did all this *before* God first spoke to him. Abraham, in short, finds God before God discloses himself to Abraham. Some Second Temple Jewish literature even claims that Abraham observed the Mosaic law generations before Moses![70] All these ideas will later make their way into rabbinic literature (and all but the last into Islam as well) and become well known to Jewish schoolchildren for centuries afterward. They make Abraham into a special person on his own and before God singled him out and gave him the extraordinary promises that started him on his way.

Similar things happen elsewhere in rabbinic literature. A good example concerns the gift of the Torah itself. In midrash we find the idea, again altogether absent from the Bible, that God offered the Torah to the Gentiles. And why? "So that they would not have an excuse to say, 'Had we been asked, we would have accepted it.'" But, of course, each of the nations finds something in the Torah that contradicts its characteristic inclination as the Torah itself defines it, while Israel alone accepts the gift and does so without inquiring into its contents in advance, thus demonstrating their superior devotion and obedience.[71]

Such narratives not only justify Abraham and the Jewish people, respectively; they also justify God, going a long way toward exonerating him of the charge of arbitrariness.[72] For, as the poet John Dryden said of great wits and madness, grace and arbitrariness are also "near allied / And thin partitions do their bounds divide."[73] It often happens that the beneficiary of good fortune identifies the cause as divine grace and, accordingly, feeling an enormous sense of gratitude, praises God for what has come to him. The apparently equally deserving person who experiences *mis*fortune is tempted to brand his fate as arbitrary, to feel cheated, and as a result either to doubt the justice of God or to challenge him to do justice.

A favor that is *merited* is no favor. But why then is it done? A gift that is earned is not really a gift. But why then is it given? There is something in *hesed* that offends our sense of fairness. God's *hesed* is no exception.

Before we condemn the idea out of hand, however, it would be worth asking about the positive moral effects of this ethically problematic notion.

We turn first to the passage in Deuteronomy on which we have been concentrating. "It is not because you are the most numerous of peoples that the LORD set His heart on you and chose you—indeed, you are the smallest of peoples," Moses goes out of his way to say; "but it was because the LORD loved you" (Deut 7:7–8). The Israelite inclined to attribute his nation's lofty status to its own greatness would surely be disappointed to hear that whatever greatness it may possess does not lie in numbers. And lest he think it lies in some other attribute instead—intelligence, innate spirituality, superior ethics, or whatever—the next clause, as we have seen, rebuffs any such notion. Instead, it ascribes Israel's specialness to God's love.

This is important because it makes it impossible for the attentive hearer of the text to identify chosenness with superiority—a mistake that is very common today, especially among those who find the whole idea of chosenness distasteful. For, like Abraham when God first speaks to him, Israel does not work its way into the role of the beneficiary of God's concern. As the text in Deuteronomy goes on to say, the very liberation of its hearers from the Egyptian house of bondage is not the result of anything the people did or even of the unmerited favor they have directly received from their divine redeemer: it results instead from the oath that God made to the patriarchs generations earlier (Deut 7:8).[74]

The descendants, then, have inherited their lofty status. They have not *achieved* it. It is a gift, not a reward. In response, they should feel not pride but gratitude, not satisfaction with their performance in the past but a profound challenge to live up to their divine benefactor's expectations in the future: "Therefore," the same passage goes on to say, "observe faithfully the Instruction—the laws and the rules—with which I charge you today" (Deut 7:11).

And so, one positive moral effect of God's gift of love is that it encourages humility. The people Israel would be making a catastrophic theological error to attribute their unique and unparalleled status to anything but God's act of grace. In modern times there has been a tendency to classify the chosenness of the Jews alongside various doctrines of racial superiority, but in the biblical thinking it is a matter neither of race nor of superiority. The people Israel is not racially or ethnically different from the peoples abutting them, any more than Abraham is racially or ethnically different from his unchosen brothers, or Jacob/Israel from his unchosen twin, Esau. The origin of the difference lies in a mysterious and gracious—and, to some, infuriatingly arbitrary—gift of God: it is motivated by his love for them.

As we have seen, the notion that Israel's very existence and good fortune were unmerited, a pure gift of grace, troubled the Talmudic sages. Interestingly, however, their efforts to mitigate it, to reduce the apparent arbitrariness and injustice of God that it implies, did not come at the expense of the biblical ethic of humility and self-effacement. On that key verse, "It is not because you are the most numerous of peoples that the LORD set His heart (*ḥašaq*) on you and chose you [—indeed, you are the smallest (*meʿaṭ*) of peoples]" (Deut 7:7), we find this:

The Holy One (blessed be He!) said to Israel: I set My heart on you (*ḥošeqeni*) because even when I bestow greatness on you, you make yourselves small (*mema'aṭim*) before Me. I bestowed greatness on Abraham, and he said, "I am but dust and ashes" (Gen 18:27); on Moses and Aaron, and he [Moses] said, "We are nothing" (Exod 16:8); on David, and he said, "But I am a worm, less than human" (Ps 22:7).

But that is not the way it is among the idolaters. I bestowed greatness on Nimrod, and he said, "Come, let us build a city for ourselves [and a tower with its top in the heavens, to make a name for ourselves]!" (Gen 11:2); on Pharaoh, and he said, "Who is the LORD [that I should heed him and let Israel go]?" (Exod 5:2); on Sennacherib, and he said, "Which among all the gods of [those] countries [saved their countries from me, that the LORD should save Jerusalem from me]?" (2 Kgs 18:35); on Nebuchadnezzar, and he said, "I will mount the back of a cloud [— / I will match the Most High]" (Isa 14:14); on King Hiram of Tyre, and he said, "I sit enthroned like a god in the heart of the seas" (Ezek 28:2). (*b. Ḥullin* 89b)[75]

This midrash contrasts the self-effacement of Israelite figures with the self-aggrandizement and self-deification of various non-Israelite rulers, most of whom are among the violent oppressors of the Jewish people: Pharaoh, the Assyrian ruler Sennacherib, and the Babylonian emperor Nebuchadnezzar, who destroyed the temple and drove the elite of the Kingdom of Judah into exile. The Jews do not allow their good fortune and high status to go to their heads; they recognize their continuing unworthiness. The idolaters do the opposite: they seek to challenge God himself; some think they are themselves God.

We must not miss the subtle two-sidedness here of God's love for the people Israel. On the one hand, Deuteronomy 7:7 denies that Israel's greatness accounts for their unique status in God's eyes. Rather, that status, that special-ness, is owing to God's love for them, the fact that he conceived a passion (*ḥašaq*) for them, as it were, and (the next verse goes on to say) took them out of Egypt because of his covenantal love for their patriarchs. On the other hand, the midrash on Deuteronomy 7:7 interprets that favor, that passion, as itself God's reaction to Israel's receiving their good fortune in humility and self-effacement. It imagines his saying, in effect, "I set My heart on/take a passion to (*ḥošeqeni*) the Jews precisely because they do not imagine themselves to be great."

The greatness of Israel is thus their recognition that their greatness comes from God, not themselves. The merit of Israel is, paradoxically, that they do not ascribe their success to their merit. In its own way, this midrash serves to rationalize the chosenness of the Jews by showing that it is not arbitrary, yet it does so in a way that continues to uphold God's love for Israel and the surpassing importance of humility for those who experience his grace.

RESPONDING IN GRATITUDE

The virtue of gratitude, which is a key component of covenantal theology and one that I have now mentioned several times, is closely associated with that of humility. It deserves more sustained attention, for it is the source of some major objections to the whole notion of covenantal obligation. We begin again with a text from Deuteronomy:

> [10]When the LORD your God brings you into the land that He swore to your fathers, Abraham, Isaac, and Jacob, to assign to you—great and flourishing cities that you did not build, [11]houses full of all good things that you did not fill, hewn cisterns that you did not hew, vineyards and olive groves that you did not plant—and you eat your fill,

[12]take heed that you do not forget the LORD who freed you from the land of Egypt, the house of bondage. [13]Revere only the LORD your God and worship Him alone, and swear only by His name. [14]Do not follow other gods, any gods of the peoples about you—[15]for the LORD your God in your midst is a jealous God—lest the anger of the LORD your God blaze forth against you and He wipe you off the face of the earth. (Deut 6:10–15)[76]

The demand for exclusive service made in verses 13–15 is familiar to us; it is, as we saw at length, intrinsic to the dynamics of covenant in general and to the covenantal love that is God's due in particular. What is noteworthy here is that covenantal service is presented as the appropriate response not simply to God's gift of liberation from slavery but also to the gift of cities, houses, cisterns, vineyards, and olive orchards from which Israel benefits but for which, significantly, it did not labor.

Here, too, there are productive analogies in ancient Near Eastern treaties. The Hittite emperor to whom we referred earlier tells his vassal this: "To be sure, you were sick and ailing, but although you were ailing, I, the Sun, put you in the place of your father and took your brothers (and) sisters and the Amurru land in oath for you."[77] In both cases, the Israelite and the Hittite, the assumption is the same: were it not for the generosity of the greater party to the covenant, the lesser one would lack the ample benefits that have been confirmed on him. The service, then, is a way of expressing gratitude: it is a "thank you" in deeds and not just words.

Here, an obvious objection arises. Is this not a case of the suzerain's "guilt-tripping" the vassal into doing his will, as my students have often put it, perhaps remembering unpleasant confrontations with parents who were overbearing, or perceived to be so? The suzerain has supposedly done a favor for the vassal, even manifested love for him, yet the suzerain's subsequent demand undercuts the very idea of favor and shows that something very far from love was at work all along. For if, as the philosopher Irving Singer puts it, "Love is sheer gratuity,"[78] then the very expectation of repayment seems to remove the whole interaction from the realm of love. Moreover, beneath the mention of the favors the greater party has done for the lesser, does there not also lurk a threat that they might be withdrawn, so that the weaker figure had better "pay up" or face bigger problems ahead? In that case, the lord in covenant, whether an ancient Near Eastern king or the God of Israel, is more like a neighborhood shakedown artist than a benevolent protector and deliverer.

Is such a charge fair?

At least in the case of the LORD, we might begin to answer by questioning the key assumption that his motivation is self-interested. Later in Jewish history, when Aristotelian ideas of divine perfection and self-sufficiency become prominent, the notion of a God who *needs* anything at all becomes a contradiction in terms. In that case, God's creating and maintaining the world and singling out the Jewish people cannot be attributed to a mercenary motive.

But even within the biblical canon, where these philosophical ideas have not taken hold, does it really make sense to say that the LORD *needs* Israel's service the same way a gang leader needs the money or power that comes from his criminal activities? The opposite would seem, rather, to be the case: a variety of sources within the Bible present God's singling out of Abraham and of Israel as what I earlier called "a bolt out of the blue"—a surprising and unexplained act of generosity for which few if any acts of service are required in return.

In fact, God's covenant with Abraham, like the covenant of Sinai, has its own ancient Near Eastern analogues, but they are different in a critical way from the ones we have discussed so far. In Moshe Weinfeld's particular terminology, Sinai is a "treaty," whereas the Abrahamic covenant (and others like it) falls into the category of a "grant." "While the grant is a reward for loyalty and good deeds already performed," he writes, "the treaty is an inducement for future loyalty."[79]

This means that within the structure of the Torah narrative as it now stands, the very existence of the people Israel is owing to that reward to Abraham, to God's gracious fulfillment of his surprising and unexpected promise to make of him "a great nation" (Gen 12:2), made to Abraham when he was childless and married to an infertile woman. It also means that when, after about another seven generations, Israel stands at Sinai to accept the covenant that will be "an inducement for future loyalty," they are anything but an autonomous and independent party who are in a neutral position relative to God and thus entitled to decline his offer of covenant with impunity. In fact, at that moment they are already in a covenant with him—the covenant with Abraham, renewed for Isaac and Jacob in turn. God's gracious and unmerited promise accounts for the existence of the people Israel in the first place. After all, they are not one of the original seventy nations of Genesis 10, but (again as the biblical narrative has it) come into existence in fulfillment of God's covenantal pledge to their childless ancestor. The covenant also accounts for their liberation from Pharaoh and escape from Egypt and thus their ability to negotiate in the first place.

All this is very far from our modern experience, and, as a result, our first inclination is to discount the narrative as it stands and to replace it with something more familiar: those overbearing parents manipulating their teenaged child or that criminal shaking down the defenseless storekeepers on his block.[80] But however convenient these analogies may be, they not only show a depressing lack of religious imagination but also do violence to the biblical narrative—precisely because they miss the moral implications of gratitude.

As the psychologist Robert Emmons observes, various thinkers have "theorized that gratitude is a moral affect— that is, one with moral precursors and consequences. They hypothesized that by experiencing gratitude, a person is motivated to carry out prosocial behavior, energized to sustain moral behaviors, and is inhibited from committing destructive interpersonal behaviors."[81] If these thinkers are right, as I believe they are, then one who properly experiences gratitude for favors received has in the process incurred a moral debt to his benefactor. His failure to discharge that debt would not be a defensible option: it would indicate a moral defect. If, moreover, the benefactor wishes the best for his beneficiary, he will discourage him from persisting in the ungrateful behavior that has disrupted the relationship.

The analogy with the guilt-tripping parent or the shakedown artist thus does not do justice to the biblical text. A better analogy would be one that involved our relationship with a person who has done us a large and unexpected favor out of the goodness of his or her heart.

Imagine that your car has broken down on a busy, dangerous road, and somebody stops and fixes it for you. Now imagine that a few weeks later you happen to see that same person in line at the supermarket, where, finding he is a few dollars short of the tab, he asks to borrow the difference from you. Legally, you can, of course, turn him down flat. But would doing so be morally appropriate? Were he a total stranger, there might be nothing wrong with simply saying "no" and walking away (and if you did lend him the money, you surely could not be accused of conniving to put him in your debt). But he is not a total stranger: a relationship already exists between you. If you treat him as a stranger, you will not only be violating that relationship but also acting in a morally shoddy manner.

This is only an analogy and an imperfect one at that. In principle, you could have turned down the offer of assistance on the road, whereas Israel never seems to have been in a position to turn down its covenant with the LORD. For the covenant with Abraham is only announced, never offered, and although Israel at Sinai, even before learning the stipulations of the covenant, respond immediately, "All that the LORD has spoken we will do!" (Exod 19:8), they were, according to the biblical story, hardly in a position in the desert to forgo divine protection and try to take the Promised Land without the help of the one who promised it. It is also surely true that whereas the person who assisted you on the road asks for the loan only from you, not from your descendants, the biblical covenantal relationship extends through all the generations: Israel is never released from it.

Partly, this is because the characteristic biblical concept of the self is familial and intergenerational and thus very different from the individualistic alternative that has become dominant in the modern West.[82] But partly, it is also because covenant in the Bible is a kind of existential stance and not simply a historical phenomenon confined to the past. In fact, Deuteronomy is especially eager to have its hearers participate personally in the renewal of covenant and not view it and the gifts upon which it rests as confined to an irrelevant past. Although those hearers are the post-Sinai Israelites who have survived the wilderness and are about to face warfare in the Promised Land, it is hard not to perceive in the narrative an address to future generations who, like them, did not stand at Sinai (which Deuteronomy calls "Horeb") and may therefore think they are not obligated by their ancestors' covenant:

> [2]The LORD our God made a covenant with us at Horeb.
> [3]It was not with our fathers that the LORD made this covenant, but with us, the living, every one of us who is here today. (Deut 5:2–3)

Still, even when allowances are made for the limitations of our analogy with the helpful driver-turned-borrower, we can still see that God's demand for covenantal service is something much more subtle than guilt-tripping or extortion. And if we see that clearly, we should not be surprised that the response of Israel in the biblical narrative, and of countless Jews through the centuries, has been one not of bitterness and resentment but rather of joyful acceptance, gratitude, and humility—in a word, love.

Once we understand the role gratitude plays in covenantal love, we must qualify Singer's claim that "Love is sheer gratuity." In the Deuteronomic vision, God's love for Israel is indeed gratuitous: Israel did nothing to merit it and, in fact, chronically acts in defiance of it. "Well I know how defiant and stiffnecked you are," Moses admonishes Israel at the end of his life: "even now, while I am still alive in your midst, you have been defiant toward the LORD; how much more, then, when I am dead!" (Deut 31:27). The fact that God bears with them nonetheless, honoring his unconditional promise to the patriarchs, testifies to the sheer graciousness of his relationship with them.

But graciousness does not mean normlessness, and if love is to be a relationship and not just an ephemeral and episodic sentiment, it must impose norms of its own (even if violating them does not terminate the relationship). Perhaps the norms are best seen as the expectations that the lover has of the beloved. For surely we all want those we love to be the best they can be and the relationship of love to be the highest relationship it can be.

In short, love may originate as "sheer gratuity," but unless it is to be chaotic and endlessly frustrating, it must also harbor moral expectations within it. We have already mentioned one obvious expectation of genuine love, namely, that it be reciprocal. Unrequited love may not terminate a relationship—so great may be the "sheer gratuity" of the lover's gift—but it certainly degrades it and deeply disappoints the lover. With regard to covenantal love, Singer is thus both right and wrong when he writes: "In loving another person, however, we enact a nonmoral *loyalty*—like the mother who stands by her criminal son even though she knows he is guilty."[83] God stands by Israel even when they breach the covenant in the most egregious and defiant ways, and Israel (ideally) stands by God even when they plausibly accuse him of gross injustice, as indeed they do at times.[84] But standing by does not mean approving, failing to correct, or being unwilling to discipline. In other words, it does not mean accepting something less from the beloved than the best he can do. Covenantal love includes both a nonmoral loyalty and a passionate insistence that the other partner live up to the terms of the covenant and make himself worthy of the gratuitous love he has received. More than a few loving mothers have no doubt insisted on the same from their criminal sons.

As a broad generalization, we might say that in the covenantal theology of the Bible, the element of sheer gratuity and nonmoral loyalty is found in the Abrahamic covenant, and the element of conditionality and moral demand in the Sinaitic. But, as we have seen, the two covenants interpenetrate, and, in the text as it stands, they cannot be disengaged. The gratuity endures even as the stipulations of Sinai are stated, then violated, and finally—

> [6]The LORD has called you back
> As a wife forlorn and forsaken.
> Can one cast off the wife of his youth?
> —said your God.
>
> [7]For a little while I forsook you,
> But with vast love I will bring you back.
> [8]In slight anger, for a moment,
> I hid My face from you;
> But with kindness everlasting
> I will take you back in love
> —said the LORD your Redeemer.
>
> *Isaiah 54:6–8*

and graciously—offered anew to a repentant and restored Israel.

From a more abstract perspective, we can see the Abrahamic covenant and its element of gratuity reflecting the giftedness of life: we do not invent ourselves but at best continually reorient ourselves in the context of a reality we did not choose. As a rabbi of the second century CE put it, "Without your consent you have been formed; without your consent you have been born; without your consent you live; and without your consent you will die; and without your consent you are destined to give an account before the Supreme King of Kings, the Holy One (blessed be He!)" (*m. Avot* 4:22). We come into the world in a particular body, a particular family, a particular culture, and a particular historical moment: we do not choose any of them, and although we can change some of them to an extent, we can never fully replace them. We do not (to give some obvious examples) select our natural parents, our birthday, or our mother tongue; we become aware of them as we grow and achieve our particular identities; but we cannot change them. Discovering ourselves to be in relationships that we never chose is a key component in the process of becoming responsible adults.

Similarly, as the Torah has it, the people Israel did not select and cannot change the fact that they come into the world in a certain relationship with God. They can, of course, betray that relationship and defy that God, and, as the Torah presents the matter, they have a long history of doing exactly that. But betrayal and defiance are not neutral; they attack but do not defeat the relationship of the people and their God. The gifts that helped establish the relationship in the first place (especially the gift of existence itself) make a claim of their own; there is no way of sending them back. Israel can honor the giver or dishonor him; there is no third option. In this thinking, the characteristically modern hope that we can be exempt of all obligations that we did not freely accept proves false. The very "we" who so hope came into the world in a tissue of relationships that impose moral demands of their own.

As we mature, we become aware of the gifts and can no longer simply accept them without consciousness of the ethical obligations they entail. Our parents, to return to one obvious example, gave us life and (ideally) much else, but at some point we become capable of giving to them in return and, in most cases, are eager to do so. This is not a repayment in a crude financial sense, as if we could somehow acquit ourselves of our debt to them and move on, all obligations between the parties having been duly discharged. Rather, the mutual gift-giving is an aspect of the ongoing relationship in which we and they stand, a relationship that has now become more reciprocal (though not equal: child and parent are not interchangeable roles). The gift-giving has become part of the relationship of love. The gifts remain gratuitous—they come without strings attached—yet they deepen, widen, and enrich a relationship of reciprocal obligation.

And so, when at Sinai/Horeb God makes his great claim on Israel's service and Israel immediately accepts it, we have a powerful narrative representation of the dynamics of covenantal love—not law as the antithesis of love, or love as a substitute for law, but love made practical, reliable, reciprocal, and socially responsible through law, divine law observed in love.

The Unending Covenant

The relationship of the people Israel and their God as they are about to receive his covenant in the book of Exodus is portrayed as an idyllic one. God has redeemed his "treasured possession among all the peoples" and now offers to perpetuate the relationship in a formal covenant, and Israel accepts without hesitation (Exod 19:5, 8). The relation, of course, soon sours: Israel repeatedly proves ungrateful, and God repeatedly threatens to annihilate them and must be talked out of so drastic an act by Moses's appeal to his reputation, to his irrevocable promise to the patriarchs, or to the prospect of the prophet's own resignation in protest.[85] Were we to judge by those moments of catastrophe, we would have to say that the original relationship of love had surely been terminated.

But to do so would be to miss the crucial fact that there is something about biblical covenant that locks in the dispositions characteristic of the idyllic situation and makes them normative for both parties. That is why, to the surprise of some, the horrors that follow never cancel the pertinence of God's initial love, and though the covenant repeatedly seems on the verge of dissolution, it is never, in fact, ended but always renewed.[86] The idyllic past has become foundational, and covenantal loyalty—the unqualified love with which we began this chapter—proves able to withstand the horrors of the present.

In chapter 2, we shall see texts that portray Jews' love of God withstanding even the most hideous and undeserved experiences of suffering and even death.

TWO

Heart, Soul, and Might

Rabbi Elazar of Bartota says: Give Him what
is His, for you and what you have are His. As
David says in Scripture, "It is all from You,
and it is Your gift that we have given to You."
Mishnah[1]

$\mathscr{W}$e have now seen that the love of God as conceived
in the Shema and the Deuteronomy theology that underlies it is in the first instance a duty owed by Israel to their
lord in covenant. It expresses a central element in the covenantal institution as it was understood in ancient Israel
and in the Near Eastern cultures in which the institution
was devised. That element is faithfulness in alliance, the
vassal's reliable loyalty to his suzerain, a loyalty discharged
in specific actions the vassal performs, or refrains from
performing, in response to the will of his lord. In this
framework, the love of God is both legal and relational:
legal, because it requires and describes specific mandatory
behaviors, and relational, because those behaviors flow not
from some abstract, universal moral code, philosophical
proposition, or process of nature but from a particular—
and very personal—relationship, the experience the two

parties have had of each other and the expectations that it elicits.

If we bear the legal dimension in mind, we shall avoid the reflexive modern temptation to see the love in question as a matter of mere sentiment or as an idiosyncratic gesture. If we remember the relational dimension, we shall avoid the pitfall, especially common in Christian and post-Christian cultures, of seeing the love of God in Judaism as defining a burdensome set of dry legalisms, devoid of vitality and spirit. Both of these misunderstandings can, truth to tell, appear at times in the life of practicing Jews. But both are deformations of the classical Jewish ideal of the religious life, and neither does justice to that ideal or to Judaism as its practitioners have described it over the millennia.

The legal dimension of the love of God explains the anomaly (anomalous, that is, for moderns but not for the ancients) that love can be commanded. The explanation is that, covenantally conceived, love is defined, first and foremost, by a set of deeds. The deeds are not dependent on emotion: whether or not individuals feel a sentiment that they name as "love," they are always obligated to serve their lord. In this way of thinking, the deed is far more than an outpouring of a feeling into the world of action, and the publicly observable religious life is far more than the externalization of an inner state. Indeed, in the absence of a feeling of love, people may perform the practices instead from habit, social conformity, or acceptance of certain traditional theological claims. One such claim is that practitioners will be rewarded but violators punished—a claim that is very prominent in biblical covenant texts and their Near Eastern antecedents and contemporaries.

But, in chapter 1, I also pointed out that deeds, however motivated, can themselves produce motivations: the flow between the two is not one-directional. And when the deeds are described in language that also describes more primal relationships—for the language of love also describes the relationship between parents and children and between husbands and wives—and when that language is ritually repeated every day, the deeds can play a role in creating the emotion, or in sustaining it in periods of spiritual dryness.

The promise of blessing and the threat of curse in covenant texts can suggest that the relationship of the master and the servant begins in self-interest, even if it ideally ends in a transcendence of self-interest. At the level of individuals, this is no doubt often the case. But in the national story, as narrated and sung in biblical texts, the relationship begins with the suzerain's unprovoked love for the vassal, specifically with the LORD's falling in love (rather mysteriously) with Israel or their originating ancestors. In the biblical telling, this love was manifested in the benefits the LORD conveyed on Israel before entering into the covenant of Sinai with them. Principal among those benefits is the exodus from Egypt and the rescue of Israel at the sea. The narratives about those events (however much or however little validity they have as objective history) undergird the key theological claims that the LORD is possessed of unparalleled and indisputable power, exercises sovereignty over the world and all who dwell in it, and, most important for our purposes, holds a perpetual claim upon the specific people he has liberated. The service of the liberated is the condign response to the generosity of the liberator. It is their response of love to his antecedent love for them, without which they would not have come into being or survived.

Within the structure of covenantal love, the relationship between the two parties is, on the one hand, familiar to anyone who has truly loved, especially anyone who has truly loved and been loved by a parent. But, on the other hand, it seems very complicated and difficult to state in ordinary prose. For one thing, the relationship is both unconditional and conditional. It is unconditional in that the love comes into, and remains, in force even when nothing has been done to deserve it. (Some would say such unconditionality is part of the definition of true love.) But the relationship is also conditional in that it involves expectations and stipulations, and suffers and turns sour if they are not met. To adopt the terminology of Christian theology, love as conceived here may seem a matter of both grace and works. But efforts, like those found in some streams of Christianity, to render one or the other of these absolute, and the other only a consequence, fail to do the relationship justice.

Why do we have such difficulty stating the relationship in simple expository prose? The reason is actually not hard to find. It is that the relationship is between *persons*—the divine Person who is God and the human person who is the people Israel: a group, to be sure, but one often understood in the classical biblical and rabbinic sources as an individual. Were we dealing not with a personal God but with an impersonal force, an ideal, a moral principle, a scientific law, a mathematical formula, or the like, our task would be different and, however technical, ultimately easier to accomplish.

Perhaps this is one of the reasons for the eagerness of some to define God in impersonal terms. The alternative to this is less manageable because it is less predictable and controllable. After all, titles ("supervisor," "CEO," "assistant") and terms of relationship ("father," "mother," "son," "cousin," "friend," "partner") tell us something that is useful in a formal legalistic sense, predictable and manageable. But if one's relationship with the other person has any depth or longevity, these words seem dreadfully inadequate and simplistic. The same is true for the declaration, frequent in its various forms in the Bible, "I will be your God, and you shall be My people" (Lev 26:12). The declaration only gestures at the covenantal relationship. It may summarize it; it can never adequately convey it.

SELFLESSNESS AND SELF-INTEREST

Let us now return to the question of self-interest in the covenantal relationship, a particularly difficult point in biblical thinking about the love of God. We have repeatedly seen that appeals to self-interest play a prominent role in the biblical covenant texts. Those faithful in covenant are promised ample reward: health, long life, fertility, wealth, and sovereignty over their own land and peace within it. Those who breach the covenant are threatened with the reverse: disease, death, loss of children, impoverishment, national subjugation, war, and exile.[2]

In rabbinic theology, this duality remains, though it has a more individualistic character; the rabbis are more likely to speak of the righteous person and the sinner, though both still stand solidly within the collective that is the Jewish people. (Rabbinic moral theology comprehends other types than just these two, including the person in the middle who could break in either direction and the ex-sinner who has repented.) The ancient rabbis are also likely to speak less of covenant and more of Torah and mitzvot (commandments).

But most strikingly, in rabbinic literature the question of motivation, the *subjective* dimension to the observance of objective law, is a matter of much greater importance and much more explicit attention than it is in the Bible. A good example of this are the midrashim on the key verse, "love the Lord your God with all your heart and with all your soul and with all your might" (Deut 6:5):

> *You shall love the Lord your God* (6:5): Perform (God's commandments) out of love. Scripture makes a distinction between one who performs out of love and one who performs out of fear. He who performs out of love receives a doubled and redoubled reward, as it is said, *You must fear the Lord your God: only Him shall you serve*

(10:20): A may [serve B] because he is afraid of him, but when B needs him, A abandons him and goes his own way. You, however, must perform out of love. Only in regard to God do we find love combined with fear and fear combined with love. (*Siphre Deut* 32)[3]

Here, the midrash makes a distinction between the love and the fear of God—fear understood not as the proper response to the overwhelming glory and majesty of God but rather as dread of punishment. This distinction between love and fear is one that, as we noted in chapter 1, the Hebrew Bible on its plain sense does not make. And, also unlike the case in the biblical usage, love and fear here refer to *motivations* for observance rather than to the state of being observant. To secure the new distinction, the midrash utilizes Deuteronomy 10:20, in which "fear" parallels "serve," a verb that derives from the same root as the noun for "slave" (*'avad/'eved*).

The reasoning seems to be as follows: whereas the one who loves "performs" (*'aśah*) God's commandments from a motivation of love, the one who fears God "serves" (*'avad*) in the manner of a slave. And how does a slave serve? He does so only because he is afraid of his master, so that when the tables are turned and the master becomes dependent on the slave, the slave walks away from his service.[4] In other words, because it depends on external circumstances, the service does not survive those circumstances. The implication is that love, because it is internalized and independent of circumstance, is more enduring. And so, because the Jew's performance of the commandments needs to be enduring and not episodic, it must ultimately be motivated by the love, not the fear, of God.

It is interesting that this text, like rabbinic theology in general, stops short of dismissing the fear of God altogether. Though its last sentence ("Only in regard to God do we find love combined with fear and fear combined with love") seems out of place, the point is clear—a ringing endorsement of the need for both love and fear in the religious life, despite the tension between them.

Perhaps the conjunction of the two was suggested by the next clause in Deuteronomy 10:20—"to Him shall you hold fast (*tidbaq*)"—which uses a verb (*davaq*) that suggests a relationship of powerful love.[5] Or perhaps the conjunction of love and fear in regard to the service of God was prompted by a verse that appears very soon thereafter: "Love, therefore, the LORD your God, and always keep His charge, His laws, His rules, and His commandments" (Deut 11:1).[6] Either way, we see a case in which rabbinic literature insists, as did the Bible beforehand, that both love and fear are necessary and neither can be summarily dispensed with. Even as the rabbis distinguish between the two, prioritizing love over fear, as the Bible did not, they nonetheless retain them both.

But why? Why not just discard the slavish fear and replace it with the nobler and hardier love of God altogether? The answer that first comes to mind is simply that the fear of God so pervades the Bible and is there regarded so positively that the ancient rabbis could not do away with it even if they had so desired. For all their creativity and for all the changes they wrought (including the fear/love dichotomy), they did not see themselves as starting a new religion. Rather, they regarded themselves as standing faithfully under the authority of the Torah, and Torah for them was not an infinitely elastic phenomenon or one whose ostensibly distasteful features could be altogether nullified at will and thus brought into comfortable conformity with the preferences of one generation or another.

A midrash puts this point well. On the words, "For this is not a trifling thing for [literally, 'from'] you: it is your very life" (Deut 32:47), it comments, "If it is 'a trifling thing,' it is 'from [that is, because of] you.' Why? Because you are not laboring over it ... When is it 'your very life'? When you labor over it" (*y. Pe'ah* 1:1). To apply this reasoning to the matter at hand: if we think the fear of God is dispensable, we need to think again—and to apply ourselves to the Torah with greater rigor and investigate it in greater depth.

There is also another and more philosophical reason for the rabbinic retention of the fear of God. As we saw in chapter 1, the rabbis were none too optimistic about human nature. They admired and advocated selfless service but saw the need for incentives, positive and negative, to bring people into a proper relationship with God and to keep them there if they are not perfectly saintly, and perhaps even if they are. If one respects only love and not fear, or selfless giving and not self-interested service, the chances fall drastically that people will observe the commandments and attain to the best motivation for doing so.

All this yields a subtle and complex picture of the relationship of self-interest to divine service. The rewards and punishments exist: the Torah affirms them, human nature needs them, and, we may add, the notion that God is just requires them (for what kind of judge disregards the merits of those who stand before him?). The goal, though, is to perform the mitzvot without concern for the rewards, as stated in a famous Mishnah in the name of a very early, in fact prerabbinic, authority:

> Antigonus of Sokho received [the teachings of Torah] from Simon the Just. He used to say: Do not be like servants who serve their master in order to receive a reward, but be like servants who serve their master not in order to receive a reward; and let the fear of Heaven be upon you. (*m. Avot* 1:3)

On the one hand, the servants are to ignore the prospect that the master will reward them. On the other hand, they are to have "the fear of Heaven"—a rabbinic euphemism for "God"—upon them: a fairly clear acknowledgment that misbehavior carries consequences.

No term for "love" appears in Antigonus's saying, but Rashi, the most influential commentator on the Bible and the Talmud (Northern France, 1040–1105), interprets the point of serving not in order to receive a reward as meaning, "You should not say, 'I will carry out the commandments of my Creator so that He will supply me with all my needs,' but, instead, serve out of love" (to *b. Avot* 5a). In his commentary on the Mishnah, Moses Maimonides, the great Sephardi legal authority, philosopher, and communal leader (Spain, Morocco, and Egypt, 1138–1204),[7] interprets the end of Antigonus's saying as reiterating the classical rabbinic theology in which the love and the fear of God both have a place: "Though you are serving out of love, do not set fear aside altogether, for the commandment to fear [God] was already stated in the Torah, 'the LORD your God you shall fear' (Deut 6:13), and the sages said, 'Serve from love, serve from fear' (*y. Ber.* 9:7)."[8] Here, as in rabbinic literature, the fear of God is understood not as awe in the face of God's infinite majesty but rather as the dread of punishment. Even the one who serves out of love must not neglect divine justice.

Although the saying of Antigonus of Sokho makes no reference to love, other rabbinic literature explicitly associates the disregard of external inducements with the commandment to love, such as this comment on "to love the LORD your God" in Deuteronomy 11:13:

> You might say, "I am going to study Torah in order to become rich," or "in order to be called Rabbi," or "in order to receive a reward in the world-to-come"; therefore Scripture says, *To love the LORD your God*—whatever you do should be done only out of love. (*Siphre Deut* 41)[9]

An augmented version of the same text articulates the paradox of divine service explicitly and succinctly: "Study [Torah] out of love, and in the end honor will come" (*b. Nedarim* 62a).

Rooted in the morality of gratitude, the love of God so conceived should not be classified as a mere reciprocal exchange, tit for tat. In contemporary terms, the paradox underlying it can be stated this way: the selfless disregard of reward brings the greatest reward. There is room for reward and punishment within a structure of covenantal love, but there is no room for genuine covenantal love premised on reward and punishment alone.

The Martyr's Love

Now we must return to our key verse ("You shall love the LORD your God with all your heart and with all your soul and with all your might" [Deut 6:5]), only this time to inquire into how the rabbis of Talmudic times understood those three key nouns, "heart," "soul," and "might."

The word for "heart" (*levavekha*) is written with two *v*'s here, whereas an alternate form of the same word (*libbekha*) would have been written with only one (the Hebrew *v* and the *b* are graphically the same). From this ostensibly meaningless fact, our midrash derives its weighty lesson that one is to love God "with both your Inclinations, the Inclination to Good and the Inclination to Evil" (*Siphre Deut* 32).[10] But how can one's inclination to evil be directed to the love of God? Is that not a contradiction in terms? A midrash suggests an answer:

> Naḥman [said] in the name of Rabbi Samuel: "[God saw all that He had made,] and found it very good" (Gen 1:31). "Found it good"—this is the Good Inclination. "Found it very good"—this is the Evil Inclination.
>
> But is the Evil Inclination "very good"?
>
> Actually, were it not for the Evil Inclination, a man would never build a house, marry a woman, or beget children. (*Genesis Rabbah* 9:7)

In this case, the interpretation turns on the fact that whereas on the other occasions in which God approves of his handiwork in Genesis 1 only the single word "good" is used, after the creation of human beings, the term "very good" appears. In the framework of the plain sense, the change would seem to reflect the fact that this time the statement comes at the end of the entire six-day process of creation and serves as its final summation. This midrash, however, exploits the difference to make a homiletical point: the inclination that might have gone to evil purposes—to sexual perversion or exploitation, for example, or to enhance one's own creature comforts or social status—can also have positive consequences, consequences that would be unlikely to appear were people to act exclusively on their noblest impulses.

In other words, raw psychic energy can be disciplined and directed to morally positive ends. And that same process of disciplining and redirecting seems to be precisely what our Mishnah has in mind. The human heart is neither altogether good nor altogether bad, and both its good and its bad impulses can, and should, energize the love of God. Or, as *Siphre Deuteronomy* again puts it, "Your heart should not be divided in regard to God" (pisqah 32).

It also bears mention that biblical psychology associates the heart at least as much with thought as with emotion. Whereas our modern idioms locate passions in the heart and thoughts in the brain, the ancient Israelites frequently placed thought in the heart. In that case, Deuteronomy 6:5 is enjoining Israel to love God with their minds, with their thought processes.[11] As for the passions, biblical psychology tends to locate them elsewhere, in the liver, for example, or the *nepheš*, the second noun in the heart-soul-might triad of Deuteronomy 6:5.

But what exactly *is* the *nepheš*? At the level of plain sense, the traditional translation "soul" is highly problematic, since, as usually construed, it starkly contradicts the general ancient Israelite understanding of human identity. Beginning in ancient Greece, Western philosophers and theologians have generally understood the soul to refer to an immortal component of the human self that is at odds with the perishable component that is the body. But in the Bible, as Hans Walter Wolff puts it, *nepheš* "is never given the meaning of an indestructible core of being, in contradistinction to the physical life ... [that is] capable of living when cut off from that life."[12] As I have observed elsewhere,

> The biblical *nepheš* can die. When the non-Israelite prophet Balaam expresses his wish to "die the death of the upright," it is his *nepheš* that he hopes will share their fate (Num 23:10), and the same applies to Samson when he voices his desire to die with the Philistines whose temple he then topples upon all (Judg 16:30). Indeed, "to kill the *nepheš*" functions as a term for homicide in biblical Hebrew, in which context, as elsewhere, it indeed has a meaning like that of the English "person" (for example, Num 31:19; Ezek 13:19).[13]

Within the original context of Deuteronomy 6:5, then, *nepheš* refers to the life force, and the commandment to "love the LORD your God ... with all your soul" means one should love him with all one's vitality, vigor, energy, selfhood, inner forcefulness, and the like. It does not mean that one should love him with some immortal and spiritual dimension of the self that is divorced from one's bodily and social identity.

In rabbinic Judaism a body-soul dichotomy, though alien to the Bible, does develop. Even then, however, *nepheš* continues to have "life" or "life force" among its senses. Thus, the midrash on Deuteronomy 6:5 in *Siphre* continues with this:

> *And with all your soul* (6:5): Even if God takes away your soul, as it is said, *It is for Your sake that we are slain all day long, / that we are regarded as sheep to be slaughtered* (Ps 44:23). R. Simeon ben Menasya says: How can a man be slain all the day? Rather, the Holy One, blessed be He, credits the righteous as if they were slain daily.

> Simeon ben Azzai says: *With all your* soul: love Him
> until the last drop of life is wrung out of you. (*Siphre Deut*
> 32; italics in the original)

Here, not only is soul (*nepheš*) understood as "life," but
much emphasis lies on the adjective "all" (*kol*). The underlying question for the rabbis is, how can we love God with
all our life? Their answer is that we should love God even
to the very end of life, love him with the last drop of life
in us, and do so even if he is the cause of our death—not
simply because he has created us as mortals but because
we die as a consequence of being in his service. Hence the
employment of Psalm 44:23, which in the rabbinic understanding alludes to martyrdom: every day (*kol* can mean
either "all" or "every") we are slain for the sake of the LORD.
The medieval Provençal commentator Rabbi David Qimḥi
adds a gloss: "for Your sake": we die "for the unification of
Your name, for we were not willing to deny You, and they
are killing us because of that" (Radaq on Ps 44:23).

As is usual in midrash, the plain sense arguably lies
elsewhere: the words might mean, "it is Your fault that we
are dying all day / every day."[14] This would comport well
with the taunt in the very next verse, "Rouse Yourself; why
do You sleep, O LORD?" (Ps 44:24), which suggests something quite different from the martyr's faithful and sub-
missive acceptance of his imminent demise. But so much
for the likely plain sense. The complication is that, as we
shall soon see, martyrdom was already both an ancient
and a contemporary reality in the time of the early rabbis,
and the notion that the threat of death overrode the Jews'
obligation to love God with all their life force was one they
could not brook. In the rare and extreme situation in which
the possibility of martyrdom confronted them, Jews were
rather to demonstrate their ultimate commitment with all
their life, enacting their conviction that even the prospect
of certain death could not deter them. Theirs was to be a
love as strong as death. (We shall deal with the concluding

comment of Rabbi Simeon ben Menasya at the end of this chapter.)

We come, finally, to the last noun in the triad of Deuteronomy 6:5, "with all your might (*me'odekha*)." As an adverb, *me'od* is extremely common in the Bible; it means "very" or "much." As a noun, though, it occurs only in this verse and in its echo in 2 Kings 23:25, and its meaning is thus far from clear. Probably, we should think of it as signifying one's "muchness." But what exactly is that? Rabbi Hezekiah ben Manoah, a thirteenth-century French commentator commonly known as "Hizquni," stresses the connection with the adverb: "Very, very much (*bim'od me'od*) set your heart and your soul to love him" (Hizquni to Deut 6:5).[15] So understood, *me'od* is not a third noun at all but serves, rather, to intensify the command to "love the LORD your God with all your heart and with all your soul." The love of God is not to be lukewarm, lethargic, or perfunctory. It must mobilize all the capacities of the self and do so to the highest possible degree. Otherwise, either it is not love or it is the love of something other than God.

This seems to be the plain sense of the term, but here again rabbinic literature suggests other interpretations, and with far-reaching moral and theological implications. Our midrash from the *Siphre Deuteronomy*, for example, continues with this:

> Rabbi Eliezer says: Having said *with all your soul*, why does Scripture go on to say, *with all your might*? And if it says *with all your might*, why does it say *with all your soul*? There are men whose bodies are more precious to them than their wealth, and *with all your soul* is directed to them. There are other men whose wealth is more precious to them than their bodies, and *with all your might* is directed to them. (*Siphre Deut* 32; italics in the original)[16]

The idea of persons who value their property above their bodies (understood as the meaning of "soul" in the Shema) may seem comical at first. It recalls the old Jack Benny routine, in which a mugger demands, "Your money or your life," and the miserly comedian, after a long and pregnant pause, calmly replies, "I'm thinking it over." In fact, though almost nobody would acknowledge regarding his property as more precious than his very body, it is not unusual to hear of people who are "working themselves to death" or otherwise injuring their health in the pursuit of something that brings them the joy and satisfaction that affluent people often derive from their wealth.[17] The examples of those addicted to drugs, alcohol, tobacco, sex, over- or undereating, and inordinately risky occupations or avocations come readily to mind.

As this midrash sees it, such people, no less than those for whom self-preservation is the highest good, must subordinate their own instincts to the love of God, redirecting themselves and their assets to his service. For just as the love of God is more precious than one's own life, so is it more precious than one's property. And from this it is reasonable to infer a further point: just as it is possible and sometimes necessary to serve God with one's very life, so it is possible and sometimes necessary to serve him with one's property, however difficult that may be. Otherwise, though misers do not use the word "gods" to name the things that claim their ultimate concern, they are akin to the biblical idolaters, preferring something else to the service of God or attempting to combine the service of something else with the service of God, as though the two were on the same plane.

As our midrash in *Siphre Deuteronomy* 32 continues, however, it becomes clear that the opinion that some people value their property over their own lives is not universally shared. To Rabbi Akiva, if the text of Deuteronomy 6:5 has said "with all your soul," it has no reason to add "with all your might." So why, then, does it say *bekhol me'odekha*? Because, he goes on, the actual message is that one should love God "in whatever measure (*middah*) God metes (*moded*) out to you, whether of good or of punishment."

Here the sage connects *me'od* with a word to which it is etymologically unrelated (*moded*) in order to make a key theological point.[18] That point is one we have seen before: Jews' love of God must be independent of the circumstances in which they find themselves. It must not, in other words, be conditional upon their immediate experience. But, in this instance, both Rabbi Akiva's wording and some of his scriptural examples make it clear that the negative experience he has in mind is not some sort of neutral bad luck. Rather—and more problematically—it comes from the hand of God himself.

With all my heart, in truth, and with all my might,
I have loved You, outwardly and inwardly.
Your name is before me: How could I walk alone?
He is my beloved: How could I sit solitary?
He is my lamp: How could my light go out?
How could I slip? He is a staff in my hand.
They have held me in contempt, who do not understand
That the shame I endure for the glory of Your name is my glory.
Fountain of life to me, I shall bless You while I live,
My song, I shall sing to You as long as I exist.
Yehudah Halevi[19]

The scriptural example that speaks most strongly to this point relates the response of Job, a paradigmatic "blameless and upright" man who "feared God and shunned evil" (Job 1:1). When Job hears of all that he has lost—even his sons and daughters have all been killed—he responds with this: "Naked came I out of my mother's womb, and naked shall I return there; the LORD has given, and the LORD has taken away; blessed be the name of the LORD" (Job 1:21). In the next chapter of the book, he is also afflicted with "severe inflammation ... from the sole of his foot to the crown of his head" (2:7), so that, to recall the language of Rabbi Eliezer's midrash above, both his body and his property have been attacked. In the biblical story, however, Job's extraordinary misfortune is not punishment. Rather, it is a test of whether his exemplary service is freely given or rooted in a self-interested and heavily conditioned behavior that continues only because it has always paid off.

It is impossible to say for certain whether the midrash attributed to Rabbi Akiva presupposes this reading of the book or another according to which Job deserves his misfortune. But the theology that derives from the requirement in the Shema to love God with all one's *me'od*, understood as "whatever measure (*middah*) God metes out to you," fits with the general rabbinic insistence that a Jew's stance toward God should be foundational and thus independent of circumstance. It should, in other words, remain the stance of a servant, even if the servant is suffering and rightly seeking redress.[20] A related text in the Mishnah puts it brilliantly, playing not on two but on three unrelated but similar-sounding Hebrew roots:[21]

> One is required to say a blessing over the bad, just as one says a blessing over the good, as it is written, "You shall love the LORD your God with all your heart and with all your soul and with all your might" (Deut 6:5) ... "With all your might (*me'odekha*)"—for whichever measure (*middah u-middah*) that he metes (*moded*) out to you, give him thanks (*modeh*) very, very much (*bim'od me'od*)." (*m. Berakhot* 9:5)

SUFFERING AND LOVE

For all the similarities, there is an important difference between the response to bad fortune exemplified by the verses the midrash quotes from the book of Job and the response mandated as law (*halakhah*) in the Mishnah quoted just above.

Job endures the afflictions to his property, his progeny, and his body with unflinching fortitude.[22] "For all that," the narrator summarizes his response, "Job did not sin nor did he cast reproach on God" (Job 1:22). He accepts his adversity with submission and recognizes its ultimate origin in God (even if the whole story of how it came about remains unknown to him).[23] But there is no indication that he actively thanks God for it or thinks that his suffering, painful though it is, also serves some higher purpose. He refrains from the sin of speaking ill of God—"Job said nothing sinful" (Job 2:10)—but he does not find anything of benefit in his excruciating and compounded misfortune. To recall the words of the Mishnah above, he is surely not giving thanks very, very much for what he must endure.

As the midrash on the love of God in *Siphre Deuteronomy* 32 goes on, however, we also hear of the *positive* aspects of suffering. "One should rejoice more in suffering than in good fortune," it counsels.[24] In fact, it asserts, without suffering "no sin of his will be forgiven." Suffering is, in a word, expiatory: it brings about the priceless state of reconciliation with God. "Indeed sufferings appease even more than sacrifices," another comment here reads, "for sacrifices involve one's money, while sufferings involve one's own body." Suffering also brings one into the presence of God: "Precious is suffering (*yissurin*) [or discipline], for the name of the Omnipresent One rests upon him who suffers, as it is said, 'the LORD your God disciplines you (*meyasserekka*; Deut 8:5).'"

In an extended story in the same chapter of *Siphre Deuteronomy*, four of Rabbi Eliezer's students attempt to comfort him as he lies gravely, and probably terminally, ill. The first three spin out rhetorically powerful tropes about the greatness of their master as a teacher of Torah. But their ailing teacher does not respond. Then Rabbi Akiva addresses him with just two words (in Hebrew): "Precious is suffering." This, by contrast, prompts Rabbi Eliezer to ask that he be propped up and that Rabbi Akiva go on.

Rabbi Akiva's words of comfort take the form of a midrash on the figure of Manasseh, an evildoing king who was the son of King Hezekiah; the latter is a doer of good in the Bible and, in the rabbinic mind, a patron of Torah as well. The Torah that Manasseh must have learned from his devout father obviously availed him not, yet we discover that after all his sinning, Manasseh "entreated the LORD his God and humbled himself greatly before the God of his fathers" (2 Chr 33:12). What brought about this reversal, making a righteous man out of a sinner, as the study of Torah obviously did not? It was, in a word, the suffering Manasseh endured at the hands of the Assyrians, who captured him and led him off in manacles and fetters to exile in Babylon. Intense suffering induced Manasseh's submission before God, who in turn restored the penitent king to his throne in Jerusalem. "Hence," Rabbi Akiva concludes, "precious is suffering."

Although we never hear Rabbi Eliezer's response, the climactic positioning of Rabbi Akiva's speech suggests that it did indeed finally bring comfort to his ailing master. And well it should have. The other three disciples attribute vast meaning only to Rabbi Eliezer's teaching of Torah—what he did in the past—while Rabbi Akiva attributes meaning to what he is doing at the moment. That lonely, passive, silent action of suffering, Rabbi Akiva claims, can surpass even the teaching and study of Torah in its positive effects. It can bring about the forgiveness of sins, reconciliation with God, and even personal restoration when even Torah, sadly, has failed to do so.

The story of Rabbi Eliezer's illness makes no reference to the Shema or to the love of God; there is no reason to think it originated in the context in which we now find it in *Siphre Deuteronomy* 32, a text that begins, it will be recalled, with an interpretation of the words "You shall love the LORD your God" (Deut 6:5).[25] Within the redacted text, though, it and other passages that speak of the preciousness of suffering are bracketed by passages on exactly this theme of the love of God. On one side lie the comments on what it means to love God with all one's heart, soul, and might. On the other side lies a midrash that connects those three nouns with the three patriarchs of Israel: Abraham, Isaac, and Jacob.

In scripture, God speaks of "Abraham My friend" (or "lover," 'ohavi [Isa 41:8]), thus (in this midrash) one who loves God with all his heart. As for Isaac, who in this midrash (in contrast to the biblical telling in Gen 22:9) "bound himself upon the altar" as a kind of martyr, he is a paradigm of one who loves God with all his soul, that is, his life. And Jacob, finally, who confesses to God that he is unworthy of the great wealth he has amassed (Gen 32:11), thus shows that he loves God with all his might. The theological message of this arrangement is to give suffering, and even death, a positive role in the love of God commanded to all Jews in the Shema. Suffering has become a

May my sweet song be good in Your eyes,
    and the best part of my praise,
Beloved One, who has flown far from me,
    for the evil of my deeds.
But I have held fast to His garment of love,
    For He inspires awe and wonder.
Enough for me is the glory of Your name:
    That alone, of all my labor, is my portion.
Add more sorrow; I'll add more love,
    for marvelous is Your love to me!

    Yehudah Halevi[26]

moment—and a highly productive and meaningful one at that—within the life animated by the love of God.

The Love that Transcends Death

This brings us back to the subject of martyrdom. For, in the history of ancient Judaism, too, martyrdom changed from something to be endured stoically (if triumphantly) to something positive—in fact, to a mode of fulfillment of the commandment to love God with all one's heart, all one's soul, and all one's might.

The English term "martyr" comes from the Greek word for "witness": martyrs, in brief, are those who refuse, even on pain of death, to change their testimony. The more general sense of martyrs as persons, especially religious ones, who die as innocent victims is not precise enough for our context. In the classical sense of the word, martyrs must choose to die rather than to renounce, by word or deed, the highest truth they know.

Martyrdom seems first to have come to the fore in Judaism in the time of the persecutions that led to the Maccabean uprising (167–164 BCE). The literature from and about this period presents us with striking images of Jewish martyrs as they stoutly withstand torture and die unsullied. Although the accounts of these martyrs are heavily stylized and often baroque, it is likely they were composed to fortify the will of the Jewish people in the sorts of situations they describe. They do so through powerful appeals to noble paradigms for imitation. Here, for example, is an excerpt from the last words of an elderly Jewish leader named Eleazar, who refused to obey the king's order to eat pork as a sign of his renunciation of Judaism:

[24]"Such pretense is not worthy of our time of life," he said, "for many of the young might suppose that Eleazar in his ninetieth year had gone over to an alien religion,

[25]and through my pretense, for the sake of living a brief moment longer, they would be led astray because of me, while I defile and disgrace my old age. [26]Even if for the present I would avoid the punishment of mortals, yet whether I live or die I will not escape the hands of the Almighty. [27]Therefore, by bravely giving up my life now, I will show myself worthy of my old age [28]and leave to the young a noble example of how to die a good death willingly and nobly for the holy laws."

When he had said this, he went at once to the rack. [29]Those who a little before had acted toward him with goodwill now changed to ill will, because the words he uttered were in their opinion sheer madness. [30]When he was about to die under the blows, he groaned aloud and said: "It is clear to the Lord in his holy knowledge that, though I might have been saved from death, I am enduring terrible suffering in my body under this beating, but in my soul I am glad to suffer these things because I fear him."

[31]So, in this way he died, leaving in his death an example of nobility and a memorial of courage, not only to the young but to the great body of his nation. (2 Maccabees 6:24–31)[27]

Although the regime inflicting these tortures was of Greek origin, it would be grossly inaccurate to describe the Maccabean conflict (commemorated in the holiday of Hanukkah) as a clash of Greek and Jewish culture, or Hellenism and Hebraism, as is too often done today. Not only is the text above preserved in Greek (a major language of Jews in those days and the source of much of their literature), but to a significant degree, the ideas it expresses have their origin in Greek culture, though adapted in important ways to the immediate Jewish context. These larger cultural affinities can tell us something important about crucial changes that the love of God underwent in this key period of Jewish history.

Greco-Roman culture often celebrated individuals who had chosen to die rather than to betray their highest convictions or most sacred cause. Unlike those whom we may think of as victims of suicide, these heroes died a noble death, a consciously chosen and principled death, not a shameless or hopeless one.[28] In fact, their choice accomplishes something more than making death into something meaningful: it brings about a transcendence of death, a triumph over the meaninglessness and the passivity of what would otherwise be a mere biological event, an expression only of our lowest, animalistic nature.

Here, for example, is the Roman philosopher Cicero's reflection upon the death in 46 BCE of Cato the Younger, who took his own life rather than to submit to the rule of Julius Caesar:

> Did Marcus Cato find himself in one predicament, and were the others, who surrendered to Caesar in Africa, in another? And yet, perhaps, they would have been condemned, if they had taken their own lives; for their mode of life had been less austere and their characters more pliable. But Cato had been endowed by nature with an austerity beyond belief, and he himself had strengthened it by unswerving consistency and had remained ever true to his purpose and fixed resolve; and it was for him to die rather than to look upon the face of a tyrant. (*De Officiis* 1:112)[29]

To be sure, the case of the Jewish elder Eleazar is somewhat different: he submitted to death at the hand of his persecutors, while Cato took his own life. (History also records instances of Jews' committing mass "suicide" rather than submit to defeat or conversion.) It is also true that, unlike 2 Maccabees, Cicero allows for exceptions on the basis of personal character: for some, a chosen death might be an indefensible contradiction to how they have lived their lives rather than the logical consummation of it. Still and all, the commonalities of the two texts are striking; they derive from a discussion that had been going on in the Hellenic world for centuries before either text was written.

The reality of Jewish martyrdom, along with the theology that undergirds it, gives the lie to the oft-heard cliché that Judaism values life above all else. The Jewish tradition does indeed value life (especially human life) highly. But traditionally, it has also taught that death is not the worst thing that can happen to a person. Self-preservation, whether of the individual or the community, is not the highest good. Just as there are things worth living for, there are things worth dying for.

Another apparent difference between the Greco-Roman and the Jewish instances deserves attention. Much of the Greco-Roman discussion centers on the outstanding *advantage* of death: the fact that through death the deeper part of the self, the soul, attains liberation from the body that constrains and limits it. In one of Plato's dialogues, Socrates (the account of whose death exerted enormous influence on this whole tradition) teaches "that death is the separation of the soul from the body and that the state of being dead is the state in which the body is separated from the soul and exists alone by itself and the soul is separated from the body and exists alone by itself." According to Socrates and Platonic tradition, it is through the soul that we attain valid knowledge and perceive truth, for the body may be capable of sensation but not of perception: it cannot know anything. And that is why the true philosopher will welcome death and not dread it. As Socrates puts it in the same dialogue, "so long as we have the body, and the soul is contaminated by such an evil, we shall never attain completely what we desire, that is, the truth ... For, if pure knowledge is impossible while the body is with us, one of two things must follow, either it cannot be acquired at all or only when we are dead; for then the soul will be by itself apart from the body, but not before" (*Phaedo* 64c, 66b).[30]

Given what we have seen about the *nepheš* (the "soul" in Deut 6:5) in the Bible, it might seem that there would be no Jewish parallel to this important stream in Greco-Roman thinking about death, and especially no parallel to the case of the philosopher who, through death, can attain knowledge of the higher truth denied him in the flesh. For if human beings are a psychophysical unity, as they are for the most part in the Bible, then such talk of the liberation of the soul, or the mind, from the body would seem alien. In point of fact, however, the notion that humans have an immortal soul, or can acquire one through right practice, can certainly be found in Jewish sources.[31]

In the case of the martyrdom narrative of 2 Maccabees, importantly, the expectation is not of immortality but of something different: a resurrection of the dead. This is the expectation that God will *reverse* death, restoring the whole person (body and soul, if we must use that dichotomy). Whereas the focus of immortality is on the nature of human beings—the fact that they have an invisible, incorporeal soul—the focus of resurrection thus lies on a future act of God, a miraculous reconstitution of the departed individuals. The martyred mother of seven heroic sons, slain one after another before her eyes, puts it memorably: "Therefore the Creator of the world, who shaped the beginning of humankind, and devised the origin of all things, will in his mercy give life and breath back to you again, since you now forget yourself for the sake of his laws" (2 Maccabees 7:23).[32]

This brings us to another oft-heard cliché about Judaism: that it is altogether this-worldly in its focus and has no doctrine of the hereafter. The truth is that the belief in God's resurrection of the dead at the end of time was a key community-defining tenet of rabbinic Judaism, and the traditional liturgy to this day includes an affirmation, recited at every service, that "You are faithful to revive the dead." It is also true, however, that the cliché is accurate as a description of the empirical reality of most modern Jews: often in the past two hundred years or so, the affirmations of resurrection (*teḥiyat ha-metim* in Hebrew) in the traditional prayer book have been softened or abolished in the non-Orthodox liturgies.[33] Even in Orthodox Judaism, which retains the traditional liturgy, the powerful world-denying and ascetic dimensions of the premodern tradition are often downplayed or ignored altogether, and resurrection is not infrequently identified with immortality, in a subtle and ironic accommodation of the older tradition to modern doubts about an active, intervening, and miracle-working Deity.

It might be argued that the existence of these doctrines of immortality and resurrection (the two, though different, can and do coexist) undermines the heroism of the Jewish martyrs. For how big a sacrifice were they actually making if they knew that their souls would survive their deaths or that God would eventually return their full, embodied selves to them?

Part of the answer is that they did not *know* these things at all. They had a *faith* in God that he would receive their souls favorably or restore their persons: a basis for hope grounded in the reliability of God to fulfill his promises. Their deaths would thus be a testimony not only to their unwavering fidelity to God but also to their confidence in his promise of life. But that he would honor that promise was by no means self-evident or a matter of settled knowledge. For not only was a belief in the resurrection of the dead rare in the Greco-Roman world, it was also hotly disputed among various Jewish sects. To be prepared to die for the God of Israel and his Torah with an explicit expectation of eventual resurrection was itself a massive existential risk.

Another part of the answer is simply that there is no evidence in these texts that the self-sacrifice of the martyrs was exclusively premised upon their belief in immortality or resurrection, as if they would have flinched if they had thought God would not raise them from the dead. Indeed, a story of religious persecution in the book of Daniel makes it explicit that the Jewish heroes were committed to honoring their God whether he rescued them or not:

> [16]Shadrach, Meshach, and Abed-nego said in reply to the king, "O Nebuchadnezzar, we have no need to answer you in this matter, [17]for if so it must be, our God whom we serve is able to save us from the burning fiery furnace, and He will save us from your power, O king. [18]But even if He does not, be it known to you, O king, that we will not serve your god or worship the statue of gold that you have set up." (Dan 3:16–18)

As in the case of Job, and as in the advice of Antigonus of Sokho that we saw earlier, the service the martyr offers is to be selfless and not conditioned on some variety of cost-benefit analysis. For, as in the covenantal theology of the Bible, the service of God is not a relative good to be weighed against others: either God's claim is absolute, or it is not God whose claim is being honored.

The attentive reader may have noticed that there is something missing in these stories of the Jewish martyrs, namely, that same absolute claim in its biblical articulation: "You shall love the LORD your God with all your heart and with all your soul and with all your might" (Deut 6:5). Like Job in the first two chapters of the book bearing his name, these martyrs withstand their suffering and resist the temptation to allow it to undermine their faithfulness to God, but there is no notion that their heroism fulfills that commandment or is itself an expression of the *love* of God.

In rabbinic literature, this changes. The outstanding examples come again, interestingly, from stories about Rabbi

Akiva, this time the legends of his death at the hands of the Romans in the time of the Bar Kokhba war (ca. 135 CE):

> Rabbi Akiva was on trial before Tineius Rufus [a Roman official]. The time for reciting the Shema came. He began the recitation of the Shema and smiled.
>
> He [Tineius Rufus] said to him, "Old man, either you are deaf or you scoff at suffering."
>
> He said, "May the spirit of that man [Tineius Rufus] give out! I am neither deaf nor do I scoff at suffering. Rather, all my life I have recited the verse, 'You shall love the LORD your God with all your heart and with all your soul and with all your might,' and I have felt pained and wondered, When will the three come to me? I have loved him with all my heart, and I have loved him with all my property, but I didn't know I loved him with all my soul. Now that the opportunity [to love him] with all my soul has come, and the time to recite the Shema has arrived, I am not ambivalent. Therefore, I am reciting and smiling."
>
> No sooner did he succeed in saying this than his soul took flight. (*y. Berakhot* 9:5)[34]

Rabbinic literature displays significantly different versions of this story of the martyrdom of Rabbi Akiva. In the more baroque version that appears in the Babylonian Talmud (and is therefore the best known), the Roman torturers rake his body with iron combs, leading his disciples to ask, "Our Master, even to this point?"—that is, how can you resist this much agony? The question elicits the same response about wanting to fulfill the divine command to love God "with all your soul" (*b. Berakhot* 61b). The point of Rabbi Akiva's answer is one that, in a different idiom and a different situation, we saw as early as Deuteronomy itself: one's love of God must be total and absolute.[35] The commonsensical consideration of cost versus benefit implicit in his disciples' question drastically misses the point.

And yet the commandment remains fragmentary if performed for its own sake *alone*. For if such performance discloses the human neighbor, and ourselves, too, as beings of intrinsic value, it is ultimately *because the divine commanding Presence so discloses them*. That is why, even if beginning with the acceptance of the disclosure only, a man is finally led to confront the divine Discloser; why performance of the commandment for *its* sake points to its performance for *God's* sake. Both are certainly part of Jewish teaching. And they exist not contingently side by side, but in an internal and necessary relation. . . . In the hour of his martyrdom, Rabbi Akiva knew that the love of God is not one commandment side by side to others. It is the life of all.

Emil L. Fackenheim[36]

Even those who generally accept the theology of martyrdom evident in these ancient sources may recoil from one implication in Rabbi Akiva's answer—the implication that without martyrdom one cannot fulfill the requirement to love God with all one's soul, and therefore that (going beyond what Rabbi Akiva says explicitly) a Jew should actively seek out martyrdom. Indeed, one scholar writes that rabbinic efforts to define precisely (and thus to limit) when martyrdom must take place "seem to have been intended not only for the protection of the people but possibly also for the discouragement of the too daring."[37]

In this connection, we can also note a comment on Psalm 44:23 quoted but not discussed earlier: "R. Simeon ben Menasya says: How can a man be slain all the day? Rather, the Holy One, blessed be He, credits the righteous as if they were slain daily" (*Siphre Deut* 32). Whether one translates the Hebrew *kol-hayyom* as "all day" or "every day," in an exceedingly literal reading it makes no sense: no one is slain either all day or every day. The effect of Rabbi Simeon ben Menasya's comment is to interpret the humdrum life of the upright as the equivalent of martyrdom in God's calculus. In the context of *Siphre Deuteronomy* 32, the implication is that they, too, love God with all their soul. That possibility is not restricted to the few who are confronted with the gruesome alternative of renouncing their faith or dying for it; it is open to anyone committed to Jewish practice. Later, what Louis Jacobs terms "the idea of imaginative martyrdom" will grow out of this same notion, and with it will come spiritual exercises in which the practitioner visualizes torments that his devotion overcomes, thus strengthening his love for God in the absence of the literal test a martyr endures.[38]

Regarding the use of Deuteronomy 6:5 in the stories of Rabbi Akiva's death, one scholar writes this: "What was new in martyrology was the eroticization of death for God, in the representation of martyrdom as the consummation of love."[39] The use of the language of love and the employment of that verse from the Shema are indeed new (so far as we know), but one may doubt whether "eroticization" is the right term. As we saw in chapter 1, in the Bible love characterizes many relationships—most important for our purposes, the relationship of suzerain and vassal, or king and subject. There is no reason to think of love as exclusively or even primarily sexual. Rabbi Akiva experiences *eros* in the sense of desire—an intense longing to fulfill a commandment and demonstrate fully his love for God—but the term "eroticization" introduces connotations that may mislead.

In the case of the Akiva traditions, I think we are seeing instead a natural and perhaps inevitable merger of two streams of thought, the Greco-Roman ideal of the patriot or philosopher who dies for his highest convictions and the biblical requirement to love God without reservation or calculation of self-interest. Inasmuch as one of the salient characteristics of rabbinic Judaism is its focus on the Torah and its commandments, it makes sense that a figure like Rabbi Akiva, famous for deriving interpretations from even the smallest points in the biblical text,[40] would understand "with all your soul" (meaning, "life") as the words with which the Torah validates martyrdom. Deuteronomy 6:5 is simply the best verse to serve that purpose, and one who prefers self-preservation over the total fidelity to God that it commands may well be thought to have dishonored that all-important mitzvah.

Which is not to suggest that the love of God in Jewish thought lacks an erotic dimension. To this we turn in chapter 3.

THREE

The Once and Future Romance

> Whenever Israel would make a festival
> pilgrimage, they would roll back the curtain
> [of the Holy of Holies] for them and show
> them the Cherubim—who were embracing
> each other—and say to them, "Look! God's
> love for you is as the love of a man and a
> woman."
>
> *Talmud*[1]

*I*n our discussion so far, I have been at pains to offer scant comment on the erotic understanding of the love of God, that is, the interpretation that places it in the category of love that is most familiar to people today, with sexuality at the very center. The reason for my reticence bears restatement: the sexual is but one variety of love, and it is not the one that is most central to the Torah (in the sense of the Five Books of Moses), nor does it today convey adequately key elements of the love of God in that most foundational and authoritative of Jewish texts.[2] These are the elements that I have been calling obedience, service, law, and the like, though really all such terms simply refer to various aspects of what is actually the same dimension in the God-Israel relationship.

To speak of God and Israel as the lover and the beloved (in either order) in the familiar, sexual sense too easily causes us to miss other key metaphors, some of which, in fact, are at least equally prominent in the Hebrew Bible— the metaphors of king and subject, for example, father and son, shepherd and flock, master and servant, or vineyard-keeper and vineyard. It is not the case, of course, that these other metaphors convey only dry, formal relationships and lack any emotional intensity. Far from it. In chapter 1, I argued that the love owed by the covenantal vassal to his lord (or by the subject to his king) is both active and affective: the fact that it denotes specific deeds of service and a general stance of obedience in no way precludes, or even diminishes, its emotional dimension. In the Hebrew Bible, the love of God and the fear of God (understood as keen recognition of his infinite majesty and taut attentiveness to his will) are not at odds; they work in tandem.

By contrast, where love is understood as primarily a sentiment, the dimension of deeds and of the service that the deeds bespeak is lost or radically transformed. And when that happens to any form of love, love is eviscerated and lightened beyond recognition, and its days become numbered. When it happens to the love of God in partic-ular, the result is the perception that all talk of God's love or of loving God is, at base, a treacly thing that appeals only to the emotionally weak—a crutch, perhaps, to help them avoid facing the lovelessness, or some kindred defi-ciency, in their own lives.

And yet, precisely because it is manifestly artificial to sever the two dimensions, the active and the affective, in the Hebrew Bible, we have already, in fact, heard the note of eros (again in the sense of the sexuality) in our discus-sion of covenant. We saw it, for example, in chapter 1 when we examined Deuteronomy 7, which speaks of God's hav-ing "set His heart" (ḥašaq) on Israel in language that can be reasonably interpreted as connoting an erotic passion and not simply a platonic favoring (v. 7). The same verb appears in the account of Shechem's crush on Dinah in Genesis 34:8 and in the law of the beautiful captive whom the Israelite warrior desires to wed in Deuteronomy 21:11. In rabbinic theology, this erotic language becomes more prominent, so much so that, as we shall see at length, the great biblical *chanson d'amour*, the highly erotic Song of Songs, becomes a central vehicle for rendering the relationship of God and Israel.

This change, this movement of erotic language from the periphery to the center, may seem to have come out of the blue, as it were. But if we turn our attention away from the Torah and to the prophets, we shall find that it has a long prehistory—and a deeper resonance in the Torah than at first seems the case.

A FAMILY RUINED AND RENEWED

We begin with the opening oracle of God to Hosea, a prophet active in the northern kingdom (Israel, as distinguished from Judah) in the eighth century BCE:

> [2]When the LORD first spoke to Hosea, the LORD said to Hosea, "Go, get yourself a wife of whoredom and children of whoredom; for the land has been straying from following the LORD." [3]So he went and married Gomer daughter of Diblaim. She conceived and bore him a son, [4]and the LORD instructed him, "Name him Jezreel; for, I will soon punish the House of Jehu for the bloody deeds at Jezreel and put an end to the monarchy of the House of Israel. [5]In that day, I will break the bow of Israel in the Valley of Jezreel."
>
> [6]She conceived again and bore a daughter; and He said to him, "Name her Lo-ruhamah, for I will no longer accept the House of Israel or pardon them ..."

⁸After weaning Lo-ruhamah, she conceived and bore a son. ⁹Then He said, "Name him Lo-ammi, for you are not My people and I will not be your [God]." (Hos 1:2–9)³

Words from the root of the Hebrew term translated as "whoredom" in verse 2 (*zenunim*) refer in their primary sense to "sexual activities conducted outside marriage, mainly by women."⁴ Adultery (that is, marital infidelity), too, can therefore fall within the semantic range of that root. It is therefore not surprising that, two chapters later, in what is evidently a variant of the same text, we find an oracle in which the prophet is instructed to love an adulterous woman (*mena'ephet*, Hos 3:1).

In this context, the difference between a prostitute and an adulteress is not so great as it may appear. In fact, "harlotry" and "adultery" appear in synonymous parallelism in Hosea 2: "And let her put away her harlotry (*zenuneyha*) from her face / And her adultery (*na'aphupheyha*) from between her breasts" (v. 4). Although in ancient Israel prostitution did not carry the stigma it was to acquire later, a married woman who acted like a prostitute was morally objectionable in the extreme. And yet it is just such a woman whom the prophet is instructed to wed: one who continually misdirects her own love and thus abuses the love shown to her.

Although it is sometimes said that Hosea inferred his message to Israel from his own failed marriage,⁵ the direction represented in the text is the reverse: he marries the unfaithful women as a dramatization of the problematic relationship between the LORD and Israel. We are dealing, in other words, with what scholars call a "prophetic sign-act," in which the prophet embodies and acts out key aspects of his message, often in ways calculated to shock his audience. Isaiah, for example, who preached slightly later than Hosea and in the southern kingdom (Judah), is said to have gone naked and barefoot for three years at the LORD's command in order to depict the coming treatment of Egypt and Nubia at the hands of Assyria (Isa 20). In Hosea's case, as is usual in the prophetic sign-act, the message is explicit: "the land has been straying (*zanoh tizneh*) from following the LORD" (Hos 1:2). The root of the verb here (*z.n.h.*) is the same as the one in the noun translated above variously as "whoredom" and "harlotry," and the doubled form adds intensity to the act portrayed. The clause would be more accurately (if less elegantly) rendered, "instead of following the LORD, the land has been whoring it up outrageously."

The children to whom Hosea's meretricious wife gives birth are to bear names that reflect her character, which is, of course, the character of the people Israel in their defection from their God. The name of the first son, Jezreel, may have had a meaning for the original hearers that we cannot recover. The only event in the Hebrew Bible to which it might refer is the revolution reported in 2 Kings 9:15b–37, which resulted, among other things, in the death by defenestration of the corrupt, idolatrous, and violent queen Jezebel, her flesh then devoured by dogs, "just as the LORD spoke through His servant Elijah the Tishbite" (v. 36). Here, the reference is to the great prophet's prediction that "the dogs shall devour Jezebel in the field of Jezreel" (1 Kgs 21:23).

The leader of the bloody revolution was Jehu, the very figure whose own dynasty is about to be punished according to Hosea 1:4. And, indeed, the last king of the House of Jehu with a reign of any significant duration was none other than Jeroboam II (ca. 786–746 BCE), the king of Israel at the time of Hosea's oracles, according to the superscription in Hosea 1:1. As is usual for the prophets of Israel, events in the political realm are taken as indications of the pleasure or (as in this case) the displeasure of the LORD with the doings of his people. Meaning: the line of the sanguinary revolutionary is fast coming to an end.

The symbolic names of the prophet's other children are more transparent (Hos 1:6–9). "Lo-ruhamah" means "Unloved," "Unpitied," or the like. Speakers of Modern Hebrew may be inclined to prefer "Unpitied" because the root of this girl's name (*r.ḥ.m.*) is different from the one that today is associated more readily with love (*'.h.v.*), but, if so, their instinct would be mistaken. The root *r.ḥ.m.* usually means "love" in languages related to Hebrew. In fact, the Targum Onqelos, an Aramaic translation of the Torah, renders "You shall love" (*ve'ahavta*, Deut 6:5) in the Shema with *vetirḥam* (from *r.ḥ.m.*), and "love" rather than "pity" or "mercy" is the more natural rendering of some instances of the root *r.ḥ.m* in the Hebrew Bible as well. The difference is not great and may be artificial in any event, for, either way, Hosea is instructed to give his daughter a name that signals the end of God's love for Israel, his refusal to accept them or to pardon them (here the notions of pity and mercy come to the fore) for their massive infidelity. Having abused its love and directed it toward a host of improper recipients, Israel now finds itself not more loved than ever but less—in fact, Unloved.

Finally, Lo-ammi means "Not-My-People," just as verse 9 indicates. The process of naming Hosea's three children ends in a crescendo: the last name symbolizes the end of the relationship of the LORD and Israel. No longer are they his people. Betrayal has, to all appearances, canceled the covenant arrangement. "Now then, if you will obey Me faithfully and keep My covenant, you shall be My treasured possession among all the peoples," God had proclaimed in Exodus 19:5. But now Israel has strayed from him, violated the covenant, and become Not-My-People. The nation God once lovingly adopted into sonship through covenant now finds itself disowned, its covenant annulled. Israel is now unloved, no longer his people.

In contemporary society, at least in America, an unhappy situation like this would have an obvious remedy:

divorce. The promiscuous wife and her cuckolded husband would go their separate ways by mutual consent, probably to seek fulfillment with other partners more to their liking. In ancient Israel, this option would not come to mind for several reasons. The first is simply that in Israelite law, the wife becomes a member of her husband's household.[6] If there is to be a divorce, it must therefore be at his instigation, not hers. And, in ancient Israel, unlike modern America, there remains an enormous dimension in the situation at hand that divorce cannot remedy: the grave sin of the adultery committed (in this case) by the wife.[7] The notion of a permanent separation of the partners, so familiar in our modern society, with its high estimation of personal independence and autonomy, cannot resolve this problem. When marriage is used to convey the *covenantal* relationship, as in Hosea, there is still another dimension to be considered. When this is the case, a permanent separation of the partners is again inadequate. For, as we saw in chapter 1, in the way covenant is developed in the theology of the Hebrew Bible, permanence and unconditionality are major elements of the relationship; the rejection and punishment of the faithless vassal for violation of the conditions are not the end of the story, though it often seems that they surely will be.

In Hosea, too, it might sound as though the marriage of God and Israel has terminated in divorce, just as God seems to disown his children by the adulterous wife. "For she is not My wife / And I am not her husband," he says, and "they are now a harlot's brood, / In that their mother has played the harlot" (Hos 2:4, 6–7). But the oracle in which we find these harsh words follows another that speaks of restoration and recalls the promises of national greatness made to Israel's forefathers in Genesis:

> The number of the people of Israel shall be like that of the sands of the sea, which cannot be measured or counted;

and instead of being told, "You are Not-My-People," they shall be called Children-of-the-Living-God. (Hos 2:1; cf. Gen 13:16, 15:5, 22:17, and 32:13)

And so, whereas the cheating wife might have met with divorce as a consequence of her adultery (or even, as the law specifies, death), and the children might have been disowned, in actuality the nation that both she and they symbolize is renewed and restored, and the children's names are changed accordingly.[8]

It bears mention that we are not dealing here with cheap grace—forgiveness without reform, restoration without repentance. Instead, God commands the children to rebuke or dispute with their mother, lest he punish her by stripping her naked and turn her land into a wilderness and a desert where she will die of thirst.

For his part, God will block her paths to her lovers so that she cannot reach them, forcing her instead to recognize at long last just who her real benefactor is:

> [9]Then she will say,
> "I will go and return
> To my first husband,
> For then I fared better than now."
> [10]And she did not consider this:
> It was I who bestowed on her
> The new grain and wine and oil:
> I who lavished silver on her
> And gold—which they used for Baal. (Hos 2:9b–10)

Behind these verses one hears not simply a competition between two suitors for Israel's wifely attentions but, much more momentously, one between two gods for her ultimate loyalty: Which one gave her the grain, wine, oil, and silver—Baal or the Lord? In taking these goods away from her, along with the wool and linen with which she clothes

herself, the Lord challenges her reliance on Baal and ex-
poses it as not merely adulterous but idolatrous:

> [11]Assuredly,
> I will take back My new grain it its time
> And My new wine in its season,
> And I will snatch away My wool and My linen
> That serve to cover her nakedness.
> [12]Now will I uncover her shame
> In the very sight of her lovers,
> And none shall save her from Me.
>
> ■ ■ ■
>
> [15]Thus will I punish her
> For the days of the Baalim,
> On which she brought them offerings;
> When, decked with earrings and jewels,
> She would go after her lovers,
> Forgetting Me—declares the Lord. (Hos 2:11, 12, 15)

The closest analogy to this contestation of deities is probably the test that Elijah is said to have set up on Mount Car-
mel, where he challenges the prophets of Baal to induce
their god to prove his divinity by consuming offerings by
fire.[9] Just as we (but not they) might suspect, they fail but
Elijah succeeds. For in response to his petition, the Lord
sends fire that consumes not only the sacrificial offerings,
but also the wood and stones of the altar and the earth
beneath it; it even laps up the water that his prophet has
placed in a trench to make the supernatural character of
the event all the more undeniable. Beyond the pyrotech-
nics of the scene, the deeper theological message becomes
clear at the end: "When they saw this, all the people flung
themselves on their faces and cried out: 'The Lord alone is
God, The Lord alone is God!'" (1 Kgs 18:39). His rival Baal
is unworthy to replace him or to receive Israel's worship
alongside him, as if it were acceptable to "hop between the

two branches," as the staunch purist Elijah memorably characterizes his hearers' syncretism (v. 21).[10]

The LORD's punishment of his errant wife in Hosea 2 is thus also a demonstration to her—and, more important, to the people Israel, whom she personifies—of his unique claims on her, based in the benefits that he, and he alone, has graciously conferred. It is, in other words, an aspect of the structure of the covenantal relationship that we explored in chapter 1. To what extent it also reflects the actual treatment of an adulteress in ancient Israel is less clear. Nothing in the various collections of Israelite law that survive in the Bible suggests that the faithless wife was to be subjected to the severe deprivations and humiliations that the LORD inflicts on Israel in Hosea[11]—though she was indeed to be subjected to something that many would consider worse: capital punishment. From this Israel is, strikingly, spared.

The severity of the punishments that Hosea's symbolic wife is to endure has understandably attracted the attention of feminist scholars. Gerlinde Baumann, for example, who has made a thorough study of the marriage metaphor in the Hebrew Bible, sees the impact of the metaphor on the two sexes as disparate. "Both sexes can identify with female Israel," she writes, "but only men can have an 'escape' from this proffered identification: they can recognize their situation also in that of the wounded and revenge-seeking husband, who is in the right. This opportunity for identification is not open to women."[12]

It is, however, much to be doubted that men hearing Hosea's oracles (or the analogous ones of other prophets) would have identified with God rather than with the Israelite nation that was being indicted and to which they belonged. The whole point of the oracle is that their situation is that of the wayward wife, not that of her wronged husband, who is, in fact, a unique and unparalleled divinity. Another feminist scholar, Phyllis Bird, thus gets it exactly right: "It is easy for patriarchal society to see the guilt of the 'fallen woman'; Hosea says, 'You (male Israel) are that woman!' "[13]

Another feminist critique, though, points to a deeper issue and to an important divide between biblical and some common modern concepts on which we touched in chapter 1. The critique is again based on a disproportion in the way biblical law treats the violation of marriage: in order for there to be adultery, a married woman must be involved. A married man who has sex with a single woman is not an adulterer (however improper his action may have been deemed); nor, for that matter, is the single woman.[14] To apply this to the case at hand, if Hosea had cheated on his wife, he would have incurred no legal culpability, and he would thus presumably have been spared the severe deprivations and humiliations to which his wife—really, God's wife—is subjected in Hosea 2.

However we are to understand the inequality of men and women in biblical marriage law (and understanding it is not simple), it is, ironically, precisely the inequality of the relationship that makes Hosea's sign-act appropriate. For if the relationship were one of equals, it would prove grossly inadequate as a metaphor to convey the covenantal arrangement that underlies these passages in Hosea. As Tikva Frymer-Kensky observes, the marital relationship is anything but unique in the repertoire of biblical metaphors for the relationship of God and his people:

A shepherd disciplines his flock, it does not discipline him. A master punishes a slave, and never the slave the master. The king punishes his servants, and not the servants the king. A father disciplines his child, and not the child the parent. And a husband in a hierarchical marriage always has the power (physical, political, and economic), and may be expected to use it to enforce his dominion over his wife.[15]

And yet the intimacy and tenderness of the husband-wife relationship give it a depth of resonance that the shepherd-flock and master-slave relationships lack (in Hos 11, the prophet shifts artlessly to the father-son metaphor to make his theological point).[16] As Frymer-Kensky again puts it, "Through this imagery, the people of Israel are enabled to feel God's agony.... As a result, the image of God as betrayed husband strikes deep into the psyche of the people of Israel and enables them to feel the faithless nature of their actions."[17] They can do so, we should note again, because the marital metaphor requires Israel to identify *themselves* with God's heedless, whoring wife.

Today, some will think that any difference between husbands and wives in the degree of legal power and recognized social authority precludes the possibility that the marital metaphor could ever convey a relationship of genuine love. Here we meet again, as we did in chapter 1, the very contemporary notion that love requires equality, and here again we must note that whatever is to be said for that proposition, it is nowhere to be found in the Hebrew Bible. In fact, if the proposition is true, then it would seem that precious few husbands and wives ever loved each other until just a few decades ago, despite the multitude of ardent protestations over the centuries in many literary genres that indeed they did, and powerfully.[18]

In the case of covenantal love, the relationship is inherently unequal, not only because one party is the lord and the other the vassal, but also because of the deeper disparity on which that obvious difference is itself based: only one of the parties (the vassal) has been the recipient of unmerited gifts. To lose sight of the source of the gifts, as Hosea's wife Gomer or the LORD's wife Israel has done (Hos 2:10, 14), is to reject the benefactor's love and thus to strike violently at the covenantal relationship. Indeed, within the covenantal thinking, to seek to level out the power disparity is to act *against* love, not for it. It is to evade the dimension of altruism, the acting on behalf of the other, that is at the heart of covenantal service. In the covenantal paradigm, there is no love without service, and service demands sacrifice.

The harsh treatment of the wife in Hosea 2 serves not only a punitive role but an educative one as well. It teaches her that it is the LORD and not Baal in his various manifestations who is the source of her bounty, and it thus prepares her for the reconciliation with the LORD and the renewal of covenant with him, with which, in fact, the chapter ends. His banishment of her to the wilderness is actually a way to rewind the tape of history in order to restore her to the condition of the exodus, thus to begin the romance anew, without the defections that have soured it:

> [16]Assuredly,
> I will speak coaxingly to her
> And lead her through the wilderness
> And speak to her tenderly.
> [17]I will give her her vineyards from there,
> And the Valley of Achor as a plowland of hope.
> There she shall respond as in the days of her youth,
> When she came up from the land of Egypt.
> [18]And in that day—declares the LORD—
> You will call [Me] Ishi,
> And no more will you call Me Baali.
> [19]For I will remove the names of the Baalim from her mouth,
> And they shall nevermore be mentioned by name.
> (Hos 2:16–19)[19]

Here the devastation of Israel's homeland is interpreted as the restoration of the wilderness through which her ancestors wandered on their trek from Egypt to the Promised Land. Here, too, the endpoint is a land of fertility for a people devoted to the LORD, and him alone, with all their heart. Now she will employ the term *'iši* to mean "my husband" and not its synonym, *ba'ali*, which contains the name of his great rival and her erstwhile paramour. In the new era of marital reconciliation, Israel will once more heed the substance of the law in the Torah that tells them, "Make no mention of the names of other gods; they shall not be heard on your lips" (Exod 23:13).

In sum, the travails of Israel's new journey in the wilderness cannot be separated from the renewal of her romance with the LORD. The new exodus, like its ancient predecessor, will be a new beginning for Israel, one marked by enhanced intimacy with her divine lover.

This new exodus, like the first one, will also lead to an event of divine covenant-making:

> In that day, I will make a covenant for them with the beasts of the field, the birds of the air, and the creeping things of the ground; I will also banish bow, sword, and war from the land. Thus I will let them lie down in safety.
> (Hos 2:20)

The covenant with the wild animals would seem to be a restriction that God places upon them, securing the safety of Israel from attack. It is, in other words, a reversal of the covenant curse in which God threatens to "loose wild beasts against you, and they shall bereave you of your children and wipe out your cattle" (Lev 26:22). Similarly, the banishment of the implements of war from Israel's land nullifies the well-known curses in which the nation, should it breach the covenant, is threatened with military defeat.[20] More immediate to the context, this promise also reverses the prediction in Hosea 1:5, "In that day, I will break the bow of Israel in the Valley of Jezreel."[21] The verbal root in the word translated above as "banish" (*'ešbor*, Hos 2:20) is, in fact, the same one as in the verb rendered "break" in the earlier verse (*vešavarti*, Hos 1:5). The term "covenant" as used in the phrase "a covenant for them with the beasts of the field" is a duty, an obligation, or, as phrased above, a restriction. But the resonances of this passage with texts about covenant in the larger sense of a relationship analogous to the suzerainty treaties we explored in chapter 1 show that the context here is also covenantal in that more capacious—and spiritually profounder—sense.

The theological message is clear: God is healing the relationship, the divorce is over, and the romance of yesteryear is about to begin anew. Curse will give way to blessing: the covenantal blessing that "you shall ... dwell securely (*laveṭaḥ*) in your land" (Lev 26:5) comes into effect when God, remarrying his once wayward wife Israel, "will let them lie down in safety (*laveṭaḥ*)" (Hos 2:20).

The grand finale of Hosea 2 is God's promise to rebetroth his wife whom he divorced, or seemed to divorce, and the prediction of the redeemed cosmos that marriage to her is to inaugurate. The passage thus adds a strong note of expectation, the expectation of nothing less than a transformed world when the LORD and Israel have resumed their intimacy:

> [21]And I will betroth you forever:
> I will betroth you with righteousness and justice,
> And with goodness and mercy,
> [22]And I will betroth you with faithfulness;
> Then you shall know the LORD.
> [23]In that day,
> I will respond—declares the LORD—
> I will respond to the sky,
> And it shall respond to the earth;
> [24]And the earth shall respond
> With new grain and wine and oil,
> And they shall respond to Jezreel.
> [25]I will sow her in the land as My own;
> And take Lo-ruhamah back in favor;

And I will say to Lo-ammi, "You are My people,"
And he will respond, "[You are] my God."
(Hos 2:21–25)[22]

In antiquity, betrothal, which took place before the actual wedding, corresponded roughly to what English-speakers call "engagement." (Even today, in a traditional Jewish wedding service, betrothal, known as *'erusin*, precedes and is formally separate from the marriage service proper, which is called *nissu'in*.) In biblical times, betrothal involved the groom's payment of a bride price to the bride's family.[23] If that is how we are to understand verses 21–22 above, then "righteousness," "justice," "goodness," "mercy," and "faithfulness" are gifts with which the LORD endows Israel in exchange for her exclusive fidelity to him.[24] In other words, he confers on her what she needs in order to become, and remain, his proper spouse after her long period of promiscuity. Alternatively, in those five nouns we can see well-known characteristics of the LORD himself, so that, as one commentary puts it, "They constitute at once what the groom contributes to and expects from the relationship,"[25] and thus characterize the success of the second marriage in contrast to the failure of the first. Either way, these five nouns describe what is necessary for a successful marriage within the structure of covenantal love.

"Then you shall know the LORD" in Hosea 2:22 (above) also tracks the reversal of serial infidelity and its replacement with a lasting marriage. Before, Israel "would go after her lovers, / Forgetting Me" (v. 15); now, when the new betrothal takes place, she will instead have knowledge of the LORD.[26] We must remember, though, that the Hebrew root *y.d.'.* has resonances that English terms like "know" and "knowledge" do not normally convey.

One of those resonances has to do with treaty obligation—that is to say, once again with covenant. A Hittite emperor, for example, enjoins his vassal, "Another lord ... do not ... know ... The Sun [alone] know," the Sun being the emperor himself, the suzerain in the relationship. In a letter to an Assyrian emperor, the correspondent, employing the Akkadian cognate of Hebrew *y.d.ʿ.*, delivers this complaint about a certain group: "They are nomads, they know neither an oath by the god(s) nor a sworn t[reaty]."[27] Here, to "know" means to respect and honor the relevant legal obligations, as it does in more than a few biblical texts as well.[28] Consider, for example, this famous verse from a prophet contemporary with Hosea:

> You alone have I singled out
> Of all the families of the earth—
> That is why I will call you to account
> For all your iniquities. (Amos 3:2)[29]

The translation "singled out" in the Jewish Publication Society *Tanakh* is a good one but obscures the fact that the verb is *yadaʿti*, which in other contexts is properly rendered "I knew," "I have known," or "I know." Underlying this verse is the belief that the LORD has a special relationship with Israel, one that entails a higher level of responsibility—and culpability—on its part.

Another example, with a closer verbal connection to Hosea 2:21–22, comes from the book of Psalms:

> Bestow Your faithful care on those devoted to You,
> and Your beneficence on upright men. (Ps 36:11)

Once again, the JPS *Tanakh* captures the sense well enough with "devoted to," but we should not miss the key fact that the Hebrew *yodeʿeykha* is the participle of *y.d.ʿ.*, so that the word might have been (too literally) rendered as, "Your knowers." These knowers of God are identified with "upright men" in this verse and contrasted with the "arrogant," "wicked," and "evildoers" in the next two. They are, in short, associated with a moral stance and the deeds that befit it and not simply with an affective attachment. It is also noteworthy that two of the endowments mentioned in Psalm 36:11, "faithful care" (*ḥesed*) and "beneficence" (*ṣedaqah*), recall two of the gifts or attributes associated with the LORD's rebetrothal of Israel in Hosea 2:21–22, "righteousness" (*ṣedeq*) and "goodness" (*ḥesed*). In both the psalm and the prophetic book, these endowments are associated with the devotion characteristic of the faithful covenant partner.

In the context of the marriage of Hosea, the cognitive and the covenantal sides of Hebrew *y.d.ʿ.* must stand alongside another, the sexual, perhaps best known from Genesis 4:1, "Now the man knew (*yadaʿ*) his wife Eve, and she conceived and bore Cain," though, in fact, the usage is not rare. Hosea 2:22 thus promises that the wife who had once acted as a prostitute, betraying her marriage to chase compulsively after a variety of men, will now experience sexual love in its proper and genuinely beneficial mode— within marriage and surrounded by righteousness, justice, goodness, mercy, and faithfulness.

The promiscuous wife and her cuckolded husband, then, have not gone their separate ways after all or found fulfillment with other partners more to their liking. If human practice alone, including biblical law, governed the relationship, the LORD could have divorced Israel, had her executed for adultery, and taken a new wife in her stead. And, to judge by the cases of various powerful men in the Hebrew Bible, he could all along have taken other wives in addition to Israel and thus all the more easily have cast her off when she went astray. Similarly, if we consider Hosea's paternal metaphor instead of the marital, we can evoke the case of the "wayward and defiant son" who refuses to heed his parents (Deut 21:18–21). The law allows the aggrieved mother and father to take the miscreant to the elders to be stoned to death. To be sure, the text in question speaks of the out-of-control son as "a glutton and a drunkard" (v. 20) and not as a sex addict, but the point still stands: the wayward son, no less than the errant wife, might in theory have been renounced.

But here a problem arises with the analogy: the theory derives from human legal practice and not from covenant theology as it is developed in the Hebrew Bible, and it is hazardous in the extreme to extrapolate uncritically from one to the other. In the book of Hosea, the wife's straying has proven disastrous, and her divine husband has ensured that her infidelity would meet a sorry fate—but he has also ensured that the covenant, though violated, would not be canceled, nor would the love in which it originated come to an ugly end. The LORD's covenantal love for Israel is absolute, but it is also responsive to her behavior and to the norms that enable covenant—and the love that it reflects— to thrive. It is a matter of grace, but—again—not cheap grace; of commitment, but not amoral commitment.

The words of God's rebetrothal of Israel in Hosea 2:21– 22 appear in the Jewish weekday liturgy. The worshipper recites them as he wraps the *tephillin*, or phylacteries, around his middle finger. The tephillin are two little boxes that are secured to leather straps and contain scrolls of the four passages from the Torah on which the practice is based (two of them, in fact, are from the Shema, Deut 6:4–9 and 11:13–21). One set is placed on the head, and the other on the arm and hand. By reciting the moving verses from Hosea, the worshipper, in effect, accepts God's offer of remarriage, pledging himself individually to faithfulness within the larger relationship of God to Israel. The strap around the finger has become, as it were, a wedding ring. The ancient marriage is renewed each weekday morning.

The Impossible Possibility of Return

Hosea is the first to give evidence of an interpretation of the history of God's relationship to Israel as a marriage. As he tells the story, the union began well: Israel responded appropriately "in the days of her youth … When she came up from the land of Egypt" (Hos 2:17), but soon the wife turned meretricious and adulterous. Ungrateful to her one legitimate lover—and apparently sex-crazed as well—she pursued a multitude of men, to her own ruin. The story powerfully underscores the hardiness of Israel's impulse to stray, or, to state the same point in reverse, the fragility of Israel's willingness to prove faithful. As the same book puts it later:

> What can I do for you, Ephraim,
> What can I do for you, Judah,
> When your goodness is like morning clouds,
> Like dew so early gone? (Hos 6:4)[30]

In fact, another passage in Hosea, one that uses the father-son rather than the husband-wife metaphor, seems to speak at greater length of the period of love and faithfulness before the catastrophic betrayal:

> [1]I fell in love with Israel
> When he was still a child;
> And I have called [him] My son
> Ever since Egypt.
> [2]Thus were they called,
> But they went their own way;
> They sacrifice to Baalim
> And offer to carved images.
> [3]I led Ephraim,
> Taking them in My arms;
> But they have ignored
> My healing care.
> [4]I drew them with human ties,
> With cords of love;
> But I seemed to them as one
> Who imposed a yoke on their jaws,
> Though I was offering them food.

⁵No!
They return to the land of Egypt,
And Assyria is their king.
Because they refuse to repent,
⁶A sword shall descend upon their towns
And consume their limbs
And devour [them] because of their designs.
⁷For My people persists
In its defection from Me;
When it is summoned upward,
It does not rise at all. (Hos 11:1–7)[31]

In his use of the marital metaphor, Hosea only hints at an initial period of love and faithfulness. In an oracle from a later prophet—Jeremiah—we find the same idea developed at greater length:

²Go proclaim to Jerusalem: Thus said the LORD:
I accounted to your favor
The devotion of your youth,
Your love as a bride—
How you followed Me in the wilderness,
In a land not sown.

■ ■ ■

⁵Thus said the LORD:
What wrong did your fathers find in Me
That they abandoned Me
And went after delusion and were deluded? (Jer 2:2, 5)

In Jeremiah, the LORD begins his marriage not with a faithless wife, as Hosea himself did, but with a devoted bride. Yet here again the marriage turns sour as she abandons him for other deities, to his great grief and with catastrophic consequences for her. The honeymoon is over. And just as Hosea initially depicts the marriage as terminated and the wife banished, so does Jeremiah at first insist that the law does not allow the divine husband to reunite with the cheating wife:

> If a man divorces his wife, and she leaves him and marries another man, can he ever go back (*yašuv*) to her? Would not such a land be defiled? Now you have whored with many lovers: can you return to Me?—says the LORD. (Jer 3:1)

The allusion to Israelite law is obvious: a man may not rewed his divorced wife if she has been married to anyone else in the interim. She cannot, in other words, return to him.[32] But what is forbidden to a human husband is permitted to Israel's God, and so great is his devotion to the people Israel that he pleads with them to do what that law forbids:

> [1]If you return (*tašuv*), O Israel—declares the LORD—
> If you return (*tašuv*) to Me,
> If you remove your abominations from My presence
> And do not waver,
> [2]And swear, "As the LORD lives,"
> In sincerity, justice, and righteousness—
> Nations shall bless themselves by you
> And praise themselves by you. (Jer 4:1–2)

To be sure, there is no reason to think this text presupposes the marital metaphor; "Israel" here (as always) is grammatically masculine, not feminine. Yet just as in the previous passage (Jer 3:1) the LORD had seemed angrily to preclude return, here he passionately pleads for just that.

The return in question is not simply a homecoming, but also a thoroughgoing change of heart, a self-purification and commitment to reform, on the order of what the rabbis, using the same Hebrew root, will later call *tešuvah*, a term conventionally (if inadequately) rendered as "repentance." And characteristic of Israel's new and reformed life in Jeremiah are traits that revealingly overlap with those that

Hosea had associated with the promised rebetrothal of the LORD and Israel: righteousness (*ṣedeq*), justice (*mišpaṭ*), goodness, mercy, and faithfulness (*'emunah*) in the case of Hosea (2:21–22), and, in the case of Jeremiah, sincerity (*'emet*, of the same root as *'emunah*), justice (*mišpaṭ*), and righteousness (*ṣedaqah*, of the same root as *ṣedeq*) (4:2).

Whatever the metaphor—and both prophetic books use a variety of metaphors—the theological message is essentially the same: Israel's behavior has gravely ruptured their intimate relationship with God, but the relationship can be reinstated and, as both books proclaim, in the future it indeed will be.

Why is my Beloved angry and disdainful of me?
My heart, longing for Him, shakes like a reed.
Has He forgotten the time when I, yearning,
Followed Him in the desolate wilderness?
How can I call out today and He does not answer?

Though He slay me, yet will I trust in Him,
And though He hide His face, I will contemplate His grace
And turn my face towards it.
The lovingkindness of the LORD will not pass away from His servant:
For how can fine gold lose its luster or suffer change?

Moses ibn Ezra[33]

The model of the relationship of the LORD and Israel as it appears in the marital metaphor in Hosea and Jeremiah (and, in fact, elsewhere in the Hebrew Bible) is a subtle one. Are God and Israel currently in love with each other? Are they, albeit metaphorically, married to each other? The texts we have been examining speak powerfully for a negative answer to both questions.

Hosea's own marriage begins with a promiscuous and adulterous woman, who then acts according to character and can be reformed and readied for marriage only through a grueling period of purgation. (Even when Hosea uses either the marital or the father-son metaphor and speaks, as we have seen, of an initial period of deep devotion, that soon comes to a crashing end when the bride or the boy rebels.) For Jeremiah, the romance began, as most do, on a high note: Israel was a devoted and loving bride, following her groom in the wilderness, "in a land not sown" (Jer 2:2). But in the present this romance, too, is dead because, as God tells Israel in the words of an oracle from the same chapter, "On every high hill and under every verdant tree, / You recline as a whore" (Jer 2:20). In fact, it is so dead that Israel's very law forbids it to be revived. And yet in both prophetic books, revived it indeed shall be: reform, though anything but easy, is possible, and return and reconciliation lie in the future—not simply as pious hope but as nothing short of divine promise.

This point is crucial: to speak of the romance of God and Israel as a settled and unchanging doctrine without regard to the flow of the narrative—to the history of the two parties as the prophets understand it—is to make a grave error. The people Israel addressed in the oracles that we have been examining are neither a devoted bride nor an obedient son. They are, rather, a people acting like a wife who flagrantly and chronically cheats on her husband, manically pursuing sexual gratification at the expense of covenantal fidelity, or like a son who ungratefully and obstinately refuses to serve his loving, giving father.

Thus, the reader of these books can hardly luxuriate in the comforting thought, "God loves me," so familiar from certain strains of American Christianity. For one thing, that "me" is too individualistic: it is the nation as a whole that is addressed, not atomized, disconnected individuals within it rehearsing their personal experience. For another thing, even within a less individualistic and more corporate understanding of Israel, of the sort appropriate to the

Hebrew Bible (and Judaism generally), the audience of these oracles exists neither in the romantic moment of the honeymoon (that is, the childhood of the nation) nor in the time of the promised reconciliation when love will at last be renewed. The audience exists, rather, in the moment of the *rupture*, when the oversexed bride regularly betrays her husband or the rebellious ingrate of a son acts out his unrealistic and irresponsible idea of independence.

The love, then, between the divine husband and the nation who is his wife is real but only in the past and in the future. The present is grim: the marriage is not terminated, to be sure, but it is, as it were, suspended. The couple has separated, but the power of the love that brought them together in the first place—the power of the LORD's ardent passion for Israel—prevents that separation from ever becoming amicable, or, more important, permanent. Only reunion can bring the current miserable moment to an end. The marriage is an ideal recollected from the idyllic past and a possibility promised for the restored future. It is not the current reality, but reality it surely is and shall be again.

The language in which I have just described this subtle relationship is the language of time: the marriage was beautiful in the past, is ugly and, in fact, suspended in the present, but will be reinstated when the future redemption comes about. This portrayal of the relationship between God and Israel as a narrative taking place over time, as all narratives do, fits the rhetorical purposes of the prophets well. For they seek to call errant Israel back to a period when she was profoundly faithful to God and behaved accordingly, and they do so in part by holding out the prospect of future reconciliation and renewal and describing the marvelous things that will attend the hoped-for redemption.

But this story playing out over time can also be seen as a dramatization of the deeper theology portrayed in the Torah in terms of the relationship between the Abrahamic and the Sinaitic covenants. As we saw in chapter 1, the

Those who have despoiled you shall themselves be despoiled,
And all who have devoured you shall go far away.
Your God shall rejoice over you,
As a groom rejoices over his bride.
  Come, my beloved, to greet the Bride:
  Let us welcome the Sabbath!
    Shelomoh Halevi Alqabets[34]

Abrahamic covenant is unconditional. It is a solemn pledge from God to Israel's forebear and comes without legal stipulations that the nation to descend from him must fulfill. It is not that their straying and failing to keep faith with him is excusable—far from it—but the straying is not fatal to that relationship and to God's fulfilling his promises to them.

The characteristic focus of the Sinaitic covenant, by way of contrast, lies on a set of conditions that Israel must meet. Literarily, this covenant serves as the framework or envelope in which various collections of law are now found. Theologically, it serves to recast the observance of the laws as acts of personal fidelity to the divine lawgiver, who is also Israel's lord in covenant.

If we put the interaction of these two significantly different types of covenant together (as the Torah itself does), we find that the violation of the laws constitutes a serious breach of covenant and thus brings in its train the harsh consequences promised to vassals who prove disloyal. Nevertheless, although those harsh consequences may prove fatal to individual Israelites, they do not prove so to the God-Israel relationship as a whole, and in large part precisely because of the note of unconditionality underlying the Abrahamic covenant.

The sheer gratuity of God's establishment of a covenant with Israel—the fact that the existence of covenant in the first place is a gift, not a reward—portends that it will survive Israel's malfeasance. The people's sins may suspend the intimacy and invert the favor characteristic of the covenantal bond, and they may move the relationship from one of blessing to one of curse. But they do not cancel the bond, and they do not terminate the relationship or make future blessedness unattainable.

Although the books of Hosea and Jeremiah nowhere refer to the specific covenant with Abraham, their portrayal of the marriage of the LORD and Israel can be seen, mutatis mutandis, as taking the same general shape as the covenantal theology just described. In their version of the marital idiom, the tender affections of an idyllic honeymoon give way to adultery and punishment, but the last word is one of favor and intimacy restored in a remarriage or reconciliation. In the past, Israel's capacity to sin may have proved more powerful than their love for God, but now God's love for them proves more powerful than sin.

National History Becomes an Extended—and Stormy—Romance

The depiction of the relation of God and Israel as a marriage began most likely as a prophetic sign-act, employed to dramatize graphically the nature of Israel's defection from her covenantal lord in favor of his rivals, whether the latter be other gods or empires. (The prophets do not tend to make a distinction between the two; however unrealistic from a practical political point of view it may be to do so, they tend to condemn international alliances as inevitably idolatrous.) The one metaphor, marriage, thus grows out of the other, covenant.

But covenant is not merely a matter of law; it comes with a narrative. Its authority, as we saw in chapter 1, rests in the history of benefits with which the suzerain, and he alone, has graced his vassal. Hosea and Jeremiah both represent that history through the image of a devoted bride following her groom in the wilderness on the way up from Egypt.[35] When devotion gives way to defection, however, the history of benefits turns into a history of horrors; the blessings of covenantal fidelity give way to the curses that attend betrayal. And so, the marital metaphor, still an out-growth of covenant, is easily extended to another phase in Israel's history: the sad phase marked by her defeat in battle, her attempts to secure herself through alliances, and thus her subjugation to great empires.

In Hosea, the marital metaphor encompasses the sign-acts with which the book begins and the evocations of love and the knowledge of God that are to be found throughout the book. In Jeremiah, the same metaphor appears in a few passages that speak of the honeymoon period, the betrayal and promiscuity in which the people have engaged, and the LORD's commitment to remarry them nonetheless. In Ezekiel 16, however, a book named for a younger contem-porary of Jeremiah, the gaps fill in to the point that we can discern the outlines of a coherent portrayal of the relation-ship of Israel and her God in marital terms.[36]

Ezekiel 16 begins with a savage address to Jerusalem—the capital of Judah, the sole remaining Israelite kingdom at the time—the site of the temple, the holiest place on earth, the very locus (ideally) of God's presence. Jeremiah, too, had addressed Jerusalem in this context, when he evoked her devotion as a young bride following God through the wilderness.[37] But Ezekiel takes the diametrically opposite tack, describing her as a female foundling of mixed blood (an Amorite father and a Hittite mother) on whom no one took pity: "on the day you were born, you were left lying, rejected, in the open field" (Ezek 16:5). Indeed, when the LORD found her, she had not been accorded the routine cleaning and swaddling of a newborn; her umbilical cord had not even been cut.

As in Jeremiah, Jerusalem here serves as symbol for the entire people, or to put it more accurately, as the most con-centrated and central part of the people and thus a fitting representation for the whole. But if Jerusalem and the people it represents are to manifest holiness and purity, the image of them as the abandoned and bloody child of two Canaanite parents (of different Canaanite groups, to boot)[38] already suggests that something has gone very wrong. Certainly, the image of Israel as originating in Canaan and not, as in Genesis, in Mesopotamia (the birthplace of their forefather Abraham) would have suggested intense moral and religious degradation to Ezekiel's hearers. This is not Jeremiah's faithful bride; it is a girl with nothing to her credit.

Yet, amazingly, the LORD takes an interest in her. More than that—he saves the life of the abandoned child on whom no one else had compassion: "When I passed by you and saw you wallowing in your blood, I said to you: 'Live in spite of your blood'" (Ezek 16:6). Soon, the child, perhaps to be understood as God's adopted daughter, has reached puberty, and his interest in her now takes a different turn:

> [7]You were still naked and bare [8]when I passed by you [again] and saw that your time for love had arrived. So I spread My robe over you and covered your nakedness, and I entered into a covenant with you by oath—declares the LORD GOD; thus you became Mine. (Ezek 16:7b–8)

The "love" (*dodim*) in question is clearly sexual, and God's spreading his robe is just as unmistakably an act of matrimony.[39] It is tempting to think that the words "I entered into a covenant with you by oath" demonstrate that marriages were understood as covenants in ancient Israel and sealed by oaths, rather like the vows that Christians (but not Jews) have traditionally taken at their weddings. The evidence against this surmise is powerful, however,[40] and we should be much better advised to see these words as Ezekiel's explicit incorporation of the covenant tradition into the marital metaphor. Or, to state the same point in reverse, we should see Ezekiel's words here as his application of the marital metaphor to the covenant theology out of which it had once emerged and which it had, by his time, long served. As in Genesis, the LORD graciously brings Israel—or at least their capital and temple city Jerusalem—into covenant with him, except that this time Israel is represented as an indigenous woman of disgraceful origins, not as the Mesopotamian immigrant Abraham and his chosen heirs, Isaac and Jacob.

Jerusalem's marriage to God elevates her dramatically, as he showers her with gifts of precious jewelry, fine fabrics, and choice foodstuffs. He even treats her as a queen, placing a glorious crown on her head.[41] "You grew more and more beautiful," the prophet summarizes, "and became fit for royalty. Your beauty won you fame among the nations, for it was perfected through the splendor which I set upon you—declares the LORD GOD" (Ezek 16:13b–14). In the background of these verses lie the fabled beauty and international fame of Jerusalem, but perhaps we can also detect here an analogy to the great wealth that Abraham, Isaac, and Jacob are all reported in Genesis to have amassed, and perhaps even an echo of it.[42] In any event, in both Genesis and Ezekiel the covenantal suzerain has proven enormously generous to his faithful vassal, and, as always, much to the suzerain's benefit.

But just as in Hosea, so here in Ezekiel the people lose the sense of gratitude essential to the covenant and with it (to revert to the marital metaphor) the sexual fidelity essential to marriage. "But confident in your beauty and fame," Ezekiel admonishes Jerusalem, "you played the harlot: you lavished your favors on every passerby" (Ezek 16:15). And in keeping with his perfervid imagination and baroque style, the prophet provides details vastly more graphic than what we saw in Hosea or Jeremiah, such as this: "You took your beautiful things, made of the gold and silver that I had given you, and you made yourself phallic images and fornicated with them" (v. 17). In fact, Ezekiel claims, Jerusalem was even worse than a prostitute: whereas a prostitute accepts payment for her services, Jerusalem bribed her lovers to make use of her.[43] In this, it is not hard to hear an attack on the kingdom of Judah for paying tribute to the great empires around her when, in her military vulnerability, she accepted vassalage to them at the expense of her covenant with the LORD. Forgetful of her humble origins and of her husband's generosity as well, God's metaphorical wife has lost all sense of her dependence on him: "In all your abominations and harlotries, you did not remember the days of your youth, when you were naked and bare, and lay wallowing in your blood" (v. 22).

The results are again—and predictably—catastrophic. The cheating wife once more loses her splendid jewelry and is left "naked and bare" (Ezek 16:39)—just as she was when God first took notice of her. Here again, the political referent is easy to spot: the horrific destruction of Jerusalem and its temple by the Neo-Babylonian Empire in 586 BCE, which brought to an end the independence of the southern kingdom of Judah and inaugurated the Babylonian Exile. (The northern kingdom, Israel, had met a similar fate in 722 BCE.) But, as in Hosea and Jeremiah, the punishment—intense, even bloodcurdling though it is—is not the last word. After the retribution has been rendered, God's anger subsides, and restoration eventually replaces retribution:

> [59]Truly, thus said the LORD GOD: I will deal with you as you have dealt, for you have spurned the oath and violated the covenant. [60]But I will remember the covenant I made with you in the days of your youth, and I will establish it with you as an everlasting covenant.... [62]I will establish My covenant with you, and you shall know that I am the LORD. [63]Thus you shall remember and feel shame, and you shall be too abashed to open your mouth

again, when I have absolved you for all that you did—
declares the LORD GOD. (Ezek 16:59–60, 62–63)[44]

Although Jerusalem has perjured herself and proven
disloyal to the God who had "entered into a covenant with
[her] by oath" (Ezek 16:8), he, by contrast, will uphold his
pledged word and show himself to be faithful to the self-
same covenant. God will not, in other words, commit per-
jury and destroy his reputation, as Jerusalem shamelessly
destroyed hers. Instead, he reinstates his desecrated covenant and perhaps even implies, in the term "everlasting
covenant" (v. 60), that the pattern of betrayal and punishment shall never recur. If so, this is an implication that fits
well with Ezekiel's prophecy that after the judgment and
the punishment, God will give the House of Israel "a new
heart ... and a new spirit": "Thus," he quotes God to say, "I
will cause you to follow My laws and faithfully to observe
My rules" (Ezek 36:26–27). To the extent that the covenant
depends on the human partners' meeting its conditions,
covenant is exceedingly fragile. To the extent that it depends on God's reliability, it is rock-solid.

Ezekiel depicts his majestic and eerily remote God without any of the tender feelings we saw in Hosea; he does
not quote the LORD as proclaiming, as the latter does, "I
will betroth you forever" (Hos 2:21). In fact, when Ezekiel
speaks of restoration after punishment, he seems to drop
the language of marriage and sexual experience altogether.
But he, too, speaks of "the days of your youth" (Ezek 16:60;
cf. Hos 2:17) and of the survival of the covenant after its
hideous desecration. In each case, Israel can violate the
covenant; they cannot nullify it. They can divert it from
its proper course and invert it against themselves; they
cannot terminate it. Whatever their own preferences and
impulses, the sworn covenant will never be defeated. The
"time for love" that they once knew may tarry, but it shall
surely return.

The book of Ezekiel returns to the marital metaphor, though with some differences, in chapter 23. We need not explore this version in detail, but one aspect is worthy of mention. Here, there are two whoring women, Oholah and Oholibah, representing the northern kingdom and the southern, respectively. Underlying both names is the Hebrew word for "tent" (*'ohel*), a term that is well known and widely used in connection with temple traditions. Hence, the name for the southern kingdom (Judah), Oholibah, means, appropriately, "My tent is in her" and thus makes a clear allusion to the surviving and uniquely legitimate temple in Jerusalem.

This temple connection is not surprising, given Ezekiel's manifest association with priestly traditions. He is, after all, a priest (*kohen*) himself,[45] and much of his preaching centers on the Jerusalem temple. The first eleven chapters of his book thus tell of the LORD's departure from his defiled sanctuary as he headed into exile in Babylonia; the last nine focus on the new (and very different) structure that will be rebuilt to replace it when the exile has ended and the Judeans have returned from Babylonia.[46] The fact that Israelites have performed idolatrous rites within the walls of their holiest site, the very palace of the LORD, is especially offensive to Ezekiel and his God. Women bewailing the loss of the Mesopotamian dying-and-rising god Tammuz at the north gate of the temple, men in its inner court bowing low in homage to the sun[47]—these are the sorts of things that have alienated God from his chosen home on earth and exiled his people from the land he has given them.

In Ezekiel 23, the idea of temple desecration has come to be expressed in the now-familiar image of the whoring wife. Or, to put the point somewhat differently, the sins of Israel, especially (but not exclusively) those involving foreign alliances and the worship of gods other than the LORD, are interpreted as attacking the temple itself, defiling and ultimately destroying it:

> ³⁶Then the LORD said to me: O mortal, arraign Oholah and Oholibah, and charge them with their abominations. ³⁷For they have committed adultery, and blood is on their hands; truly they have committed adultery with their fetishes, and have even offered to them as food the children they bore to Me. ³⁸At the same time they also did this to Me: they defiled My Sanctuary and profaned My sabbaths. ³⁹On the very day that they slaughtered their children to their fetishes, they entered My Sanctuary to desecrate it. That is what they did in My House. (Ezek 23:36–39)

Viewed from one angle, Ezekiel 23 tells us that the *temple* of the kingdom of Judah has gone astray through the deviant cultic activities that have gone on in it; hence, the symbolic names of the two meretricious sisters who have committed the many atrocities the chapter details. From another angle, though, it tells us that the *people* of both Israelite kingdoms have historically acted in such an abominable way as to invalidate the temple, and from this angle we again see that the real malefactor is not the two sisters of the parable but the men and women whom they represent—the Israelites who have committed the abominations. From this latter vantage point, the temple is not the perpetrator of the abuses: it is their victim. As in the case of the women lamenting the death of Tammuz or the men bowing to the sun, the temple community has polluted its own sanctuary, befouling the terrestrial home of the true lord of the universe and making it unfit for his continued residence.[48] The presence of God in Jerusalem has become a casualty of Israel's evildoing.

In the next chapter, Ezekiel performs a sign-act that underscores the temple theology but also the marriage metaphor. The passage begins with God's ominous announcement to him:

> [16]O mortal, I am about to take away the delight of your eyes from you through pestilence; but you shall not lament or weep or let your tears flow. [17]Moan softly; observe no mourning for the dead: Put on your turban and put your sandals on your feet; do not cover over your upper lip, and do not eat the bread of comforters. (Ezek 24:16–17)

The "light of [Ezekiel's] eyes," it turns out, is his wife, and when the people ask the prophet the meaning of his strange failure to observe the usual mourning rituals for her, he has his reply ready. It is, in fact, one that extends the ominous tone of God's announcement:

> [20]I answered them, "The word of the LORD has come to me: [21]Tell the House of Israel: Thus said the LORD GOD: 'I am going to desecrate My Sanctuary, your pride and glory, the delight of your eyes and the desire of your heart; and the sons and daughters you have left behind shall fall by the sword. [22]Accordingly, you shall do as I have done: you shall not cover over your upper lips or eat the bread of comforters; [23]and your turbans shall remain on your heads, and your sandals upon your feet. You shall not lament or weep, but you shall be heartsick because of your iniquities and shall moan to one another. [24]And Ezekiel shall become a portent for you: you shall do just as he has done, when it happens; and you shall know that I am the LORD GOD.'" (Ezek 24:20–24)[49]

Ezekiel's loss of his wife serves as a representation of Israel's loss of its temple, and his abstention from the accustomed rites of mourning underscores the gravity of their loss: at this point there can be no comfort, only heartfelt remorse for the sins that brought about the unspeakable catastrophe. The prophet's marriage has thus become a parable of the relationship of God to his people, much as we saw in the case of Hosea, but with a key difference. As Larry L. Lyke puts it, "Whereas in the former [that is, the marital sign-act of the sort we have seen] God was understood to be married to Israel or Judah, here it is implied that God's spouse is not the people but the temple."[50]

I would add that here God's wife is not the temple as an agent of sin—there is no reason to think that Ezekiel's wife's death was punishment for anything she did—but rather as that which is lost as a result of the people's chronic wrongdoing. What they have lost is their pride and glory, the delight of their eyes and the desire of their heart—the place, that is, in which they are most ennobled, closest to God, and most likely to attain intimacy with him. The romance that he had known is now unavailable; the lovers have been separated.

With the sign-act attending his wife's death, Ezekiel has again extended the marriage metaphor so as to take into account the catastrophe of 586 BCE, but this time he has done so in a new way. Now the emphasis falls not on the community in its sinfulness, chronically and compulsively breaching covenant, but rather on the community in its ideal state, a locus of purity and majesty, as befits the palace of God. The ideal Israel associated with the temple has indeed been lost, but, as we have seen, in the book of Ezekiel the loss is not permanent. The ideal and the real will yet reunite. The unavailable lover will return.

"MY BELOVED IS MINE, AND I AM HIS"

Of all the books in the Bible, none concentrates more on love than the Song of Songs. A work of a mere 117 verses in eight chapters, the book presents us with a collection of related songs of erotic longing and fantasy, all spoken by the lovers themselves in exquisite poetry, much of it among

the most memorable in scripture. Unlike the prophetic
texts we have been examining, in this book it is the woman
who does most of the speaking. It is she who, as one
scholar puts it, "dominates speech and takes most of the
sexual initiatives—at least in terms of words."[51] And it is
her words, not her lover's, that begin and end the book.[52]
Here is the beginning:

> [2]Let him give me of the kisses of his mouth,
> For your love is more delightful than wine.
> [3]Your ointments yield a sweet fragrance,
> Your name is like finest oil—
> Therefore do maidens love you.
> [4]Draw me after you, let us run! (Song 1:2–4a)[53]

And here is the ending, again in the woman's voice:

> [13]O you who linger in the garden,
> A lover is listening;
> Let me hear your voice.
> [14]"Hurry, my beloved,
> Swift as a gazelle or a young stag,
> To the hills of spices!" (Song 8:13–14)[54]

The woman introduces herself as a humble country girl,
sun-darkened because "My mother's sons quarreled with
me, / They made me guard the vineyards" (Song 1:6). At
other times, though, she seems to be a figure of the royal
court, or at least known there, as her lover passionately
attests:

> [8]There are sixty queens,
> And eighty concubines,
> And damsels without number.
> [9]Only one is my dove,
> My perfect one,
> The only one of her mother,
> The delight of her who bore her.

Maidens see and acclaim her;
Queens and concubines, and praise her. (Song 6:8–9)

The description of her lover betrays a similar ambiguity. On the one hand, he is a shepherd boy on the move with his flocks, as seen in the following exchange. She speaks in verse 7 and he in verse 8:

7Tell me, you whom I love so well;
Where do you pasture your sheep?
Where do you rest them at noon?
Let me not be as one who is veiled
Beside the flocks of your fellows.
8If you do not know, O fairest of women,
Go follow the tracks of the sheep,
And graze your kids
By the tents of the shepherds. (Song 1:7–8)[55]

On the other hand, there are passages like this, voiced by the female lover:

12While the king was on his couch,
My nard gave forth its fragrance.
13My beloved to me is a bag of myrrh
Lodged between my breasts.
14My beloved to me is a spray of henna blooms
From the vineyards of En-gedi. (Song 1:12–14)

Is the shepherd boy also "the king"? The references to Solomon, not only in the superscription (1:1) but in other verses as well, speak (though perhaps not definitively) for a positive answer:

9King Solomon made himself a palanquin
Of wood from Lebanon.
10He made its posts of silver,
Its back of gold,
Its seat of purple wool.
Within, it was decked with love

By the maidens of Jerusalem.
[11] O maidens of Zion, go forth
And gaze upon King Solomon
Wearing the crown that his mother
Gave him on his wedding day,
On his day of bliss. (Song 3:9–11)[56]

Perhaps the ancient Mesopotamian description of kings as the shepherds of their people plays a role in this dual portrayal of the male lover; note that in the Bible, Joseph, Moses, and David all tended flocks before assuming political power. (Solomon did not.) In any event, although some scholars have suggested that there are two men involved, one humble and pastoral and the other mighty and regal, the description of the male figure as both king and shepherd seems more likely to be a literary device that advances a key theme of the whole book—the transience of the lovers' availability to each other. As Francis Landy puts it, "the king cannot escape his role. Throughout the Song there is a tension between his humanity and his function, between his inaccessibility, behind his curtains (1:5), and his attempt to woo the Beloved.... The lovers can only find or imagine an enclosure, secluded from the world: a garden, a forest bed, or the poem itself."[57]

One of the reasons that the lovers seek seclusion is that the community cannot understand the love they feel for each other and, as a result, inflicts abuse upon them. The woman's allusion to her brothers' quarrels with her is probably an example, and her allusions to watchmen hitting and bruising her surely is.[58] Most memorable, though, are these verses:

[6]Let me be a seal upon your heart,
Like the seal upon your hand.
For love is fierce as death,
Passion is mighty as Sheol;
Its darts are darts of fire,

A blazing flame.
7Vast floods cannot quench love,
Nor rivers drown it.
If a man offered all his wealth for love,
He would be laughed to scorn. (Song 8:6–7)

Putting this social rejection together with the prominence of the woman's voice (she is again the speaker in the passage above) and her willingness to take the sexual initiative, some scholars find in the Song of Songs a protest against what has in recent decades come to be called "patriarchy," and a corollary advocacy of sexual equality. As Phyllis Trible puts it, "In this setting, there is no male dominance, no female subordination, and no stereotyping of either sex."[59]

We should be careful, however, not to extrapolate excessively from the situation that sets the tone for the entire book and the moment in the human life cycle from which it derives: the situation of courtship and intense sexual love between two people who have yet to build families of their own. There is no reason to believe that the youthful speakers in the Song of Songs, when they have finally married and settled into domestic life, will adhere to anything other than the traditional gender roles of their society or that they will abstain from making their own contribution to the succession of generations, remaining instead forever in the mode of unencumbered lovers longing only for each other's presence and each other's body. Trible has a point when she writes, "to the issues of marriage and procreation, the Song does not speak. Love for the sake of love is its message, and the portrayal of the female delineates this message best."[60] But the assumption that there is a significant dichotomy between love for its own sake, on the one hand, and love leading to marriage and children, on the other, is false to ancient Israelite culture. There is no reason to think that, by focusing on youthful romance, the author of the Song of Songs sought to offer a critique of marriage, procreation, parenthood, or the structures that went with them in ancient Israel.

The celebration of sexuality in general and female initiative in particular in the Song of Songs may seem to stand in stark contrast with the relentless indictments of God's wayward wife in Hosea, Jeremiah, and Ezekiel. The contrast, however, is ill considered. It is not at all the case that the Song celebrates female sexuality and the prophets condemn it. Note that in the prophetic metaphor, Israel is a married woman who "whores," that is, one who is promiscuous, giving sexual favors to a series of lovers and thus proving faithless to her husband. In the Song of Songs, the woman, still single, longs only for her lover, and he only for her: "My beloved is mine," she famously sings, "and I am his" (Song 2:16). Whatever social taboos she may have violated to incur the wrath of her brothers and the town watchmen, she has not betrayed her relationship with the singular object of her libido. If an analogy to her must be found in the prophetic metaphor, it is to Israel not as a whoring wife but as a faithful bride or as the wife redeemed, restored, and remarried to her faithful and loving husband, the LORD, God of Israel.

But Who Are the Speakers?

So far, we have spoken of the Song of Songs as a freestanding composition, without regard to the implications of the fact that we find it in the collection we have been calling the Hebrew Bible. If we treat the book this way, we surely need to guard against any interpretation that claims to know more than the text can reasonably support. Rather than seeking to identify the speakers in the Song of Songs with specific figures, or their actions with particular historical situations, for example, it would be wiser to see them as what J. Cheryl Exum calls "archetypical lovers—

composite figures, types of lovers rather than any specific lovers." "By providing access only to the voices of the lovers," she observes, "to what they say [and] not who they are, the poet is able to identify them with all lovers." This is precisely what "makes it easier for readers to relate the Song's lovers' experience to their own experience of love, real or fantasized."[61]

There is no question that the Song of Songs can be profitably read this way, as a freestanding composition, disconnected from the great story of Israel. It is highly doubtful, however, that most ancient Jews actually interpreted it apart from the other literature that defined their culture and dominated their education—that is, from the rest of the Hebrew Bible, or whatever parts of it existed at the time.[62] It is one thing, in other words, to say that the Song of Songs *can* be read in isolation or was so intended by its author or authors; it is quite another to argue that it *ought* to be so read, that it is best so read, or that ancient Jewish culture would not most naturally have sought to place it in a larger framework, something roughly on the order of the biblical canon in which it has, in fact, come to us. To be sure, some Jews did indeed treat the book in a more secular fashion, singing it at wedding banquets or in taverns; we know this because the great Rabbi Akiva is reported to have anathematized the practice.[63] But, as a matter of historical fact, the ancient Jewish interpretations of the Song that we actually have in our possession place it securely within a more capacious and more culturally resonant framework.[64]

Within that larger context, the question of the identity of the speakers takes on greater urgency than when the book is viewed in isolation. Who, in this larger framework, could these two passionate lovers possibly be? Let us put the question in terms of the rest of the Hebrew Bible: Where in that set of books do we find an intense love in which the lovers are separated much of the time, the male of the two is not continuously accessible, the identities of the lovers seem to shift in various situations, powerful external forces oppose and threaten the romance, and the consummation of the relationship seems to be continually, maddeningly postponed?[65] Put that way, the question nearly answers itself: the only such romance is that of God and Israel. To be sure, not every detail matches up, and much imaginative interpretation is necessary to sustain the identification. That very process of imaginative interpretation, though, is highly productive theologically and spiritually. It places both the marriage metaphor of the prophets and the poems of erotic longing in the Song of Songs in a new framework in which love is again the central term in the relationship of God and Israel. But now it is a love that is not only covenantal but also deeply passionate and, or, to put the point more precisely, it is a love simultaneously covenantal and deeply passionate, even erotic, a love that draws from, and enriches, both frames of reference by refusing to keep either in isolation from the other.

Conventionally, this interpretation of the Song of Songs as the love song of God and Israel is described as "allegorical" and thus faulted for the arbitrariness characteristic of that genre.[67] Both that convention and the criticism that accompanies it are unfortunate, however, for the identification of the speaking voices in the Song with Israel and her God, while not defensible as the plain sense of the Song considered in isolation, is far from arbitrary. It derives, rather, from the logic of midrash, which seeks to bring different scriptural texts into productive relationship with each other and, in the process, to bring the deeper unity of the scripture to light. Unlike the allegorist, Daniel Boyarin writes, the midrashist "does not translate the images of the verse into ideas, but says this verse was said as a metaphoric interpretation of another text and that the reading of the two texts together will already interpret both of them."[68] And unlike the allegorist, for whom the particu-

[2]I was asleep
But my heart was awake.
Hark, my beloved knocks!
"Let me in, my own,
My darling, my faultless dove!
For my head is drenched with dew,
My locks with the damp of night."
[3]I had taken off my robe—
Was I to don it again?
I had bathed my feet—
Was I to soil them again?
[4]My beloved took his hand off the latch,
And my heart was stirred within me.
[5]I rose to let in my beloved;
My hands dripped myrrh—
My fingers, flowing myrrh—
Upon the handles of the bolt.
[6]I opened the door for my beloved,
I was faint because of what he had said.
But my beloved had turned, had gone.
I sought, but found him not;
I called, but he did not answer.

Song of Songs 5:2–6[66]

lars of the text are but ciphers for some more abstract meaning, "When the Rabbis read the Song of Songs, they do not translate its 'carnal' meaning into one or more 'spiritual' senses; rather, they establish a concrete, historical moment in which to contextualize it."[69] In the midrashic mind, the key question, then, is, "With regard to which place in the Torah was it said?"[70]

Thus, on the opening of the first stanza in the book, "Let him give me of the kisses of his mouth" (Song 1:2),[71] one rabbi interprets the verse to have been said at the Red Sea; another tells us it was spoken at Mount Sinai; still another, that it was said in the Tent of Meeting, the shrine that accompanied the Israelites on their trek to the Promised Land;

but the majority of rabbis, this text reports, hold that it was spoken in the temple. The precise verses and verbal connections that facilitate these midrashic interpretations need not concern us here. What is relevant, however, is that the speakers are understood to be God (or his angels) and Israel, though which is the speaker and which the addressee differs in the various instances. Indeed, one famous midrash interprets the opening verse—"The Song of Songs, by Solomon (*lišlomoh*)" (Song 1:1)—as a reference not to the human king of that name but "to the king to whom peace belongs (*šehaššalom šello*)." The point is clear: "The Holy One (blessed be He!) said it himself in his great majesty."[72]

We are not, then, dealing with just another pair of youthful lovers libidinously yearning for each other. We are, instead, dealing with the longest lasting and most consequential romance ever—the unending romance of God and the people Israel, which, it now turns out, has something important in common with the relationship of young lovers in their passionate pursuit of each other. Without the application of the Song of Songs to the Torah, the depth and power of their libidinous passion might never have come to expression. And without the application of the Torah to the Song of Songs, the deeper spiritual import of erotic love would surely have gone unnoticed.

In line with this midrashic correlation of the Song of Songs with the Torah, we find a reinterpretation of Sinai as God's proposal of marriage. Thus, on the words, "Let him give me of the kisses of his mouth" (Song 1:2), we find this parable:

> Rabbi Yoḥanan interpreted the verse as applying to Israel at the time they went up to Mount Sinai: It is like a king who wants to marry a woman from a good family and with a good pedigree. He sent a messenger to her to speak with her. She said, "I am not worthy even to be his slave woman, but nonetheless I want to hear it from his own

mouth." When the messenger returned to the king, his face was full of smiles, but his conversations were not reported to the king. The king, who was very perceptive, said, "This man's face is full of smiles. It would appear that she accepted the offer. His conversations were not reported to me. It would appear that she wants to hear it from my own mouth." Hence, Israel is the woman from a good family, Moses is the messenger, and the Holy One (blessed be He!) is the king. At that time, "Moses brought back the people's words to the LORD" (Exod 19:8). So why does the text [in the very next verse] say, "Then Moses reported the people's words to the LORD"? Because, inasmuch as it says, "I will come to you in a thick cloud, in order that the people may hear when I speak with you and so trust you ever after." "Then Moses reported the people's words to the LORD" (v. 9)—he said to Him, "This is what they have asked for." He replied, "People grant a child what he asks for." (*Song of Songs Rabbah* 1:2:3)

The logic of this complex midrash demands explication. The "good family" and the "good pedigree" characteristic of the wife sought by the king refer to Israel's descent from Abraham, Isaac, and Jacob. Here, the focus is not on the irrevocable covenantal promises so prominent in Genesis but rather on the proven record of fidelity and integrity that rabbinic thought attributes to those national ancestors. Presented with God's offer, Israel protests her unworthiness—people do not, after all, *deserve* to have a specific person love them to the point of proposing marriage—but also asks to hear the proposal directly from God's lips. Hence the relevance of the plea, "Let him give me of the kisses of his mouth," in Song of Songs 1:2. But God's intermediary, Moses, though happy at Israel's apparent consent, refrains from reporting her request to God, probably because he thinks it infringes on the divine majesty: it is inappropriate for mere mortals to ask God to speak directly to them.

So "Moses brought back the people's words to the LORD" (Exod 19:8), apparently without giving the specifics. But God recognized what the response must have been and so in the very next verse promises to speak directly to the people with his own mouth, as it were: "I will come to you in a thick cloud, in order that the people may hear when I speak with you and so trust you ever after" (v. 9). And that is why that same verse ends in what may initially look like a meaningless repetition of the previous verse, "Then Moses reported the people's words to the LORD." Once Moses realizes that God knows the people's request, he "reported" the words, whereas before he had only "brought" them. Israel had asked for a direct proposal of marriage—"the kisses of his mouth"—and God obliged. It bears mention that in the next verse, God instructs Moses to "go to the people and warn them to stay pure (*veqiddaštam*)" (v. 10), using a verb (*qiddeš*, usually rendered as "to consecrate") that in rabbinic parlance will come to refer to the marriage ceremony.

In this midrash, then, Moses brokers more than a covenant understood along the lines of the suzerainty treaties we discussed in chapter 1: he brokers a marriage as well. His mission results in the holy matrimony of God and the people of Israel.

So much for God's offer of marriage and Israel's acceptance of it. What of the wedding itself?

> Another interpretation: "On the day that Moses finished (*kallot*) [setting up the tabernacle, he anointed and consecrated (*vayqaddeš*) it]" (Num 7:1). *Klt* is what is written, meaning, "On the day that the bride (Aramaic *kalta'*) entered the bridal chamber (*genuna'*)." (*Pesiqta de Rav Kahana* 1:5)

This midrash, too, requires some explanation. The verse on which it comments (Num 7:1) speaks of Moses's finishing

the building of the tabernacle: the portable, tentlike structure that served as Israel's temple during their wandering
in the wilderness and thus as the locus of God's presence
on earth and his availability to the people Israel on their
way to the Promised Land. Here it must be remembered
that Biblical Hebrew was written essentially only in consonants, and the possibility of filling in different vowels from
those supplied by the tradition was enormously fruitful
for the makers of midrash. In this instance, the consonants
of the word rendered as "finished" (*klt*) suggest the Hebrew word for "bride" (*kallah*) and, even more so, its Aramaic cognate (*kalta'*).

The implication of this slight change is momentous: on
Sinai, Moses celebrated the wedding of God to the people
Israel. What is more, the tabernacle was Israel's bridal
chamber—the place, that is, in which their union was consummated. Here again, the verb *qiddeš* (consecrate) helps
catalyze the midrashic interpretation. When, at the literal
level, Moses was anointing the tabernacle and its accoutre-
ments, transferring them from the realm of the profane to
that of the sacred, he was enacting, at the midrashic level,
the consecration of Israel to God as his bride—a condition
that in the rabbinic mind has survived both the tabernacle
and the temple that it foreshadowed, and has defined the
Jewish people through all their generations. The tabernacle served as the chuppah, the marriage canopy, for the
wedding of God and Israel.

In the distant background of this metaphor lie Jeremiah's
and Ezekiel's addresses to Jerusalem, the temple city, as a
once faithful bride who has betrayed her marriage, and,
more specifically, Ezekiel's implied equation of the temple
and his own beloved wife, which we examined earlier in
this chapter. But in the midrash the wife is not the adulterous city or nation who the prophets berate. She is rather
the *keneset yiśra'el*, the Community of Israel faithful to her

loving husband, eager to serve him, and longing for reunion with him, just as he is everlastingly faithful to her, in love with her, and committed to redeeming her.

This is, of course, a theological ideal and not at all an accurate description of the historical facts, as the prophetic and many other biblical and postbiblical texts painfully attest. But it is an ideal with a potent and enduring capacity to inspire behavior, to provoke repentance—and to ignite the love of God among Jews. Within the marital metaphor as these Talmudic rabbis extended and developed it, the Torah, both as narrative and as law, becomes a site of intense erotic passion. Its narrative tells of God's and the Jewish people's falling in love with each other, of his proposing marriage and her accepting the proposal, of the wedding itself and the intimacy and deepening commitment that followed it.

And what of the Torah's *law*? Within the rabbinic metaphor of marriage, the laws are as far as possible from being meaningless, feelingless strictures—so far, in fact, that our dry English word "law" can never do them justice. Contrary to the way the laws of the Torah have so often been described (and sometimes still are), the rabbinic tradition does not take them to be prescriptions to be grimly, if punctiliously, fulfilled by a people frightened into submission, seeking to earn their salvation like a worker's wage, or living their lives on spiritual and emotional autopilot. On the words from the opening of the Song of Songs, "For your love is more delightful than wine" (Song 1:2), where the word for "love" (*dodeykha*) is plural in form, various midrashim thus simply assume that the reference is to "words of Torah."[73]

Similarly, an early midrash makes this parable:

A king of flesh and blood said to his wife, "Beautify yourself with all your jewelry, so that you will be desirable (*reṣuyah*) to me." Thus, the Holy One (blessed be He) said

to Israel, "My children, be distinguished by the commandments, so that you will be desirable (reṣuyah) to me."
Therefore it says, "You are beautiful, my darling, as Tir-
zah (tirṣah)"—you are beautiful when you are desirable
(reṣuyah) to Me. (*Siphre Deut* 36, quoting Song 6:4)

Ideally, when Jews involve themselves in Torah, they are
singing a love song to God and responding to his love song
to them. The Torah is narrative, and the Torah is law, but
within both law and narrative lies Torah as love.[74]

Sex as Symbol

I have been at pains to argue that the logic by which the
ancient rabbis interpreted the Song of Songs is not in the
first instance best described as allegorical. Rather, it derives,
as most midrash does, from an effort to correlate and con-
nect the different parts of the sacred writings, all of which
the rabbis maintain "were given by one Shepherd" (Qoh
12:11). This is not to deny, of course, that the Song of Songs
can be appreciated in isolation. The many scholars and ordinary readers who have found in it a beautiful and profound depiction of human sexual love provide evidence
that indeed it can be so appreciated, and very profitably.
Nor is it to deny that at times the midrashic sense has
been invoked prudishly to suppress the plain sense, or, to
be more precise, the plain sense when the book is read
in splendid isolation from the larger story of Israel. "The
trouble," Marvin Pope writes in his massive and amazingly
learned commentary on the book, "has been that interpreters who dared to acknowledge the plain sense of the
Song were assaulted as enemies of truth and decency. The
allegorical charade thus persisted for centuries with only
sporadic protests."[75]

Although the adjective "allegorical" does not do proper
justice to the interpretive assumptions at work here, and

the noun "charade" fails to reckon with the theological motives of the interpreters, it is certainly true that we must
guard against altogether replacing the plain sense of the
Song of Songs with its midrashic application. For without
a sense of the power and passion of human sexual love, we
shall miss the import of the midrashic move. Ironically,
then, if we confuse the midrashic sense (*deraš* in rabbinic
terminology) with the plain sense (*pešaṭ*), as often happens today in some pious circles, we shall fail to recognize
fully the creativity and the power of the midrash itself.

The wisest course is neither to substitute a modern secular interpretation for the traditional religious one (as Pope
and many other scholars do) nor to adhere to the traditional interpretation alone as if it were the plain sense of
the book considered as a stand-alone composition. The
Song of Songs can and, in my opinion should, be interpreted with an awareness of its different contexts and the
different levels of meaning these suggest. To some people—
and this may be the cause of Pope's harsh language—to
accept the midrashic interpretation is to drain the earthy
vitality out of the Song of Songs, spiritualizing it into a
bland description of the relationship of God and Israel (or,
in the Christian version, Christ and his Church). A lusty
set of poems about real-life erotic passion evaporates into
a bloodless theological lesson about the platonic love of an
incorporeal God and his idealized people.

At best, however, this tells only half the story. For the
process actually moves in both directions. The midrashim
that we have examined not only read the Song of Songs in
the light of Exodus; they also read Exodus in the light of
the Song of Songs. Consider the effect of that latter movement. Events in the Torah that are not described as motivated by love, certainly not by anything analogous to sexual
love—events like the making of the covenant or the building of the tabernacle at Sinai—are now depicted in the
strikingly earthy, sexual language of one of the most erotic

pieces of literature of the ancient world. If indeed it is true that the midrashic interpretation drains some of the heat and blood out of the Song, it is also the case that it infuses that same heat and blood into the Torah.

To be sure, there is an analogical leap from the passion of the physical lovers to that of the bodiless God and his ideal lover, *keneset yiśraʾel*, the Jewish people in their ideal state of wholehearted faithfulness and devotion to their divine lover. But whether that leap involves a loss or a gain is a question that the study of culture, history, and language alone can never resolve. It is one that depends on the more encompassing issue of the theological and philosophical framework within which interpretation takes place.

Here an observation of Irving Singer's is apposite. Against Freud's well-known tendency to find sexual symbolism hither and yon, Singer writes this:

> The mountain or the ladder symbolizes sexual intercourse? Possibly; indeed, very likely. But what does sexual intercourse symbolize? What does sexuality signify? In calling sex an instinct, Freud thinks he has reached a physiological category beyond which analysis cannot go. But no one lives at the level of instinct.[76]

We might say similarly that the Song of Songs, including many of its specific images, is about sex. So be it. But what is sex about? What higher reality does human sexual love disclose? Or are we really to believe that human sexual love is itself the highest reality and an end in itself—so much so that there can be nothing to which it symbolically points? As Singer observes, though sex has its obvious physiological dimension, humans are more than physiological beings, and sexual *love* is therefore more than sex.

In this light, we might say that the prophetic description of Israel as a wayward wife is a critique not of sexual love, female or other, but of sex divorced from love, sex divorced from the covenantal love of the LORD and his once faithful wife, sex pursued manically and addictively and thus reduced from genuine sexual love to mere instinct. As C. S. Lewis puts it, "Without Eros sexual desire, like every other desire, is a fact about ourselves. Within Eros it is rather about the Beloved."[77]

That Jews have so long interpreted the Song of Songs to be about the sexual desire, as it were, that binds their own Beloved and themselves tells us much about both the Song of Songs itself and the Jewish people.

FOUR

The Consummation of the Spiritual Life

> What then *is* the right love? It is a love of
> God so great, surpassing, abounding and
> intense that one is bound up, heart and soul,
> with the love of God and thus ever enthralled
> by it.
>
> *Maimonides*[1]

*I*n our previous chapters, we have concentrated on the foundational sources of the Jewish idea of the love of God in the Hebrew Bible and in the rabbinic literature of late antiquity, which interprets the biblical texts but also reshapes them. Because neither the biblical nor the rabbinic sources present a systematic theology, our discussion has necessarily ranged over a wide variety of texts, drawing together their scattered remarks about the love of God to expose the connections among them and attempting to develop a rounded view of the subject.

When we come to the philosophical literature of the Middle Ages, we find ourselves in a rather different world. This is a world concerned with systematic organization, critical thinking, precision in meaning, and self-conscious articulation: a method of thought whose origins lay in ancient Greece a millennium and a half earlier, when Western philosophy first arose, and that by now has come to characterize the work of Jewish, Christian, and Muslim thinkers alike. And it is not just manners of expression and organization that have changed: now, in all three religious communities, the very content of the theology richly manifests the Platonic and Aristotelian thinking of its common philosophical antecedents. Yet in each case, even as they now interact in a new way with the demands and resources of philosophical thinking, both the underlying structure of each religious tradition and its expectations of belief and practice remain in place.

Another significant difference lies in the authorship of this body of medieval thought. In the case of biblical and rabbinic literature, the authors are for the most part unknown, and the associations of various books with specific figures are often the product of later and very shaky speculations.[2] Especially in the case of rabbinic literature, the figures named and quoted cannot be considered "authors" in any sense familiar today. The comments of Rabbi Akiva, for example, whom we have encountered in each of our previous chapters, are scattered throughout many books, none of which he can be said to have composed or edited. In the case of the medieval philosophical literature, by contrast, the authors tend to have individual identities; their works are books in the modern sense and not simply compilations and redactions of oral materials. Furthermore, their compositions are addressed to readers, not congregations or academic assemblies, and it is easier to spot the concerns and perplexities of those readers in their specific historical contexts.

Although generalization carries risk and exceptions can be found, it is safe to say that the perplexity of those medieval readers lies precisely in the tension between these two sources of knowledge: the foundational, authoritative, and prephilosophical texts specific to Judaism, Christianity, or

Islam, and the common Greco-Roman philosophical thinking that all three religions have absorbed to one degree or another. As a result, the relevant literature often falls into two ostensibly different categories—that of the spiritual guide (or manual of devotion) and that of the philosophical treatise.

But the difference between these two categories narrows considerably if we bear in mind this key point: in those days, unlike in ours, philosophy was not an academic specialization but rather (to echo the title of a famous study) "a way of life."[3] It spoke not only to professional scholars with technical expertise, but also to laymen on a spiritual journey. It offered not only knowledge but insights into practice, and it did not address disconnected individuals treating their spiritual lives as a consumer choice but rather persons committed to upholding the long-standing traditions of the communities in which they were embedded and through which ultimate meaning (they believed) came to them.

In the new philosophical environment, the way in which the practice of loving God could remain at the center of the Jew's life, where scripture and tradition had insisted it stand, became an important question. And so did the question of whether a rationally defensible conception of God must necessarily eliminate the ancient and religiously central notion that God loves the people Israel. These questions are large ones; our discussion will have to restrict itself to only a few of the works that address them and only to the most essential aspects.

A PHILOSOPHICAL AND SPIRITUAL JOURNEY

Our first example is probably the greatest reflection on the love of God in medieval Jewish literature, and perhaps in all of Jewish literature. This is Bahya ibn Paquda's *Duties of the Heart,* written in Arabic in Saragossa, Spain, around 1080 CE and translated into Hebrew a century later.

Baḥya's book—one of the most beautiful products of the great Judeo-Muslim symbiosis that flowered in medieval Spain—richly reworks both the Neoplatonic thinking of the common Greco-Roman philosophical tradition and the Sufi mysticism specific to its predominantly Muslim milieu.[4] It long served as, and for some it remains, a staple of Jewish spiritual sustenance.

From Neoplatonism, *Duties of the Heart* receives the focus on the One unique being that is at the root of all other beings, which the One brings into existence and which, in turn, depend ultimately on the One and on it alone. Indeed, all beings partake to some degree of the One and draw their energy from it. In the case of those beings that have a soul, the consummating spiritual event is the return of the soul to its origin in the One. That event may take place in this life, though in that case it is, of course, not yet permanent. Plotinus, a pagan Neoplatonic philosopher writing in Greek in the third century CE, describes such an experience in a famous passage:

> Often I have woken up out of the body to my self and have entered into myself, going out from all other things; I have seen a beauty wonderfully great and felt assurance that then most of all I belonged to the better part; I have actually lived the best life and come to identify with the divine; and set firm in it I have come to that supreme actuality, setting myself above all else in the realm of Intellect. Then after that rest in the divine, when I have come down from Intellect to discursive reasoning, I am puzzled how I ever came down, and how my soul has come to be in the body when it is what it has shown itself to be by itself, even when it is in the body.[5]

For our purposes, what is most important here is Plotinus's notion that "liv[ing] the best life" enables one "to identify with the divine," liberating the soul from those carnal forces that drag it away from "the better part." The "divine," in turn, is basically synonymous with the "Intellect" (though here the latter term obviously possesses an intense spiritual connotation that it does not have in our culture, where spirit and intellect are frequently thought to be at least different and often at odds with each other). The Neoplatonist, in sum, seeks to purify his life so as to ascend to the realm of the divine.

> You are One—the first of all numbers, the foundation of all structures.
> You are One—and at the mystery of Your Oneness the wise are astonished,
> for they do not know what it is.
> You are One, and Your Oneness neither decreases nor increases,
> lacks nothing and has nothing left over.
> You are One—but not like a unit that can be possessed and counted,
> For neither multiplicity nor change can touch You,
> Neither description nor name.
> *Solomon ibn Gabirol*[6]

Sufism, the other great influence on Baḥya, is a Muslim mystical movement that focuses on the inner spiritual life of the practitioner—though, importantly, it does so without opposing the outer legal structures that regulate and direct the life of the religious community. From the Sufis, Baḥya receives not only his focus on motivation and subjective experience but also his constant concern for the purification of the inner self and for the acquisition of those spiritual traits that draw one closer to God—again, not in opposition to objective practices ("the duties of the limbs," as he calls them) but rather as the spiritual force that directs, drives, and perfects them. As Diana Lobel puts it,

"The Sufi cultivates ethical or spiritual virtues such as patience, humility, trust, sincerity, devotion, and love, and aims not at philosophical illumination, but rather union with a being whom he or she loves."[7]

As Lobel wisely points out, it would be fruitless to make a sharp distinction between these two intellectual currents potent in Baḥya's cultural milieu.[8] Both Neoplatonism and Sufism encourage a mystical ascent powered in large part by spiritual practices that aim to qualify the self for intimacy with God. But Lobel points out one important distinction:

> What differentiates the two is the way they describe God and how this colors their understanding of the path to the divine. Although [like the Neoplatonist] the Sufi, too, undertakes a journey of return to or union with the divine, God is depicted by the Sufi as a personal, loving being.... Most Sufi thought does not describe philosophy as a prerequisite for union with God.... True learning is the fruit of experience, not a prerequisite or path to mystical union. Learning detached from experience is mere scholasticism.[9]

In sum, the Sufi influence encouraged Baḥya to transform the ancient Jewish notion of the individual's love of the personal God into a spiritual ascent, the consummation of the spiritual life. The Jew who practices the duties of the heart thinks in many ways like a philosopher, but what he approaches is not "Intellect" or some other impersonal being. What he approaches is the God of Israel—the personal God of the covenant who chose the people Israel in love and commanded that they love him in return.

Baḥya ibn Paquda's *Duties of the Heart* is divided into ten sections, or "gates." It is essential to bear in mind that the various gates do not stand alone but rather serve as, in Lobel's phrase, "mirroring aspects of a unified soul."[10] Still, the fact that the tenth and last gate is entitled "The Love of God" is significant. It suggests that practice of the love of God is especially indicative of the fact that the soul has attained the sought-for unification and has come into the presence of the One toward whom all the gates are directed. In Baḥya's own words:

> You should understand and know, my brother, that all the duties of the heart, virtuous character traits, and noble qualities of soul mentioned previously in this book are steps and stages leading to the supreme objective that we intend to explain in this gate. You should also know that every duty and virtue—whether learned from reason, Scripture, or [rabbinic] tradition—is a stage and stepping-stone by which one ascends to this, their goal and culmination. There is no level higher than this, nor any stage beyond it. (*Duties* 10, introduction)[11]

At the outset, Baḥya defines the love of God by means of a conceptual vocabulary quite distant from that of the Hebrew Bible. "It is," he writes, "the soul's yearning ... for God, so as to become attached to His supernal light" (*Duties* 10:1). Here, one sees the legacy of the Greco-Roman concept of a "soul" as a distinct and separable part of the self, in contrast to the biblical notion of the person as a psychophysical unity.[12] The legacy is already evident in rabbinic literature, but by the Middle Ages it had become a staple of Jewish philosophical thinking.

That the soul seeks to become attached to the "supernal light" reflects not only the world picture offered by medieval science but also certain quasi-mystical tendencies evident in late antiquity and prominent in Judaism by Baḥya's time. Later, the ideal of the radical and profound "attachment" (*devequt*) of the worshipper to God became central to certain currents in Jewish mysticism.[13] It may well be that the appearance here of the idea of attachment in the context of the love of God reflects a text like Deuteronomy 11:22, which speaks of "loving the LORD your God, walking in all His ways, and holding fast (*dovqah*) to Him."[14]

What all this makes clear, in any event, is that for Baḥya, the love of God consummates a spiritual journey—not in the modern sense of an open-ended and very personal quest but in the earlier sense of a metaphysical ascent of the spiritual dimension of the journeyer until it cleaves to its heavenly source, the one and unparalleled God of the world.[15]

Baḥya goes on to classify the motivations that may bring one to the love of God. Such motivations, he says, are analogous to those that move a servant to love his master. The servant may do so because of the master's kindness to him, for example, or because the master readily forgives his transgressions, or, finally, simply "because of his greatness and glory and out of reverence for his very essence and being—not because of a desire [to receive any benefit] and not because of fear." All of these can rightly apply to the love of God as well—but, Baḥya insists, the last-named form of love is the purest and the one that Moses had intended in the famous injunction of the Shema: "You shall love the LORD your God with all your heart and with all your soul and with all your might" (Deut 6:5; *Duties* 10:2). Whatever inducements God's kindness and forgiveness may offer, and whatever fearful consequences may be entailed in the refusal to love him, the highest love of God is that of those who seek no reward and fear no punishment. Rather, they love God solely for who he alone is.

In the biblical vision, as we saw in chapter 1, Israel's love for God is rooted in his own prior love for them as manifested in his acts of kindness, especially those by which he has delivered them from oppression and danger. In *Duties of the Heart*, by contrast, it is rooted, at least in the first instance, in the philosophical perception of his unique being and the awe and wonder that this act of recognition evokes.

And so here we find the mutual interaction of philosophy and religious devotion in an especially striking form. Lobel again states the import nicely:

> Philosophy is thus the first foundation of the spiritual life. Philosophy enables us to strip away our misconceptions about the divine, making room for the God of experience. Through contemplation of the wisdom in creation—the beauty with which the world is constructed—we discover traces of God everywhere around us. At the same time, we discover a living personal God as a comforter, source of strength, and inner witness.[16]

It is philosophical reflection that enables one to avoid the false notions of God that derail the spiritual quest and prevent the love that is its ultimate destination. Thus, as Baḥya observes in his fourth gate ("Trust in God"), one must learn to see beyond the proximate causes of things and to discern the ultimate and most powerful cause. Failure to do so will result in the fear of lesser things and the neglect of the ultimate cause who is the sole source of help and solace—the Creator.[17]

Unlike so much modern philosophy, this version does not lead away from the active, personal, and creative God: it leads toward him. Clear philosophical thinking is a key prerequisite for the journey of self-perfection and spiritual elevation—and for the soul to attain to the love of God.

We can go further. Recall that Baḥya, following Talmudic precedent, sees the purest love of God as one that is based neither on the quest for benefits nor on the fear of punishment but derives rather from "reverence for [God's] very essence and being" (*Duties* 10:2). The Torah, too, as we saw at length in chapter 1, offers a model of covenantal love that cannot fairly be reduced to self-interest, that is, to the pursuit of advantage and the avoidance of loss. But it is also true, and much on Bahya's mind, that the Torah does speak of reward and punishment, as befits a book that tells of a God of justice. In his mind, however, as in traditional Jewish sources generally, the rewards and punishments, though real and not to be ignored, function nonetheless at a relatively low spiritual level. There are times, to be sure, when they are the only means to reach a person, and there are persons—young children, for example—who respond to them alone and not to the more elevated motivations for service to God. But for Bahya, the true lover of God sees beyond them, just as he sees beyond the proximate causes of the things that happen to him.

In Bahya's thinking, the Torah itself is like those rewards and punishments: it is an external reality—a powerful one, of course, and one that leads to the all-important act of submission to God and ultimately to the World-to-Come (or, as he phrases it here, "the World of Rest"). But it is an external stimulus nonetheless, and for that very reason it necessarily speaks to a level of spiritual development that is less than ideal. The higher level, he maintains, is "the submission which is prompted by the [inner] urging of the mind and rational demonstration."[18] This, he insists, is the submission that God prefers.

It must not be missed that the two paths are connected. The stimulus of the Torah leads to the path of rational demonstration, but it is the latter to which the spiritual seeker should aspire. "As a philosopher," Lobel writes, Bahya "is predisposed to consider response to a natural law implanted in our reason superior to a law revealed from an external source."[19] As Bahya sees it, of course, that "natural law" derives not from an autonomous, godless natural order of things but from the Creator, to whom nature (rightly interpreted) points and to whose loving service human beings must aspire. Human nature is not a matter of nature alone: it is open to God and has the power to direct itself toward him.

To most of us today, questions of motivation still matter, as they did to Baḥya. We instinctively respect those who do what is right for its own sake and avoid what is wrong simply because it is wrong. We take a dimmer view of those who are motivated by the benefit they receive for doing what is right or by the negative consequences for themselves of doing what is wrong—for example, the price of getting caught. In Baḥya ibn Paquda's case, however, the most important point is not about doing good for its own sake or avoiding evil for the same reason. It is about recognizing the intrinsic connection between the will of God and the good, and between violating his will and evil—or, to be more precise, it is about doing good and avoiding evil as acts of love and service to God. And ideally this recognition is to come not from religious tradition (indispensable though that is) but rather from clear philosophical thinking, deeply and passionately internalized in the individual self. As Lobel puts it, "The philosopher's motivation is higher than that of a person motivated by religious tradition alone."[20]

Among today's Jews, the notion of reward and punishment is most alive and vivid for the more religiously traditional. In many cases, however, among both the more and the less traditional, the individual's motivation for practicing Judaism (however defined) derives not from philosophical commitment but from family tradition, from the memory of departed ancestors (especially those slain in the Holocaust), from a love of Jewish culture or an identification with Jewish history, or simply from the group with whom the individual socializes. The effect of sheer inertia on one's life commitments (of whatever sort) must never be underestimated.

In chapter 1, we saw that the Jewish tradition generally takes a position that is quite the opposite of T. S. Eliot's famous couplet, "The last temptation is the greatest treason: / To do the right deed for the wrong reason."[21] Better that the right deed be done for the wrong reason than not at all! There is thus no reason to think Baḥya would dismiss outright those who do good deeds from motives that are less than ideal, such as inertia or social location. But he would still say that those individuals were stranding themselves on a lower rung of the spiritual ladder than the one to which he thinks all Jews should aspire—and failing to realize fully the character of the highest rung.

Preparing to Love God

For Baḥya ibn Paquda, the love of God is a state of being for which one can prepare oneself—one does not just fall in love with God—but the preparations are no simple matter. Trying to generate and expand an experience of love will not work: "One who aims for it directly—without the requisite preparations—will not be able to reach it."[22] A principal prerequisite is the reverence, or fear, of God. "A person has no path to [the love of God]," he tells us, "unless he first has the fear and awe of God (may He be exalted!)."[23]

Another indispensable prerequisite—and one that goes against the grain of much modern thinking—is abstinence. We cannot expect to attain the love of God, Baḥya goes on to say, if we do not counteract our instinctual love of the world. We cannot devote ourselves wholeheartedly to divine service if our appetites are unrestrained and our loves are not ordered appropriately. For that reason, he explains, he has placed his gate of "Abstinence" just before his climactic gate, which is devoted to the love of God: "When the believer's heart, as a result of insight and understanding, is emptied of the love of the world and of its desires, the love of God can be established in his heart and fixed in his soul."[24] Without a large dose of instinctual renunciation, Baḥya insists, we cannot direct ourselves to the love of God. Without saying "no" to our bodily desires, we cannot say "yes" to the love of God.

Although this highly negative view of the body is foreign to the biblical and rabbinic legacies, the general notion of the "no" that underlies the love of God is familiar nevertheless. We have seen it early on, in exploring the notion of covenantal love in chapter 1. But there is a difference: it is no longer the foreign deities who are the ever-tempting distractions threatening to divert Israel from the service of the LORD and thus to undermine the love that is his due. Now, instead, it is the appetites that come with being human—the need for fame, social status, pleasure, sex, and the like. These must be disciplined and subordinated to God's will if he is to be served appropriately and his love is to be felt to the full and returned in proper measure.

The idea that our innate appetites and attractions must be tamed and redirected was hardly new in Judaism when Baḥya wrote his great book toward the end of the eleventh century. Already in the Mishnah, for example, we find a sage of the second century CE teaching, "Who is a mighty hero? One who masters his own Inclination, as it is said, 'Better to be forbearing than mighty, / To have self-control than to conquer a city'" (*m. Avot* 4:1, quoting Prov 16:32).[25] But in *Duties of the Heart*, self-mastery has become an indispensable component in a systematic grammar of spiritual ascent—and a key preparatory moment in the quest for the love of God. The point is clear: before we can engage in self-surrender, we must first own, free and clear, the self that we are to surrender. It cannot be beholden to its own attractions and temptations.

In the Islamic world in which Baḥya lived, this ancient Jewish teaching about the higher heroism resonated in a fascinating way with a famous post-Qurʾanic story (*ḥadīth*) about Muḥammad, the prophet of Islam. Indeed, Baḥya actually quotes the hadith:

It was said of one of the pious men that he encountered
men returning from a battle with an enemy whom they
had conquered after a fierce struggle. He said to them:
"You have returned, praise be to God, victorious after
a small struggle. Now prepare yourselves for the large
struggle." They said to him, "What is the large struggle?"
He said to them, "The battle against the instinct and its
armies." (*Duties* 5:5)[26]

Bahya tells his Jewish audience neither the source of
the story nor the identity of the speaker in it. He does,
however, use the same Arabic term for "struggle"—*jihād*.
In the Islamic context, this little story about Muḥammad
serves as the basis for the key distinction between the
lesser jihad (military struggle) and the greater jihad (the
struggle against one's own instincts)—a distinction that
restates in Arabic and Islamic terms the point made long
before by both the Mishnah and the verse in Proverbs that
it aptly quotes.[27]

Of course, simply mastering one's instincts and over-
coming one's temptations (which Bahya sees as a continuing struggle and not a battle won in a single moment) does
not equate to attaining the love of God. To do that, Bahya
speaks of four categories of preparation—wholehearted
dedication, humility, self-accounting, and reflection—and
he divides each of these into two subcategories.

One must have wholehearted and exclusive devotion
(1) to the affirmation of the unity of God and (2) to deeds
of obedience and service to him. One must be humble
(1) before God and (2) before God's special devotees. One
must take account of oneself (1) because of one's indebted-
ness to God as a consequence of the benefits God is constantly giving and (2) because of God's disregard of one's
sins and his forbearance and forgiveness. Finally, one must
reflect upon (1) the experience of the earlier generations
by attentively studying the Torah and the traditions those

generations have handed down and (2) the world today and the wonders and creatures one sees within it.[28]

This system shows nicely Baḥya's characteristic concern for both the outer and the inner dimensions of the relationship of God and his people Israel—that is, for what Baḥya takes to be the objective facts and for the need to internalize those facts in one's soul and to actualize them continually in one's deeds. To him, it is a demonstrable fact that God is possessed of absolute unity; has revealed himself in the Torah and the rabbinic tradition; continually demonstrates generosity and kindness as well as forbearance and forgiveness; and has created and filled with wonders the world in which we dwell. But these truths become fully realized only when the worshipper makes them the basis for a personal stance of dedication, humility, self-accounting, and reflection, and commits himself to the practices that they inevitably entail.

Do these preparations work? Do they by themselves enable their practitioners to attain to the love of God? Baḥya's answer is a qualified "yes." For those at the lowest level of the quest, who are prepared to sacrifice their money but not any part of their bodies or, even less, their very lives, it is within their power to succeed. The same is true of those who are prepared to give up even part of their bodies so long as they remain alive. But as for the highest level, the level at which the lovers of God are prepared, if necessary, to sacrifice their very lives (and here he shows the influence of the thinking on martyrdom that we explored in chapter 2), only those whom God has specially graced can attain it. Of this self-giving love of God, Baḥya observes, "It is above the capacity of human beings, for nature opposes and rejects it, and when it is found among certain special individuals from among the human race, this is only because God has helped and strengthened them, granting them victory in order that the evil impulse not overcome them."

To be sure, Baḥya immediately goes on to say that God's gift comes in response to the lovers' service to him and their observance of his commandments; it is not, in other words, a matter of caprice or totally undeserved. The implication would seem that if one perseveres in practicing the love of God at the lower levels, God will enable him to progress to the higher and purer level of self-giving love.[29] And yet the high level of service and practice of these exceptional individuals—he cites Abraham as the paragon—is itself owing in some measure to divine grace; it is not something totally under their control.

Whether or not Baḥya is altogether consistent here, I think we can safely conclude that for him the love of God is, as it is generally in the Jewish tradition, a joint product of divine grace and human effort. It has within in it an element of undeserved gift and one of human achievement. The very fact that an individual has attained it in its highest form is owing in significant measure to the action of the God who is to be loved. Once again, the love of God as subject and as object—God's love for Israel and Israel's love for God—are not to be disjoined. Even those who have successfully climbed to the highest rung of the spiritual ladder have had assistance from the one who awaits them at the top.

The note of divine grace introduced by Baḥya suggests that the preparations he details for reaching the love of God are something other than surefire techniques. There remains an element of contingency in the process. Figures like Abraham or Job (another of Baḥya's paragons) can serve as models to be imitated, but only because their motivation is so much purer than most people's. There is also ample room to wonder whether without gruesome tests like the ones these biblical figures are said to have undergone we can really know that we have succeeded in the arduous spiritual task. And even when we think we can know, we still have to reckon with the possibility that we have acted out of motivations that are less than the highest. Can martyrs know that they are choosing death over betrayal only because of the love of God and not because of the shame and social exclusion that betrayal would occasion? Can they be certain that they are not acting on the basis of an underlying psychological condition (like depression) that is causing them to devalue their lives?

I doubt it. In my opinion, we have little basis for certainty about the motivations behind the things we do, great or small. We may think our motivation has been noble and pure, only to realize in retrospect that it was other factors, unknown to us at the time, that moved us. We may flatter ourselves that we act solely on the basis of our unconditioned will, but surely that very will, our personalities, and our scale of values have long been conditioned by factors—whether biological, social, or even providential—beyond our ken and outside our control. And so the love of God remains an ideal, an aspiration, a goal—but whether anyone truly attains it in its highest manifestations, God only knows.

The Practice of the Love of God

Some of the most moving sections in *Duties of the Heart* describe the signs that a person is indeed practicing the love of God. Examining those signs will give us a more realistic sense of just what Bahya thinks the love of God entails in the Jew's daily life.

The first such sign is "the abandoning of all superfluous things that distract from obedience to God."[30] In this, we see what Georges Vajda calls Bahya's "ascetic theology,"[31] and, as in any form of asceticism, the pressing question is this: For what higher goal is the renunciation made? What is so important as to require that the bodily indulgences be restricted or eliminated? In the case at hand, the higher goal is undivided devotion to God, from which worldly luxuries are again thought to serve as distractions at best and at worst as rival recipients of service. Both divert psychic energy from the highest task and hinder the spiritual ascent. The prescription is thus the simple life, but not pursued as a goal in and of itself. It is, rather, a precondition for the higher form of life, the one in which God and his service are at the center.

Bahya's next indication that one loves God is that "the signs of the fear and awe of God are manifest on his face." I take this to mean that the lover's very demeanor reveals the depth of his ultimate commitment and the constancy of his relationship with his creator. Lest the term "fear" be misunderstood, Bahya is again quick to point out that he is speaking not of the dread of punishment but rather of the awe inspired by awareness of God's incomparable majesty. To make his point, he quotes the paradigmatic lover of God as one who says not that his service is dependent on reward and punishment—in which case it would not exist without them—but rather that "I serve Him because He is worthy of it." The reality of his service, like the reality of the God he serves, is unconditional. It is not the product of a self-interested cost-benefit calculation.

The next of Bahya's signs is that the lover's commitment to do God's will is uninfluenced by the praise or blame conferred by others. Here again, the key point is that the love of God is absolute: it relativizes everything else. This raises once more the prospect of the acid test of personal commitment—martyrdom. The lover of God, Bahya writes, is willing "to surrender his life, his body, his possessions, and his children for the will of God." Here his proof text is one that we have seen before, and, not coincidentally, in this same context: "It is for Your sake that we are slain all day long, / that we are regarded as sheep to be slaughtered" (Ps 44:23).[32]

In fact, even when the source of the affliction is God himself, the lover does not cease to love, does not sever the relationship, and does not give up the hope for restoration:

"If He bestows a benefit upon her [the soul, a feminine entity], she is thankful. If He afflicts her, she is patient. And this only increases her love for Him, her yearning to satisfy His will, and her reliance upon Him" (*Duties* 10:1). Were the putative lover of God to hold back something precious, he would be showing that his love is not absolute after all, that it is but one motive among others, pulling him in various directions. His dedication would be anything but wholehearted; it would be hedged and qualified in ways that are incompatible with the ideal of loving God with all one's heart, soul, and might.

Here, Vajda's term "ascetic theology" can be misleading. Baḥya is not suggesting—and he would not be in accord with rabbinic tradition if he were suggesting—that his readers renounce life, body, possessions, and children. He is not recommending that they seek out martyrdom, nor is he advocating monasticism. Rather, he is speaking of the priority of the love of God over all else, including one's very life, should that dire choice present itself. Life, body, possessions, and children are all goods that rabbinic tradition and the rabbinic conception of divine service seek to safeguard. But to fulfill the commandment to love God, Baḥya would say, all of these find their proper places within a larger structure centered on the love of God—the basis of the Torah itself. In the rare situation in which there is a conflict, if love of God does not emerge triumphant, then the individual obviously does not love God. Enjoying one's life, body, possessions, and children is proper. But it is not ultimate.

Another sign of the love of God is that mention of God's name is regularly on the lover's lips in expressions of thanks, blessing, and praise, but not in trivial or false oaths or in curses. Today, it is common for people to say things like "God damn him!" with no sense that they have desecrated anything or that, formally speaking, they are uttering a prayer. The idiom is a frozen expression, devoid of the religious meaning that once gave it force. More than nine hundred years ago, interestingly, Bahya observed that the masses were already resorting to such usages to a large degree, bringing (in his view) disgrace upon themselves. When the language is debased, the reality to which it points suffers as well. Care in speech indicates a proper concern for the soul and the God with whom it seeks intimacy.

On this same matter of speech, when Bahya's paradigmatic lover of God makes promises and predictions, as we all do, he is careful to condition them on the will of God. This is, Bahya observes, because he may die before he can fulfill his promise or because God may have decreed some other turn of events that the person cannot anticipate. For a human being to make promises or predictions without acknowledging such contingencies is to speak as if one were totally in control and even knew the future; it is to imply that God is not sovereign over human events and thus to deny a key basis for the love of God. What many today would see as luck or fate (good, bad, or indifferent), Bahya's lover of God instinctively sees as providence. His habit of speech prevents him, and also those with whom he interacts, from forgetting the ultimate and divine origin of events.

It is also characteristic of the Jew who loves God that he seeks actively to influence those with whom he comes into contact: "He guides and directs others to obedience to God's service, gently or forcefully as is needed according to the time and the place and different types and levels of people."[33] For all that Bahya stresses inwardness and intention, he does not confine the religious life to the private sphere or imagine his lover of God as detached from the community or unconcerned about its morals.

Indeed, lest his readers content themselves with their private spirituality alone, Bahya places special stress on this instructional dimension. "You should know, my brother," he warns, that even if a believer were to attain the utmost limit in the improvement of his own soul for the sake of God ... his merits cannot compare to those of one who guides others to the right path and directs the disobedient toward obedience to God, may He be exalted and glorified. For the merits of such a person are multiplied as the days pass and as time goes on by the merits of those [whom he has guided].[34]

The good deeds of the Jew who loves God, then, reproduce themselves in the deeds of those whom he has influenced for the good. That he has played his part in forming and renewing the conscience of his community redounds to his own continuing credit.

Another sign of the love of God is that the person takes delight in his good deeds, not, Baḥya is quick to point out, because he is proud or self-important but rather because being virtuous is what he truly enjoys. Correlatively, he experiences worry and even anguish over his sins, about which he is penitent and remorseful. As is generally the case in Judaism, the righteous person is not the one who is free of sin—as Solomon is reported to have said, there is no such individual[35]—but rather the one who is alert to his sins and committed both to repairing them and to re-orienting himself toward good deeds.

Baḥya also describes the successful lover of God as one who takes on liturgical practices beyond those required by Jewish law. In the daytime, he fasts if his health permits, and at night he engages regularly in prayer. Baḥya particularly stresses the spiritual advantages of nighttime over daytime prayer, among them the absence of distractions and the opportunity for solitude:

He can engage in solitary prayer, while remembering God, and having intimate companionship with Him at the time when every lover is wont to be alone with his beloved and when intimates enjoy solitude with each other, as it says, "At night I yearn for you with all my being (*naphši*)" (Isa 26:9); "Upon my couch at night / I (*naphši*) sought the one I love." (Song 3:1)

The word *naphši* here, as is common in Biblical Hebrew, reinforces or intensifies the first-person singular pronoun ("I"). That each of the two verses cited by Baḥya uses this word suggests that he is reading it in light of the common medieval meaning of *nepheš* as "soul." If so, for him the point is that nighttime prayer enables the devotee to attain not merely privacy with God but also something like mystical union, or at least an intense spiritual attachment, like the *devequt* mentioned earlier in this chapter.

In most Jewish circles today, this strong emphasis on private, personal devotion is seldom, if ever, heard. If prayer is stressed at all, what is highlighted is usually the communal and social dimension. Not infrequently one hears that attention to one's inner spiritual condition and personal relationship with God are non-Jewish, Judaism being allegedly communal, social, and activist rather than private, solitary, and contemplative. One of the extraordinary aspects of Baḥya's great book is precisely his concern for *both* dimensions and his keen sense that they are deeply interrelated. His discussion points to aspects of the Jewish heritage lost even to many self-identified traditionalists today.

In Baḥya's thinking, to a Jew who has successfully pursued the love of God, the commandments of the Torah seem only a privilege, not a burden. Instead of complaining about their large number, such Jews will, Baḥya insists, regard them as few "compared to the effort and exertion, forbearance and patience that they accept upon themselves as obligatory in order to obey Him."[36] As in the case of the ancient Near Eastern treaties and covenants we discussed in chapter 1, awareness of the suzerain's antecedent grace moves the vassal toward joyous and willing service. As in the case of the collections of law in the Torah, what might have proven to be dry, legalistic ordinances come alive and speak to the passions once they have been transposed into the framework of a personal relationship between covenanting parties.

Baḥya's idiom is, of course, very different from that of the Bible, and much has changed in the intervening two millennia. But the degree of continuity remains striking.

> Beloved of the soul, Compassionate Father,
>> Draw Your servant to Your will.
> Then Your servant will run like a hart
>> And fall prostrate before Your majesty.
> For Your love is sweeter to him
>> Than honey from a comb or any other taste.
>> *Yedid Nepheš*[37]

A PHILOSOPHER'S LOVE

The best known of the medieval Jewish philosophers—and, in the opinion of many, the greatest—was Moses Maimonides (1138–1204),[38] whom we have already met in chapter 2. Much of Maimonides's conception of the love of God recalls Baḥya's, and that is hardly surprising considering that both were faithful heirs of the rabbinic tradition and products of the Judeo-Muslim symbiosis.[39] For Maimonides as for Baḥya, the love of God follows from the recognition of God's own nature as it is readily manifest in the world: "When a person contemplates His deeds and His great and wondrous creations and infers from them that His wisdom is beyond value and has no end, he immediately loves, praises, and glorifies Him and experiences a powerful longing to know His great name, as David said,

'My soul thirsts for God, the living God'" (*Mishneh Torah, Yesodei ha-Torah* 2:2, citing Ps 42:3).

In comparison with Baḥya, Maimonides places less stress on the element of personal gratitude and more on the element of infinite wisdom evident in the natural order. In his great philosophical work, *The Guide of the Perplexed*, he tells his reader that the love of God commanded in the Torah "becomes valid only through the apprehension of the whole of being as it is and through the consideration of His wisdom as it is manifested in it" (3:28).[40] As Warren Zev Harvey puts it, "The love of God, according to [Maimonides] is not based primarily on the study of history, which reveals human cruelty and stupidity, but on the study of the natural sciences, which reveals divine wisdom."[41]

In fact, so necessary is the philosophical quest to the spiritual ascent that Maimonides assigns to a lower rung on the spiritual ladders "the jurists who believe true opinions on the basis of traditional authority and study the law concerning the practices of divine service, but do not engage in speculation concerning the fundamentals of religion and make no inquiry whatever regarding the rectification of belief" (*Guide* 3:51).[42] As in Baḥya's *Duties of the Heart*, so here religious and legal tradition is no substitute for clear philosophical thinking. An argument from authority does not get one very far either intellectually or spiritually, for it is not enough to hold correct opinions: one must also be able to derive and demonstrate them.

In contrast to Baḥya's conception of the love of God, though, Maimonides's is much more intellectualistic. Indeed, for him the intellect constitutes the prime connection between God and man. It is, he writes, a kind of king who connects human beings with the ultimate ruler of the universe: "This king who cleaves to [a person] and accompanies him is the intellect that overflows toward us and is the bond between us and Him, may He be exalted" (*Guide* 3:52).[43]

To acquire the love of God, then, one must hold the correct intellectual conceptions, and to Maimonides, the Torah is a key factor in the process. The love of God commanded in Deuteronomy 6:5 is achieved, he writes, "through the opinions taught by the Law, which include the apprehension of His being as He, may He be exalted, is in truth." Similarly, the fear of God, likewise commanded in the Torah, "is achieved by means of all the actions prescribed by the Law" (*Guide* 3:52).[44] As in the biblical and rabbinic legacies beforehand, and as in Baḥya's thinking as well, there is room in Maimonides's philosophy for both the love and the fear of God, with the latter understood as the dread of punishment; they are not at odds. But as in the rabbinic texts we examined in chapter 2 and again in Baḥya, it is the love of God that is the higher spiritual state. Although Maimonides conceives of that love in more intellectualistic terms, it remains the core connection between God and human beings, the bond that joins them.

It would be a capital error to take this emphasis on intellect as suggesting that for Maimonides the love of God is, to use the slang, a "head-trip," a matter of the intellect alone as we conceive intellect. On the contrary, nothing stands out in Maimonides's discussions of the love of God more than his emphasis on how it must by nature be all-consuming. Here is his interpretation of the words, "You shall love the LORD your God with all your heart" (Deut 6:5):

> With all the forces of your heart; I mean to say, with all the forces of the body, for the principle of all of them derives from the heart. Accordingly, the intended meaning is ... that you should make His apprehension the end of all your actions. (*Guide* 1:39)[45]

In an observation of Maimonides on Psalm 91:14, one sees just how far such love must go. The verse, which addresses those who "dwell in the shelter of the Most High,"

reads: "Because he passionately loves (*ḥašaq*) Me I will deliver him; / I will set him on high, for he knows My name."[46]
Now the verb *ḥašaq* is one we have seen before. It describes
God's passion for Israel in Deuteronomy 7:7, "It is not because you are the most numerous of peoples that the LORD
set His heart (*ḥašaq*) on you and chose you—indeed, you
are the smallest of peoples." It is also the verb used in an
address to an Israelite warrior who spies "among the cap-
tives a beautiful woman and you desire (*ḥašaqta*) her and
would take her to wife" (Deut 21:11).

In chapter 1, we found that in the Deuteronomic conception of covenant, God's love for Israel has a passionate
and erotic character analogous to that of the warrior in the
second passage. Similarly, Maimonides makes a distinction between "the terms *one who loves* [*'ohev*] and *one who
loves passionately* [*ḥošeq*]," with the latter term signifying
"an excess of love ... so that no thought remains that is directed toward a thing other than the Beloved" (*Guide* 3:51).[47]

In the case of the love of God, then, the Beloved must
consume all the lover's thoughts. In that sense, the love of
God, like God himself, is different from all others that one
might place in the same category, and, of course, superior

[2]Like a hind crying for water,
    my soul cries for You, O God;
  [3]my soul thirsts for God, the living God;
    O when will I come to appear before God!

    ▪ ▪ ▪

[6]Why so downcast, my soul,
    why disquieted within me?
  Have hope in God;
    I will yet praise Him,
    my ever-present help, my God.
        Psalm 42:2–3, 6[49]

to them. It is not one love among many. Rather, it is, in Harvey's splendid phrase, "the passion that includes all passions, the love of loves."[48]

In Maimonides's hands, the distinction between 'ohev and ḥošeq, then, is not that the latter denotes an erotic or sexual love. For him the point is that it denotes a love that occupies the lover's entire mind, displacing all rivals for his attention and affection. But there is an analogy with eros nonetheless, as Maimonides makes abundantly clear in his great law code:

> What then *is* the right love? It is a love of God so great, surpassing, abounding and intense that one is bound up, heart and soul, with the love of God and thus ever enthralled by it—like the lovesick, whose minds are never free of love for the woman by whom they are ceaselessly enthralled, whether sitting down or standing up, eating or drinking. Greater still should be the love of God in the hearts of His lovers, ever enthralled by it, as we were charged, "with all your heart, all your soul, and all your might" (Deut 6:5). That is what Solomon means when, speaking figuratively, he says: "For I am sick with love" (Song 2:5). Indeed, the entire Song of Songs is a figure for this theme. (*Mishneh Torah, Hilkhot Tešuvah* 10:3)[50]

Here, the Song of Songs is seen not as the love song of God and Israel, or not only as that, but as the love song of the individual for God, a figural representation of the passion that must stand at the center of the individual's spiritual life and provide its energy.

In order to realize the ideal of keeping the love of God at the center of one's life, Maimonides, like Baḥya before him, recommends various practices, most of which, to modern ears, sound rather ascetic. The pursuit of solitude (and its wise use) is again an example. Of the goal of "total devotion to Him and the employment of intellectual thought in constantly loving Him," Maimonides remarks, "Mostly

this is achieved in solitude and isolation. Hence, every ex-
cellent man stays frequently in solitude and does not meet
anyone unless it is necessary." But, again, Maimonides's
ideal lover of God is hardly a monk or a hermit. Instead,
he "achieves a state in which he talks with people and is
occupied with his bodily necessities while his intellect is
wholly turned toward Him, may He be exalted, so that in
his heart he is always in His presence, may He be exalted,
while outwardly he is with people" (*Guide* 3:51).[51] In his
law code, Maimonides identifies the norm as the ability
to earn a living, eat, drink, and engage in sex not as ends
in themselves, and not as sources of pleasure, but as the
means to maintain one's physical well-being in order to be
able to serve God all the more. The goal of this demanding
life practice is to enable the person to "direct his heart and
all of his deeds to the knowledge of God" (*Mishneh Torah,
Hilkhot De'ot* 3:2).

The life focused on the love of God as Maimonides conceives it—and, even with the ascetic notes, he conceives it
in very rabbinic terms—is a life lived actively in the world
yet focused on the Creator and drawing its energy from an
all-encompassing love for him. In that sense, for all Maimonides's enormous debt to Greco-Roman and Islamic
philosophy, he continues the covenantal theology of the
Hebrew Bible to a high degree. That, we recall, is a theology in which worldly things are not renounced or escaped
but brought within a structure of relationship with God
and service to him alone. In the Muslim world in which
Maimonides spent his entire life, the principal spiritual
danger was thought to come not, as in ancient Israel, from
other gods but rather from the human tendency to absol-
utize the relative, to pursue sensory pleasure for its own
sake, to miss the limitations and subservience of the finite
and the material. It was thought to result, in brief, from
losing sight of the ultimacy and uniqueness of God.

Maimonides insists that the person who succeeds in the difficult spiritual task that he lays out will see the error in the vulgar notion that God's "knowledge is like our knowledge or that His purpose and His providence and His governance are like our purpose and our providence and our governance." And in Maimonides's thinking, this paradoxical state, this knowledge of the unknowable God, harbors within it the answer to the great question posed in the book of Job: Why does God allow bad things to happen to good people? The answer lies in recognizing the infinite gap between divine "knowledge" and what people designate by the same term. "If man knows this," the philosopher writes, "every misfortune will be borne lightly by him. And misfortunes will not add to his doubts regarding the deity ... but will, on the contrary, add to his love" (*Guide* 3:23).[52] That is to say, a philosophically sophisticated person who experiences misfortunes will know better than to fault God. He will instead welcome lovingly all that a mysterious and unknowable divine providence sends his way.

In support of this claim, Maimonides cites the end of a Talmudic text that is worth quoting in full:

Our rabbis taught: Those who are insulted but do not insult back; who hear themselves reviled but do not answer; who act out of love and rejoice in suffering—of them the Scripture says, "And those who love Him are like the sun rising in might." (*b. Shabbat* 88b, citing Judg 5:31)[53]

What some may take to be a sign of weakness or emotional instability—the refusal to respond to insult or to be saddened by adversity—is here presented as a sign of strength and a telling characteristic of the love of God itself. Even in the most trying of circumstances, Maimonides's lover of God maintains self-control and mental balance; his inner focus on the Beloved and the joy it brings continue unabated.

Can a Perfect God Love?

The passionate language with which Maimonides describes the individual's love for God finds scant echo in his description of God's love for human beings.[54] Harvey points out that Maimonides rarely speaks of the latter type of love at all; the few exceptions tend to occur in the context of his citation of biblical verses.[55]

What could be the origin of this strange disproportion? It surely does not lie in the classical Jewish sources that Maimonides inherited and to which he devotes so much attention. For, as we have seen at length, biblical and rabbinic books present us with abundant texts in each category of love. The origin, rather, lies in the philosophical tradition to which Maimonides adhered and to which he contributed so influentially. In particular, it lies in his intense and uncompromising insistence on the incorporeality of God, the claim that God has no body and nothing even like a body.[56] All the language in the Bible that suggests otherwise—the texts that speak of the mouth of God or his eyes, ears, hand, finger, place, ascent, descent, and all the rest—must, he repeatedly insists, be taken figuratively and only figuratively.

In light of this, Harvey asks exactly the right question, "How could God have *ahavah* [love] for us? *Ahavah* is a bodily passion and God has no body." The one exception involves acts of *ḥesed*. This is a term that, as we saw in chapter 1, is conventionally rendered with words like "love," "kindness," "generosity," and "lovingkindness." Traditionally, it describes deeds in which "the strong does an act of love for the weak—with no ulterior motive and not to satisfy a need," as Harvey writes. "The paradigm of this disinterested love was for Maimonides the act of Creation by the omnipotent God who has no ulterior motives and no needs."[57] And so, when people do acts of *ḥesed*—when they clothe the naked, visit the sick, bury the dead, or comfort the mourner—they are, just as rabbinic tradition claims, imitating God.[58]

It would seem, though, that Maimonides's use of these traditions about *ḥesed* falls well short of a claim that God loves anyone. Rather, God performs *deeds* of a particular loving sort, and people can, and should, imitate those deeds. But are they imitating anything *in God* when they feel (to quote Maimonides again) that "love of God so great, surpassing, abounding and intense that one's soul is bound up with the love of God"?[59] In other words, is there in Maimonides's philosophy any counterpart in the divine realm for the all-encompassing love for God that he sees as the consummation of the spiritual life in the human realm? The answer seems to be negative, and in that sense the disproportion remains: for Maimonides the love of God means a relationship in which human beings are the only ones doing the loving. People can and should imitate the divine examples of what we classify as *ḥesed*, but God does not love.

Few of those who today believe in the biblical God would dispute Maimonides's cautions against taking literally the scriptural language suggesting that God has a body and is thus spatially and materially limited, as any embodied entity cannot but be. God, that is, does not literally have eyes, ears, hands, and the like. But what if we move from body to feelings? Here, many would be reluctant to make such a sweeping statement. They would not be altogether comfortable with the notion that God is so self-sufficient and so self-enclosed that he does not love and has no affections. To be sure, they would concede that it does not mean the same thing for God to love, communicate, and have relationships as it does for human beings, but an analogy is still in order, and the analogy is closer than the one between God's having eyes, ears, and hands and our having the same body parts. In some sense, God really does love, they would say, and people really can feel God's love for them.

What accounts for Maimonides's stringent opposition to any language (or idea) that likens God to human beings? Ultimately, it derives from his intense, indeed overwhelming sense of God's perfection. This is a phenomenon common in the history of Islam and hardly unique to Maimonides among Jewish thinkers, but a major influence on his particular articulation of it goes back to Aristotle. For Aristotle's God is, in the philosopher's own words, "eternal and immovable and separate from all sensible things [that is, things that the senses can perceive]" and "impassive and unalterable."[60] As one historian of philosophy puts it, Aristotle conceives of a being that is "eternal, unchangeable, immovable, wholly independent, separated from all else, incorporeal, and yet at the same time the cause of all generation and change. It is the *perfect Being* in which all possibility is at the same time actuality; of all that exists it is the highest and best—the *deity*." The same scholar goes on to note that in this idea "dwells a significance of mighty import for the world's history," and specifically for "monotheism" as it came to be "conceptually formulated and scientifically grounded."[61]

But a deity who is "wholly independent, separated from all else" is an exceedingly poor candidate for a relationship on the order of the biblical covenant that we have explored in chapters 1 and 3. He (better: it) is for the same reason an exceedingly bad candidate for the variety of monotheism that is associated with covenant. For, as we have seen, a covenant is a bond based on a personal relationship and has as a goal the mutual benefit of the two persons. So, while it may be, as our historian of philosophy writes, that "*spiritual monotheism* is the ripe fruit of Grecian science,"[62] covenantal monotheism—the kind that dominated in Judaism in the biblical and rabbinic periods, with wide repercussions in Christianity as well—has a different source and a very different character. To say that the

God of covenantal monotheism is "wholly independent" is dangerously misleading.

This is not to say that, in the biblical covenant theology, God is *dependent* on Israel or somehow incomplete without them. Rather, the covenant is a gift, an act of disinterested love (like creation itself in Maimonides's philosophy); so far as we can judge, at least from the biblical texts, it is not deemed to be the expression of a need or deficit. The gift itself implies an antecedent relationship between the parties, and the covenant seeks to regulate, deepen, and sustain that relationship in the future.

I suspect that if Maimonides were to read our account of covenant in the Hebrew Bible, he would judge the underlying theology to be unworthy of God and sadly unable to honor his majesty fittingly—an impairment, in other words, of God's unparalleled perfection. There is, however, another model of perfection, one drawn from the world of relationship rather than from the Aristotelian science that underlies Maimonides's thinking on this issue.

Consider a person who is like Aristotle's deity—unchangeable, immovable, wholly independent, separated from all else, and with no potential that is not actualized at all times. Such a person would not only lack relationships and feelings. He or she would also not communicate or respond to new situations and to communications from others. Would we describe such a person as perfect? I suspect we would do the reverse: we would actually describe him or her as profoundly impaired, suffering from something on the order of a crippling autism. And so, various philosophers closer to our own time—to Jews, the name of Martin Buber will be the most familiar—have argued that it would be more helpful if we conceived perfection in social and relational terms.[63] To be sure, such terms cannot do justice to God as he is in and of himself; they are only similes and metaphors and must not be taken literally. But they do communicate something about God that, from the biblical and rabbinic perspective, is real and, in fact, crucial: that he can and does love.

A Philosophical Defense of the Loving God

The language of the loving God so pervades not only the Bible of the Jews but also their liturgy that it was probably inevitable that later philosophers would find Maimonides's intellectualistic and coldly abstract thinking to be inadequate to their spiritual experience.[64]

One who did so was Ḥasdai Crescas (ca. 1340–1410/11), a Jewish philosopher in Christian Spain.[65] Against the Aristotelian notion that love results from need and is thus more appropriate to the inferior party in the relationship, Crescas argues exactly the reverse. Like Maimonides, he pays special attention to the verb *ḥašaq* and the related noun *ḥešeq*, which, as we have seen, indicate a love of a particularly intense and passionate character. But Crescas notes that in the Torah itself it is God who is the subject of *ḥašaq*, as in Deuteronomy 10:15—"Yet it was to your fathers that the LORD was drawn (*ḥašaq*) in His love for them"—whereas the human love for God is conveyed by the verb *'ahav* and its related noun *'ahavah*, which Crescas sees as denoting something weaker. The stronger love, in other words, is God's. "Since love is an essential property of perfection," Crescas writes, "and God's perfection is infinitely immense, His love for the good is more immense [than man's], even though the good [that is] loved is of a very low degree."[66]

Joseph Albo (ca. 1380–1444), Crescas's student, makes a similar point.[67] Like both his teacher and Maimonides beforehand, Albo reflects on the use of *ḥašaq/ḥešeq* to describe the love of God in the Torah. But whereas Maimonides employs the word to convey the total enthrallment of the human lover in the divine object of his affections,[68]

Albo, like Crescas, also applies it to the divine lover himself and his inexplicable passion for the people Israel. He
does so, though, with a twist. That Hebrew word, Albo
writes, indicates that God's love for Israel is an affair of the
heart without rational grounds:

> To show that God's love of Israel in preference to every
> other nation and tongue is not like the love of equals, nor
> like natural love, but a free love, due to the will of the
> lover alone and without any reason, the Bible calls God's
> love of Israel by the name ḥešeq (desire): "The LORD set
> His heart (ḥašaq) on you and chose you" (Deut 7:7). The
> word ḥešeq is applied to extraordinary love without a
> reason. Thus the love of a man for a particular woman in
> preference to another more beautiful is called ḥešeq be-
> cause it is without a reason.... So God's love of Israel is
> like that love (ḥešeq) which is without a reason. The en-
> tire book of Canticles [that is, Song of Songs] is based
> upon this analogy between the love of God for Israel and
> the love of a man for his sweetheart, which is without a
> reason." (Sepher Ha-'Ikkarim 3:37)[69]

Albo connects his theology of God's suprarational love
for Israel to what he takes to be another telling point of
biblical diction, the use of the word segullah ("treasured
possession" or the like) to describe the covenanted people
itself. His interest lies in the appearance of this term in the
same passage that describes God's passionate love for Israel that he cites above:

> [6]For you are a people consecrated to the LORD your God:
> of all the peoples on earth the LORD your God chose you
> to be His treasured people (segullah). [7]It is not because
> you are the most numerous of peoples that the LORD set
> His heart (ḥašaq) on you and chose you—indeed, you
> are the smallest of peoples; [8]but it was because the LORD
> loved you and kept the oath He made to your fathers that

the LORD freed you with a mighty hand and rescued you from the house of bondage, from the power of Pharaoh king of Egypt. (Deut 7:6–8)[70]

For Albo, the point is clear:

The meaning is that just as a property (*segullah*) pertains to a species and is inseparable from it, and yet is not to be explained either by the quantity or the quality of the thing, so this love is in the nature of a property attaching to the people not because of their quantity.... Nor is it because of their quality.... This love is like the love (*ḥešeq*) which has no reason, but is due solely to the will of the lover. And it is this love which was promised to the people at the time of the Sinaitic revelation, as a reward for accepting the Torah. (*Sepher Ha-'Ikkarim* 3:37)[71]

Albo goes on to cite, fittingly, the text in which we first meet *segullah*, in the LORD's initial offer of covenant at Sinai:

⁵Now then, if you will obey Me faithfully and keep My covenant, you shall be My treasured possession (*segullah*) among all the peoples. Indeed, all the earth is Mine, ⁶but you shall be to Me a kingdom of priests and a holy nation. (Exod 19:5–6)

And so, with this, we have come full circle. For all the manifest changes that have occurred between the time when the idea of the love of God, as the classical Jewish sources have generally conceived it, was born in the context of ancient Near Eastern covenants, and the time when Albo wrote, the continuities are nonetheless remarkable. The covenant between the LORD and the people Israel remains rooted in love, God's mysterious and (to many) scandalous love for Israel, and it demands love in return, one manifested most obviously and explicitly in Israel's undivided and heartfelt service of the LORD alone.

The two loves are not the same—Israel has more reason to love God than God has, or at least initially had, to love them. And yet they are inseparable, just as, in the theology that has been our subject throughout, God and Israel are themselves inseparable.

FIVE

"Because He has sold Himself to us with the Torah"

And love, of course, seizes both, the lover
as well as the beloved. But the beloved
differently from the lover. It originates in
the lover. The beloved is seized, her love is
already a response to being seized.
Franz Rosenzweig[1]

*B*efore concluding, we must return anew to the verse from the Shema with which we began: "You shall love the LORD your God with all your heart and with all your soul and with all your might" (Deut 6:5). But this time, our focus is not on its meaning in the ancient Near Eastern world in which it originated and whose political and cultural realities it reflects, but rather on modernity and the way two Jewish thinkers wrestled with its enduring implications and difficulties less than a century ago. So doing, we can get some sense both of the challenge of modernity to earlier religious thinking and of the ways that Jewish thinkers have sought to meet that challenge.

In chapter 1, we saw that the love commandment of this verse derives from the singular and exclusive claim of the

Lord, God of Israel, on the service of his vassal, the people Israel. The service was to be discharged in acts of obedience, namely, in the mitzvot, or commandments, that he gave them. In key biblical texts, especially in Deuteronomy, observance of those mitzvot is largely, but not completely, synonymous with the love of the God who commands them. Such observance articulates the full measure of Israel's devotion and faithfulness to him, just as their very possession of his commandments testifies to the special love that underlies his election of them to their special status.

But we cannot make a complete equation of Israel's love for God with their observance of his mitzvot because, as I have been at pains to point out, Deuteronomy insists repeatedly that the "words" it associates with covenant be repeated ceaselessly and taken very much to heart.[2] What is more, this language of feeling is more than a technical term for covenantal service. The very metaphors of covenant, at least those drawn prominently from familial relationships (principally, father-son and husband-wife), carry with them an affective connotation that is not easily reconciled with a set of merely mechanical deeds unconnected to the realm of subjective experience. An ancient Near Eastern vassal is, after all, himself a king (though not a "great king" like his suzerain): he is a servant, but he is not a slave. What the "great king" who is the God of Israel (Mal 1:14; Ps 47:3) wants from Israel is not the robotic service of an unfeeling instrument but heartfelt devotion, realized in the practice of specific norms.

So understood, however, commandments lack something that is essential to any social body, and not only to the people Israel: they lack the fixity, the public force, and the predictability of law. "Law" in this sense denotes something impersonal, a norm cast not in the second person ("Thou shalt" or "thou shalt not") but in the third: if a man does x, he shall experience y, or the like. On this understanding, law, unlike covenant, does not plead to be observed; it does not cajole or woo those to whom it applies; it neither expresses joy when it is observed nor grief or a feeling of betrayal when it is violated. Certainly, it need not express any love between those who must obey it and those who author or administer it. In this, it is markedly different from covenant.

In chapter 1, we also saw a further complication. The covenantal commandments have been incorporated into collections of law, but, correlatively, the legal norms themselves have acquired the status of covenantal stipulations. Observing the law, even when it is phrased impersonally, thus becomes an act of covenantal service; conversely, breaking the law is a breach of covenant, a failure to recognize and reciprocate the divine lawgiver's love. So, although commandment and law are conceptually different, in the Torah the two are powerfully interfused, and, in fact, in the form that the Torah takes, they are inseparable.

For most of Jewish history, moreover, the conviction was unquestioned that the Torah is, ideally, the law that should govern a polity. However much personal devotion and individual commitment were stressed—and they were stressed a great deal—the Torah and its commandments were not understood as merely personal choices made in response to inward promptings or to private religious experiences. Another way of saying this is that the people Israel, the Jews, did not understand themselves to be at the deepest level only a voluntary association of disconnected individuals who come together in response to shared inward experiences or religious convictions. Rather, they were (at least ideally) a body politic, one governed as far as possible by Torah law.

Beginning in the eighteenth century, the situation changed radically with the Enlightenment and the emancipation of the Jews that came with it. Now, gradually increasing numbers of Jews found themselves as citizens of states committed (theoretically, at least) to ideals of reason, public secularity, and freedom of religion.[3] The possibility emerged of a fully nonreligious identity for both Jews and Gentiles. In lands in which this happened, every religious community, whatever its classical theology had taught, became a voluntary association.

Wherever the new thinking penetrated and wherever it changed the practical realities of social identity, the communal force of the Torah—the expectation that every Jew would seek to practice it or at least not openly flout it—decreased exponentially. Emancipated Jews could still decide, of course, to treat the mitzvot as the necessary, loving response to God's own antecedent love for them. Or they could decide not to. If, however, they decided to do so, they were now perforce treating the Torah as a set of personal options, not as a body of binding law in the classical sense. Now, only the law of the state held sway. To obey it was a necessity; the law of the Torah was merely a personal choice.

The Jewish responses to the new situation were several and need not be described in detail here. In some instances, which can be termed "liberal," Judaism was reformulated so as to lessen the social import of the category of religious law altogether and to shift the focus toward a more abstract and philosophical understanding of virtuous behavior, one less connected to the particularities of Jewish identity and the foundational literature that had been so prominent within it. Staunch traditionalists, by contrast, tended to insist all the more doggedly that divine revelation was a historical fact, and the norms it disclosed were immune (whatever historians might say) to change or development.

In still other cases, the religious tradition was neither reformulated nor reiterated but simply abandoned as an unredeemable relic of a bygone era, a vestige of the prescientific thinking that new discoveries had discredited. Instead, Jews were urged to replace Jewish religion with

Jewish nationalism or, conversely, with an unqualified universalism that left no place for Jewish peoplehood, except perhaps as a vanguard of the coming undifferentiated humanity.

For those who sought both to speak to a wider Jewish public and to retain the notion of Torah and mitzvot in some sense, it was now all the more important to focus on the key dimension of religious *experience*, the experience of inwardness, of intuitions of higher realities. The weakening of external constraints rendered the internal perceptions all the more important. Now those who spoke of Torah and mitzvot, like their Deuteronomic forebears who sought to elicit assent to covenant from a stiff-necked and rebellious people, often found themselves cajoling and wooing their readers with visions of a self-revealing and loving God—a God in search of a renewed and deeper relationship with *them*.

MITZVAH IN CRISIS

The issue of Torah and mitzvot as they affect the modern, emancipated Jew came to the fore in the 1920s in an especially striking and instructive way through an exchange between two of the titans of modern Jewish theology, Martin Buber (1878–1965) and Franz Rosenzweig (1886–1929).

There has never been a Jewish thinker more focused on the dimension of personal relationship than Buber, best known for his aptly named classic, *I and Thou*.[4] In Buber's thinking, the post-Enlightenment world has known many gains, but also some grievous losses. Among the most grievous is the fact that the life of many in the modern technocratic world is not authentic; it is a life of alienation. How might we overcome this?

As Buber's title implies, human fulfillment lies in relationships, and the primal reality of relationship, which he calls "I-Thou" (or "I-You" in modern English), "can only be spoken with one's whole being." By contrast, its binary opposite, "I-It" "can never be spoken with one's whole being."[5]

Human wholeness, then, is not an attribute of the self in isolation. It is not to be found in disconnected individuals communing with themselves, or reflecting in solitude on the great truths, or acting as agents of a given social cause, however worthy. Nor can it be found through a stance that is instrumental, acquisitive, manipulative, or the like, whatever value such a stance may otherwise have. True wholeness comes into being only in an existential stance that has overcome the dichotomy of subject and object through relationship. As Buber memorably puts it, "All real life is encounter."[6]

For Buber, the I-You relationship also discloses a higher, transcendent reality. "Every It borders on other Its," he writes, but "You has no borders."[7] There is, in fact, something divine about the I-You relationship; or, to put it more precisely, those in the authentic mode of relationship are in a relationship with God himself, whether they name it as such or not. In the striking words that open the third and final section of *I and Thou*, "Extended, the lines of relationships intersect in the eternal You."[8]

> Feelings one "has"; love occurs. Feelings dwell in man, but man dwells in his love. This is no metaphor but actuality.
>
> *Martin Buber*[9]

All this might lead one to suspect that Buber would have great sympathy for the covenantal institution of biblical Israel, especially in the Deuteronomic iteration, with its heavy emphasis on the love and mutuality of the relationship between the LORD and his people Israel. One might even imagine that in the specific commandments of the Torah, Buber would see precious occasions for transcending the instrumental thinking he finds so problematic and for living a "real life" in relationship with God and one's fellows. But the story, it turns out, is rather different. For in Buber's mind, as he explains in a letter to his friend and collaborator Rosenzweig, law falls securely into the category of I-It, and its commandments partake of the I-You mode only if the individual person senses himself to be commanded:

> I do not believe that *revelation* is ever a formulation of law. It is only through man in his self-contradiction that revelation becomes legislation. This is the fact of man. I cannot admit the law transformed by man into the realm of my will, if I am to hold myself ready as well for the unmediated word of God directed to a specific hour of life.[10]

In sum, revelation can never take the form of law.[11] When that is attempted, law ceases to be a communication from God and becomes a product of humans alone. What is more, the very predictability and generality of law render it incompatible with the immediacy of authentic relationship. The word of God must come directly and not through any intermediary, not even a text, and it must speak to the immediate circumstances of one's life.

Given these views, Buber, for all his dislike of subjectivity,[12] has no choice but to fall back upon his own private intuitions to determine whether or not the law speaks to him and therefore obligates him:

> It is this fact which explains why I cannot accept the laws and the statutes blindly, but I must ask myself again and again: Is this particular law addressed to me and rightly so? So that at one time I may include myself in this Israel which is addressed, but at times, many times, I cannot. And if there is anything I can call without reservation a *Mitzvah* within my own sphere, it is just that I act as I do.[13]

Behind Buber's thinking here lay a long history of scholarly investigation of the Torah in which its very human, very historical character and its compositional process had been progressively disclosed, a process that has continued and, in fact, vastly accelerated in the decades between this letter and our own time. No longer was it easy for modern Western people to ignore the historical contingency of the sacred scriptures of any religion—the circumstances to which they spoke, the institutions they took for granted, the cultural world they reflected, the social structures they assumed or endorsed, the changing language in which they are composed. Thus, even when a text (from whatever culture or tradition) claims to be a divine message, transcribed from God's very mouth, the new awareness of human mediation makes it much more difficult to affirm that a divine You is speaking through the text.

Buber here accepts the fruits of this scholarship and, in its light, stakes out his position as an individual confronting, case by case, the demands made upon him by Jewish law. There is something brave and honest in his formulation. But consider the costs entailed in it.

Perhaps the most obvious cost is the loss of community that follows when every member asks, in Buber's words, "Is this particular law addressed to me and rightly so?" What happens to the identity of the people Israel as a social body when each individual within it decides whether or not to be included "in this Israel which is addressed"? And what are the prospects for "real life," for a life of authentic relationship, when the individual self, even if spiritually transformed by an authentic encounter with God, is granted such unrestricted autonomy?

Quite apart from the specific question of Jewish observance at issue between Buber and Rosenzweig in this exchange, it would seem that Buber's position both reflects and perpetuates the very thinking that led to the modern loss of personal authenticity and spiritual meaning that he laments and earnestly seeks to rectify. Instead of the connection characteristic of I-You, his response to Rosenzweig evokes, ironically, the sovereign, autonomous, and isolated self of modernity[14]—a self most at home in an I-It mode of relation.

Rosenzweig's Rebuttal (1): The Difference God's Love Makes

Whereas Martin Buber had grown up in a traditional Jewish household and moved away from observance as a young man, Franz Rosenzweig's life had gone in the opposite direction—from a high degree of acculturation and assimilation to a life of increasing involvement not only in Jewish belief but, eventually, in the lived religion of the observant Jew.[15] So, it is not surprising that Rosenzweig would find Buber's thinking on Torah and mitzvot inadequate. To understand the background of his disagreement, however, we must first return to the love commandment of Deuteronomy 6:5 and examine Rosenzweig's reflections on it in his early and best known work, *The Star of Redemption*.

Rosenzweig begins by asking the familiar question, "Can love then be commanded? Is love not a matter of fate and of being deeply touched, and if it is indeed free, is it not sheerly a free gift?"[16] His answer penetrates to the essence of love itself and how it transforms the autonomous and sovereign self into something very different, something fit to receive the love that is given:

> Yes, of course, love cannot be commanded; no third party can command it or obtain it by force. No third party can do so, but the One can. The commandment of love can only come from the mouth of the lover. Only the lover can say and does say: Love me—and he really does! In his mouth, the commandment of love is not an alien commandment: it is nothing other than the voice of love itself. The love of the lover has, in fact, no other word to express itself than the commandment. Everything else is

already no longer direct expression, but explanation—explanation of love.

But this "explanation of love," Rosenzweig continues immediately,

> is very deficient; it always comes, like every explanation, after the event; and, therefore, since the love of the lover is in the present, it really always comes too late.... The imperative of the commandment makes no provision for the future; it can imagine only the immediacy of obedience. Were it to think of a future or an "always," it would be neither commandment nor order, but law. Law reckons with times, with a future, with duration. The commandment knows only the moment: it waits for the outcome right within the moment of its growing audible, and when it possesses the spell of the genuine tone of a commandment, it will never be disappointed in this waiting.[17]

In certain ways, Rosenzweig's reflection here anticipates the letters that, as we saw above, Buber would send him a few years later. Rosenzweig, too, makes a distinction between commandment and law, to the benefit of the former, and he, too, stresses the directness and immediacy of commandment over against the fixity and predictability of law. In Rosenzweig's mind, hearing the words "Love me" coming directly from the lover's mouth communicates a reality that exists outside the psyche of the one who hears it and cannot be reduced to emotion or the like. But surely the claim that such an event took place is not publicly verifiable, and for that reason is, in practice, as much a subjective experience as Buber's authentic mitzvah, whose address is disclosed only through private intuition.

And yet lurking already here in *The Star of Redemption* is the hint of a critical difference from Buber. Against the latter's claim that he "cannot accept the laws and the statutes blindly,"[18] the early Rosenzweig would, I think, reply that an acceptance born of love is anything but blind: it is, rather, the only response that can do justice to the fact of being loved, of hearing the lover's voice speaking in "the genuine tone of a commandment." For love makes man "com[e] out of the boundaries of his ego," as Stéphane Mosès puts it in his comprehensive study of Rosenzweig's philosophy.[19] "In other words," Mosès writes,

> *Revelation is this movement through which God entrusts his own being to the experience man has of him.*
>
> It is this movement through which God brings himself toward man that Rosenzweig calls *love* .... As in the Song of Songs, human love is here the paradigm that serves as model for the description of a relation whose departure point is not accessible to experience. In fact, Revelation constitutes itself as experience only within human subjectivity, even though the nature itself of this experience requires the coming out of itself of this subjectivity.... This is the paradox of Revelation according to Rosenzweig; Revelation is an event of personal experience, but the latter, by definition, is not capable of containing it.[20]

Although *The Star of Redemption* is notoriously difficult to understand, one can suggest that in Rosenzweig's conception of revelation and God's love, the assent to the mitzvah is something other than a personal choice on the part of the autonomous self. Rather, the very fact of being loved redefines and expands the self, so that the only appropriate response to that all-important command "Love me" is a positive one. Or, as Rosenzweig himself puts it:

> God's first word to the soul that is opening itself up to him is "Love me!" And everything that he may yet reveal to the soul in the form of law turns without more ado into words that he commands it "today." It turns

into execution of the one and first commandment: to love him.[21]

In these words, it is not hard to hear an echo of words in the Mishnah uttered some seventeen centuries earlier—that in reciting the first paragraph of the Shema (in which the love commandment of Deut 6:5 is found), one "first accepts the yoke of the kingship of Heaven" and only "afterward," in reciting the second paragraph (Deut 11:13–21), does one "accept the yoke of the commandments" (*m. Berakhot* 2:2). As we saw in chapter 1, the foundation of the observant life in all its multitude of details lies in the singular and all-important act of acclaiming the LORD's uniqueness and kingship. This is an act that is inextricably tied to the commandment to love him—in the Shema, in the Mishnah, and in Rosenzweig's philosophy alike.

Rosenzweig's Rebuttal (2): Making Law into Mitzvah Again

Now we return to the response that Rosenzweig wrote, about five years after the *Star*, to Buber's letters on the subject of law and commandment. Buber, it will be recalled, had insisted that revelation can never be "a formulation of law" but must be unmediated, requiring individuals to determine for themselves whether any given practice is a mitzvah or not. Given the passages we have seen from the *Star*, it is no surprise that Rosenzweig tells his friend, "For me, too, God is not a Law-giver." But whereas Buber drove a broad wedge between law and commandment, Rosenzweig counters that Jews must instead strive to transform law *into* commandment, to find the commanding voice of the personal God behind the impersonal laws of Jewish tradition. For Rosenzweig, what needs to be restored is a keen personal awareness of the import of the words "I am the LORD," which so often serve to authorize divine commands

> Man can appropriate divine commandments if they are handed over for human appropriation. He can live by the Torah in the love and for the sake of God, if the Torah itself is a gift of divine love, making such a life a human possibility. He can participate in a three-term relationship which involves God Himself if God, Who in His power does not need man, in His love nevertheless chooses to need him.
>
> *Emil L. Fackenheim*[23]

in the Bible. The Jew must relearn the habit of approaching the classical texts and traditions with "love and fear."[22]

This, in turn, means that, as opposed to Buber's principled rejection of law, Jews must instead cultivate a stance of openness to it. Invoking the title of the most influential compendium of Jewish law, Rosenzweig affirms, "If 'On this day' becomes a *Shulhan Arukh* then I turn a bit pantheistic and believe that it does concern God. Because He has sold Himself to us with the Torah."[24]

In other words, the immediacy of commandment can be found even in what appears to be a dry, technical compendium of law precisely because there, too, God has entrusted his being to the Jewish people. The laws are not immediate revelations, but neither are they simply a product of human beings, of "man in his self-contradiction," as Buber put it. Nor does the choice lie between rote observance of the law as an impersonal, unfeeling reality, on the one hand, and the rejection of law as incompatible with the being of the loving God, on the other. There is a third position—a principled stance of openness to the Torah as the medium for encountering the loving and commanding God of Israel. As Rosenzweig put it in his letter to Buber a year earlier:

> Law must again become commandment which seeks to be transformed into deed at the very moment it is heard. It must regain that living reality in which all great Jewish

periods have sensed the guarantee for its eternity. Like *teaching*, it must consciously start where its content stops being content and becomes inner power, our own inner power. Inner power which in turn is added to the substance of the law.[25]

This transformation of law into commandment, and of external content into inner power, cannot come from study alone; the key transformative act is not a cognitive one, or at least not purely a cognitive one. What is required, rather, is the act of observance itself:

> What can be expressed, what can be formulated in terms of theology, so that a Christian too could understand it as an "article of faith," is the connection between election and the Law. But an outsider, no matter how willing and sympathetic, can never be made to accept a single commandment as a "religious" demand. We wholly realize that general theological connection only when we cause it to come alive by fulfilling individual commandments, and transpose it from the objectivity of a theological truth to the "Thou" of the benediction: when he who is called to the reading of the Torah unites, in his benediction before and after the reading, thanks for the "national" election from among the peoples of the earth with thanks for the "religious" election to eternal life.[26]

In Rosenzweig's thinking, intellectual comprehension alone can never disclose the religious dimension of Jewish law. Only by transposing law from the realm of objectivity to that of personal interaction with the living God can it become commandment; or, as Buber himself might have put it, only thus can the "It" of law be transformed into the "You" of authentic dialogue. For Rosenzweig—and here he differs sharply from Buber—it is incumbent on the Jew from the start to work at that transposition, to transcend the realm of study and objectification in order to participate through practice in the higher reality that intellectual comprehension alone cannot reach.

KNOWING THROUGH DOING

We must confront the fact that, as an answer to the problem of Jewish law in the post-Enlightenment and post-emancipation world, Franz Rosenzweig's thinking is not fully adequate. In his thought, as in Buber's, the Torah is still not a communal norm; it still lacks social force. However much Rosenzweig insists that the reality of God's love exists outside the psyche of the one who hears the command "Love me," the practical reality is that the command is known only through the personal testimony of individuals. And when Jews find, as many did in his time and as many do today, that they cannot hear the genuine voice of the loving God in the particular laws of the Torah, they are not likely to commit themselves to practicing those norms. Beyond that, some may well demand, or expect, that the laws be abolished or redefined in terms that the classic codes could not approve.

But, for all his ambitions in the realm of systematic philosophy,[27] Rosenzweig's thinking is not a comprehensive program for Jewish observance in the modern Western world. Rather, it is an effort to communicate the reality of God so that the newly awakened reader might move, in the words with which *The Star of Redemption* famously ends, "INTO LIFE."[28] Especially in his later exchange with Buber, it becomes obvious that Rosenzweig's objective is not to propose a solution to the large sociopolitical issues confronting the modern Jew but to clear a path that can draw people into the traditional life. He wants to find a place for the Jewish tradition within modern social reality, a place that represents neither an inauthentic accommodation to secular thinking nor a fundamentalist and intellectually indefensible retreat into the pre-Enlightenment world. The objective is not to deny the modern sciences but to relativize them, to unmask their claims to *total* knowledge.

One can see this in Rosenzweig's approach to the claims of such disciplines as psychology, the history of religion, and sociology when they confront the commandments of the Torah:

> Psychological analysis finds the solution to all enigmas in self-delusion, and historical sociology finds it in mass delusion.... The Law is not understood as a commandment addressed by God to the people but as a soliloquy of the people. We know it differently, not always and not in all things, but again and again. For we know it only when—we *do*.
>
> What do we know when we do? Certainly not that all of these historical and sociological explanations are false. But in the light of the doing, of the right doing in which we experience the reality of the Law, the explanations are of superficial and subsidiary importance.[29]

Whether Rosenzweig's characterization of the social sciences was altogether fair when he wrote these words or is fair today need not concern us. Of enduring value is his pointing beyond the realms in which the social-scientific explanations of documents or institutions hold true. Those explanations cannot simply be dismissed as false; nor does Rosenzweig propose that they be replaced with a narrative of direct and miraculous divine authorship of the documents and institutions that such explanations claim to explain, as if the historically contingent human dimension did not exist. But there is, he insists, another mode of knowing, the mode in which Torah speaks (to recall other words of his) with "the genuine tone of a commandment" and expresses the primal commandment of the lover: "Love me."[30] This is the mode that is realized only in the doing, in practice.

The assumptions of the psychologist, historian, and sociologist require them to miss this mode, and with it the voice of the divine lover behind the realities that these specialists study. Again, those sciences are not to be dismissed or avoided—only relativized. Without proposing that scholars in these fields bow to religion, or cease their investigations, Rosenzweig asks them only to recognize that there are more things in heaven and earth than can be dreamt of with their methodologies.

Wilfred Cantwell Smith, a historian of religion prominent in the last third of the twentieth century, provides an analogy that is helpful here. To explain what he means by "transcendence," Smith writes of the different levels at which a musical composition exists. "One may listen to one's equipment," he writes, "one may listen to the performance, one may listen to Mozart, one may listen to God."[31]

To listen to Mozart does not require one to deny that a very material thing, a violin or piano or electronic device, is producing the sound one hears or, at the next remove, that the performer is causing the instrument to make the sound, or at still another level, that the performer and the instrument are making Mozart himself available. Indeed, some may sense, in a way that Mozart himself may only have glimpsed, that they are listening to something that stands above instrument, performer, and composer alike (though making use of all of them)—something transcendent and unfathomable: Smith's "God." To acknowledge and respond to that highest reality does not require one to deny the lower ones; it requires only that one recognize they are all rendering something more, something that can be apprehended even if never grasped.

In the case of the love of God as we have explored it in this book, some will believe they hear only the voice of the ancient, medieval, or modern Jews whose writings we have discussed, speaking exclusively within the historical worlds of their own time and place and having nothing to say in our day. Others, though, may believe they hear the genuine tone of the ancient commandment "Love me," and act accordingly.

1. *m. Avot* 3:14 (note that the enumeration is different in various editions). The speaker is Rabbi Akiva, whom we shall meet in chapters 1–4. I have departed from the NJPS translations of Gen 9:6 and Prov 4:2 in order to bring out the understanding of these verses that inform the Mishnah in which they are quoted.

ONE
A COVENANTAL GOD

1. When the passage is recited liturgically, the following line is inserted after v. 4: "Blessed be the name of His glorious kingship forever and ever." The other two paragraphs are Deut 11:13–21 and Num 15:37–41.

2. The translation of Deut 6:4 is notoriously difficult and has been addressed by many scholars over the centuries. See, for example, Jeffrey H. Tigay, *Deuteronomy: The JPS Torah Commentary* (Philadelphia: Jewish Publication Society, 5756/1996), 438–40, and R.W.L. Moberly, "'YHWH is One': The Translation of the Shema," in *Studies in the Pentateuch*, ed. J. A. Emerton, Supplements to *Vetus Testamentum* 41 (Leiden: Brill, 1990), 209–15, reprinted in R.W.L. Moberly, *From Eden to Golgotha: Essays in Biblical Theology*, South Florida Studies in the History of Judaism 52 (Atlanta: Scholars Press, 1992), 75–81. See also his *Old Testament Theology: Reading the Hebrew Bible as Christian Scripture* (Grand Rapids, Mich.: Baker Academic, 2013), 7–41.

3. This translates Oxford Oppenheimer Additions folio 23. I thank Professor Bernard Septimus for his help on the textual problems here.

4. See William L. Moran, "The Ancient Near Eastern Background of the Love of God in Deuteronomy," *Catholic Biblical Quarterly* 25 (1963): 77–87; reprinted in William L. Moran, *The Most Magic Word*, ed. Ronald S. Hendel, Catholic Biblical Quarterly Monograph

Series 35 (Washington, D.C.: Catholic Biblical Society of America, 2002), 170–81. The influence of the famous essay by my late teacher and colleague on this chapter is pervasive. The references are to the version in *The Most Magic Word*. On the connection of 1 Kgs 8:23 to Deut 7:9, see 171n9.

5. W. L. Moran, "A Kingdom of Priests," in *The Bible in Current Catholic Thought*, ed. J. L. McKenzie (New York: Herder and Herder, 1962), 7–20, especially 11–17. Moran, however, thinks "kingdom of priests" ascribes quasi-royal powers to the priesthood. For a more recent discussion and one closer to the interpretation offered here, see William H. C. Propp, *Exodus 19–40*, Anchor Bible 2A (New York: Doubleday, 2006), 157–60. Propp writes, "[the LORD's] 'treasured' vassal Israel will serve as priest-king over all the nations of the Earth" (159).

6. Moran, "The Ancient Near Eastern Background," 171–72.

7. On this and the other ancient Near Eastern examples, see Moran, "The Ancient Near Eastern Background," 172–74.

8. The text can be found in J. A. Knudtzon, *Die El-Amarna-Tafeln mit Einleitung und Erläuterungen*, 2 vols. (Leipzig: J. C. Hinrichs'sche Buchhandlungen, 1915), 1:500. Henceforth, this book will be abbreviated as *EA*, and the letters in it will be identified as *EA* followed by the number and line of the reference. This is *EA* 114:68. The Akkadian verb in the first clause is *râmu*. Interestingly, William L. Moran renders it as "love" in "The Ancient Near Eastern Background," 173, but as "be loyal" in his later work, *The Amarna Letters* (Baltimore: Johns Hopkins University Press, 1992), 189. (The same variation in Moran's translations of *râmu* occurs in our next two examples as well. See "The Ancient Near Eastern Background," 173, and *Amarna*, 153 and 222.) That the verb can have both these meanings, depending on context, conforms to our understanding of the underlying conception.

9. *EA* 83:51, found in 1:402.

10. Ibid., 582, for *EA* 138:71–72. The translation follows Moran, "The Ancient Near Eastern Background," 173.

11. Moran, "The Ancient Near Eastern Background," 173.

12. Ibid., 174.

13. *Ancient Near Eastern Texts Relating to the Old Testament*, 3rd ed., ed. James B. Pritchard (Princeton: Princeton University Press, 1969), 204. The text is the "Treaty between Mursilis and Duppi-Tessub of Amurru."

14. The closest analogy comes from the first Arslan Tash plaque, a Phoenician inscription from the seventh century BCE. See Ziony

Zevit, "A Phoenician Inscription and Biblical Covenant Theology," *Israel Exploration Journal* 27 (1977): 110–18.

15. It is likely that "them" in Exod 20:5 refers not to the images mentioned in the previous verse but to the "other gods" of v. 3. The possibility that v. 4 is an interpolation has been plausibly argued by, among others, Benno Jacob, *The Second Book of the Bible: Exodus* (Hoboken, N.J.: KTAV, 1992), 548, 551. The commentary was composed in 1935–40, according to its author's grandson and translator (xiii).

16. See Jon D. Levenson, *Creation and the Persistence of Evil: The Jewish Drama of Divine Omnipotence*, 2nd ed. (Princeton: Princeton University Press, 1994), 131–39.

17. An exception can be found in the thinking of Baḥya ibn Paquda, a profound Jewish thinker of the eleventh century writing in Arabic in Muslim Spain, whose thinking we shall explore in depth in chapter 4. In *Duties of the Heart* 10:2, Baḥya counsels his readers to love only what God wills them to love and thus to make their legitimate loves part of their love of God.

18. The NJPS translation, "befriend the stranger," misses the nuance of the verb that we need here and is insufficiently precise about the meaning of the noun.

19. Rabbi Akiva's statement can be found in the *Siphra*, *Qedošim* 2:12. Here, we pass over the practical question of just how the commandment is fulfilled. On Rabbi Akiva and the question of love in rabbinic literature, see Naftali Rothenberg, *Wisdom of Love: Man, Woman & God in Jewish Canonical Literature* (Boston: Academic Studies Press, 2009), 59–126. Rothenberg acknowledges that the figure of Rabbi Akiva represented in these texts need not correspond to the historical personage (93, 127). In the New Testament, the commandment to love God in Deut 6:5 and the commandment to love one's neighbor in Lev 19:18 are conjoined (see Mark 12:28–34; Matthew 22:34–40; and Luke 10:25–28). In fact, Luke 10:27 goes so far as to present the two injunctions as if they were drawn from the same version. For this, there are Jewish precedents in the *Testament of Issachar* 5:2 and the *Testament of Dan* 5:3, as noted in *The Jewish Annotated New Testament*, ed. Amy-Jill Levine and Marc Zvi Brettler (New York: Oxford University Press, 2011), 124. To the best of my knowledge, however, there are no rabbinic parallels. Werner G. Jeanrond is thus in error when he implies that Judaism connects these two love commandments as tightly as does Christianity. See his *A Theology of Love* (New York: T&T Clark, 2010), 126. Note especially p. 246, where he speaks of "the double

love commandment in the Torah," giving Deut 6:4–9 as the reference, as if that were the location of both commandments.

20. *m. Avot* 1:12.

21. Examples of such prohibitions can be found in Exod 22:19, 23:12; and Deut 12:29–13:1, 13:2–12.

22. *Pesiqta de Rav Kahana* 4:7. The speaker is Rabban Yoḥanan ben Zakkai, who lived in the first century CE.

23. Francesca M. Cancian, "The Feminization of Love," *Signs: Journal of Women in Culture and Society* 11 (1986): 692–709, here 698. See also her *Love in America: Gender and Self-Development* (New York: Cambridge University Press, 1987), especially 69–80. The bibliography on love is enormous. For a historical perspective, with attention to literary and theological issues, see the classic work of Denis de Rougemont, *Love in the Western World*, rev. and augmented ed. (Princeton: Princeton University Press, 1983). The book was originally published in 1940. Also helpful are a number of works by Irving Singer, especially *The Nature of Love: Plato to Luther* (New York: Random House, 1966). For a more recent (and more idiosyncratic) study, see Jean-Claude Kaufmann, *The Curious History of Love* (Cambridge, U.K.: Polity Press, 2011). For the understanding of love in the Christian tradition, with special attention to modern and contemporary theology, see Jeanrond, *A Theology*.

24. Cancian, "Feminization," 692.

25. Ibid., 695. For empirical support, Cancian cites Margaret Reedy, "Age and Sex Differences in Personal Needs and the Nature of Love" (Ph.D. diss., University of Southern California, 1977).

26. Cancian, "Feminization," 703.

27. See, for example, Deut 8:5, 14:1, and 32:6 (if the last can be counted as Deuteronomic). On the theological use of father-son language in Deuteronomy, see Dennis J. McCarthy, SJ, "Notes on the Love of God in Deuteronomy and the Father-Son Relationship between [the LORD] and Israel," *Catholic Biblical Quarterly* 27 (1965): 144–47. But McCarthy's claim that the love in question "is simply a matter of reverence, loyalty, obedience, things subject to command and commanded," and not one of "tender, feeling love" (146), is not correct, as I argue later in this chapter.

28. J. W. McKay, "Man's Love for God in Deuteronomy and the Father/Teacher–Son/Pupil Relationship," *Vetus Testamentum* 22 (1972): 426–35. My discussion here relies heavily on this article.

29. I have rendered the first word as "Hear," rather than "Heed" (NJPS) to bring out the connection in the Hebrew with Deut 6:5.

30. So maintains Moran ("The Ancient Near Eastern Background," 171). But the instructional situation alluded to in Deut 6:7 ("Impress them upon your children") speaks in favor of McKay's claim that the love of God here is properly associated with the father/teacher–son/pupil relationship.

31. On this subject, see the useful studies of Jacqueline E. Lapsley, "Feeling Our Way: Love for God in Deuteronomy," *Catholic Biblical Quarterly* 65 (2003): 350–69, and Bill T. Arnold, "The Love-Fear Antinomy in Deuteronomy 5–11," *Vetus Testamentum* 61 (2011): 551–69. Arnold has a good review of literature on this point on 556–59. I thank Professor Lapsley for drawing my attention to Professor Arnold's splendid article.

32. On this, see (among many others) Dennis J. McCarthy, *Treaty and Covenant*, 2nd ed., Analecta Biblica 21A (Rome: Biblical Institute Press, 1978), especially 155–298, and Moshe Weinfeld, "The Loyalty Oath in the Ancient Near East," *Ugarit-Forschungen* 8 (1976): 379–414.

33. Frank Moore Cross, *From Epic to Canon: History and Literature in Ancient Israel* (Baltimore: Johns Hopkins University Press, 1998), 7, 8.

34. See Isa 7:4–6.

35. There are many text-critical issues and difficult points of translation in this passage, on which see A. Graeme Auld, *I & II Samuel*, Old Testament Library (Louisville, Ky.: Westminster John Knox Press, 2011), 235, 238–39, and 241–42. For our purposes, it is sufficient simply to reproduce the NJPS.

36. I am speaking of the text. Whatever the underlying history was, it is not at issue here. One of the outstanding problems in recent critical scholarship on David is its tendency to ignore or misinterpret the manifest text in its eagerness to reconstruct the historical events. Whether this results in good history is open to argument; it certainly results in bad theology. On this, see J. Randall Short, *The Surprising Election and Confirmation of King David*, Harvard Theological Series 63 (Cambridge, Mass.: Harvard University Press, 2010).

37. On this, see J. A. Thompson, "The Significance of the Verb Love in the David-Jonathan Narratives in 1 Samuel," *Vetus Testamentum* 24 (1974): 334–38.

38. The earliest attestations listed in the *Oxford English Dictionary* are to Miles Coverdale's translation of the Bible (1535), specifically to Ps 25:6 and Ps 89:34 (there listed as 89:33); the expression was

originally written as two words, "louynge kyndnesse" (*Oxford English Dictionary*, 3rd ed., March 2008; online version, March 2012).

39. Auld, *I & II Samuel*, 242. The context of Auld's remark is his discussion of a version of the text other than, and significantly different from, the Masoretic Text, which is the basis of the translation I have used. But his remark applies nonetheless. Auld's observation that in the Masoretic Text to 1 Sam 18 and 20, "it is always Jonathan who is said to love David ... but David's own attitude to Jonathan remains unstated" is valid, but the sample from which it is drawn is small, and even in that text we cannot assume that the love is unidirectional. At least in the poem in 2 Sam 1, David is portrayed as deeply appreciating Jonathan's love for him and calling him, as befits covenant partners, "my brother" (v. 26).

40. Hermann Spieckermann, "Mit der Liebe im Wort: Ein Beitrag zur Theologie des Deuteronomiums," in *Liebe und Gebot: Studien zum Deuteronomium*, ed. Reinhard G. Kratz and Hermann Spieckermann, Forschungen zur Religion und Literatur des Alten und Neuen Testaments 190 (Göttingen: Vandenhoeck & Ruprecht, 2000), 190–205, here 193 (my translation). "On your heart" is a possible (and perhaps preferable) translation of the phrase the NJPS renders as "take to heart." (Spieckermann erroneously gives the reference to Deut 6:6 as Deut 6:7.) Note also David M. Carr, *Writing on the Tablet of the Heart: Origins of Scripture and Literature* (New York: Oxford University Press, 2005), 135, where it is pointed out that "this text does not refer to discussion of the commandments, as is often implied by the translations.... Instead it commands a constant process of recitation of the texts during all activities of the waking day." It should be noted that it is quite possible that Deut 6:8–9 refers to amulets, but this interpretation need not contradict the notion that the text speaks of a process of internalization. On the relevance of amulets here, see Moshe Weinfeld, *Deuteronomy 1–11*, Anchor Bible 5 (New York: Doubleday, 1991), 341–43.

41. "Nothing entirely straight can be fashioned from the crooked wood out of which humankind is made." Immanuel Kant, "Idea for a Universal History from a Cosmopolitan Perspective," in *Toward Perpetual Peace and Other Writings on Politics, Peace, and History*, ed. Pauline Kleingold (New Haven: Yale University Press, 2006), 3–16, at 9 (the essay dates from 1784). The specific wording, "crooked timber of humanity," comes more directly from a famous collection of Isaiah Berlin's essays of that title.

42. "Uncircumcised heart" is a more literal translation of the idiom that appears (in various permutations) in Lev 26:41, Deut 10:16, and Jer 4:4, though none of these verses is rendered literally in the NJPS. The same image appears in Deut 30:6, wherein the verb translated as "open up" means more literally, "to circumcise," as the NJPS notes.

43. See the preceding text, Deut 30:1–5.

44. I have rendered *davar* in v. 14 as "word" rather than "thing" (NJPS) in order to bring out the affinities with Deut 6:6 and because it is more uplifting to have a word in one's mouth than a "thing." "Instruction" in v. 11, it should be noted, is the Hebrew word for "commandment" (*mitzvah*).

45. See n. 1 above.

46. Arnold, "The Love-Fear Antinomy," 563, 564. Note also Bernard Bamberger, "Fear and Love of God in the Old Testament," *Hebrew Union College Annual* 6 (1929): 39–53, especially 39: "Furthermore, the idea of fear or love of God as *motives for righteous conduct*, an idea of which the Rabbis made so much, is absent in Biblical literature" (italics in the original).

47. Arnold, "The Love-Fear Antinomy," 565–66.

48. *m. Soṭah* 5:1; *b. Soṭah* 31a. The biblical references are Job 1:1 and Gen 22:12. On this love-fear dichotomy and the approaches to it in classical rabbinic literature, see Ephraim E. Urbach, *The Sages: The World and Wisdom of the Rabbis* (Cambridge, Mass.: Harvard University Press, 1975), 402–9.

49. Peter L. Berger and Thomas Luckmann, *The Social Construction of Reality: A Treatise in the Sociology of Knowledge* (Garden City, N.Y.: Doubleday, 1966), 142. See also Peter L. Berger, *The Sacred Canopy: Elements of a Sociological Theory of Religion* (Garden City, N.Y.: Doubleday, 1967), especially 126–53; Gary A. Anderson, *A Time to Mourn, a Time to Dance: The Expression of Grief and Joy in Israelite Religion* (University Park: Pennsylvania State University Press, 1991), especially 95–97; and Lapsley, "Feeling Our Way," 356–57.

50. Anderson, *A Time to Mourn*, 95.

51. I have departed from the NJPS in order to bring out the midrashic understanding of the verses in Jeremiah. I thank Rabbi Yehiel Poupko for suggesting "starter dough" as a translation of *śʾor*. The image is that of a leavening agent catalyzing the rising of the dough. The point, he observes, is that "the Torah is the catalyst that moves the Jew to God." Private communication, April 29, 2012.

52. The lines are said by Thomas Becket near the end of part 1 of *Murder in the Cathedral*. T. S. Eliot, *The Complete Poems and Plays, 1909–1950* (New York: Harcourt, Brace & World, 1958), 196.

53. François, duc de la Rochefoucauld, *Reflections; or Sentences and Moral Maxims* (Gutenberg Project online edition, http://www.gutenberg.org/files/9105/9105-h/9105-h.htm). This is maxim 218.

54. I say "can" because it seems unlikely that Rav Huna (and others who cite variants of the dictum) thought the happy result was inevitable.

55. The texts are *EA* 121:61 and 123:23, of which translations can be found in Moran, *The Amarna Letters*, 200, 202 (my quote does not reproduce Moran's conventions for indicating fragmentary words). See Moran, "The Ancient Near Eastern Background," 173n17.

56. *EA* 158:36, translated in Moran, *The Amarna Letters*, 244.

57. I have rendered *'ahavat* (v. 8) as "loved" rather than "favored" (NJPS) for reasons that will become clear.

58. Deut 7:1–5.

59. *Leviticus Rabbah* 17:6; *Deuteronomy Rabbah* 5:14.

60. For a survey of the current models for the emergence of Israel and the reasons that the term "conquest" is often judged to be historically inaccurate, see Iain Provan et al., *A Biblical History of Israel* (Louisville, Ky.: Westminster John Knox, 2003), 138–93, especially 139–47.

61. See R.W.L. Moberly, "Toward an Interpretation of the Shema," in *Theological Exegesis: Essays in Honor of Brevard S. Childs*, ed. Christopher Seitz and Kathryn Greene-McCreight (Grand Rapids, Mich.: Eerdmans, 1999), 124–44, especially 134–37; Moberly, "Election and the Transformation of Ḥērem," in *The Call of Abraham: Essays on the Election of Israel in Honor of Jon D. Levenson*, ed. Gary A. Anderson and Joel S. Kaminsky (Notre Dame, Ind.: University of Notre Dame Press, 2013), 67–89; and Nathan MacDonald, *Deuteronomy and the Meaning of "Monotheism*," Forschungen zum Alten Testament, 2nd series, no. 1 (Tübingen: Mohr Siebeck, 2003), 108–22. This is not to deny, of course, that the rhetoric in Deuteronomy could inspire violence against those deemed dangerous to the Lord and his proper worship; it is only to argue that this does not exhaust the meaning of the passage or constitute its characteristic interpretation in the ancient Israelite or continuing Jewish traditions.

62. For nearly two hundred years, historical scholars of the Bible have connected Deuteronomy with the violent reform (or purge) carried out by King Josiah around 622 BCE. See 1 Kgs 23:1–25.

63. On the political and specifically covenantal resonance of "treasured people" (*segullah*), see Weinfeld, *Deuteronomy 1–11*, 368.

64. On the thorny issue of chosenness, see Joel S. Kaminsky, *Yet I Loved Jacob: Reclaiming the Biblical Concept of Election* (Nashville: Abingdon Press, 2007). See especially Kaminsky's refutation of the commonly heard but utterly mistaken notion that Christianity lacks any notion of a chosen people (169–92). Also of great use are the essays in *The Call*, ed. Anderson and Kaminsky.

65. On the common mistake of interpreting the story of the biblical exodus as an attack on slavery, see Jon D. Levenson, *The Hebrew Bible, the Old Testament, and Historical Criticism: Jews and Christians in Biblical Studies* (Louisville, Ky.: Westminster / John Knox, 1993), 127–59.

66. Note that "oath" and "covenant" can be synonyms. See McCarthy, *Treaty and Covenant*, 32–36. See chapter 4 in this volume for the similar interpretation of *ḥašaq* in the medieval Jewish philosophers Ḥasdai Crescas and Joseph Albo.

67. Gen 12:1–3. On the call of Abraham and its underlying theology, see Jon D. Levenson, *Inheriting Abraham: The Legacy of the Patriarch in Judaism, Christianity, and Islam*, Library of Jewish Ideas (Princeton: Princeton University Press, 2012), chapter 1.

68. Gen 15:7–20 and chap. 17.

69. The passage is Gen 22:15–18. See R.W.L. Moberly, "The Earliest Commentary on the Akedah," *Vetus Testamentum* 38 (1988): 302–23. On the Aqedah more generally, see Levenson, *Inheriting Abraham*, chapter 3.

70. See Levenson, *Inheriting Abraham*, chapters 4 and 5.

71. *Mekhilta de-Rabbi Išmael, Baḥodeš* 5.

72. The charge is explicit in *Genesis Rabbah* 55:1, where it is rebutted by reference to Abraham's willingness to sacrifice Isaac.

73. *Absalom and Achitophel*, lines 163–64, in *Selected Works of John Dryden*, ed. William Frost (New York: Holt, Rinehart, and Winston, 1953), 26.

74. Note also Deut 10:15, in which the chosenness of the descendants is a consequence of God's love for the patriarchs.

75. I have changed the wording in some of the biblical citations in order to bring out the meaning the rabbinic texts see in them. The ascriptions of Gen 11:2 to Nimrod and of Ezek 28:2 to Hiram derive not from the plain sense of the biblical texts but from midrashic narrative.

76. On "jealous God," rather than "impassioned God" (as in the NJPS), see our discussion of Exod 20:5, above.

77. *Ancient Near Eastern Texts*, ed. Pritchard, 204.

78. Irving Singer, *The Nature of Love*, 15.

79. Moshe Weinfeld, "The Covenant of Grant in the Old Testament and in the Ancient Near East," *Journal of the American Oriental Society* 90 (1970): 184–203, here 185.

80. The modern scholar, however, may think of another way to attribute God's demand for covenantal service to self-interest—that is, to the self-interest of the authors of the text and the social sectors from which these authors hailed (for example, the priesthood or the palace). This approach of ideology critique has become very popular in the humanities over the past several decades and has obvious validity. Surely, texts participate in the social contingencies of their time and place, just as they do in the history of the culture and language in which they are written, and scholars are wise to take those contingencies into account. The problem comes when ideology critique becomes exclusive and reductive and maintains (this often happens without explicit articulation) that the historical and social placement of the text precludes its having any larger, transhistorical meaning, a claim that extends beyond the domain of empirical investigation.

81. Robert Emmons, "Gratitude," in Shane J. Lopez, ed., *Encyclopedia of Positive Psychology* (Malden, Mass.: Wiley-Blackwell, 2009), 442–47, here 443. See also this comment of A.D.M. Walker: "In political philosophy [gratitude] appears in the earliest theory of political obligation when Socrates claims that his obligation to obey the laws of Athens is in part an obligation of gratitude for benefits received under the Athenian system." A.D.M. Walker, "Gratefulness and Gratitude," *Proceedings of the Aristotelian Society*, new series 81 (1980–81): 39–55, here 40. Walker's reference is to Plato's *Crito*, 50a–51c. Mutatis mutandis, the parallel with the (much older) Israelite covenant theology is remarkable. I gratefully acknowledge my debt to Dr. Shai A. Held for drawing my attention to these sources.

82. See Jon D. Levenson, *Resurrection and the Restoration of Israel: The Ultimate Victory of the God of Life* (New Haven: Yale University Press, 2006), 108–22.

83. Singer, *The Nature of Love*, 11–12.

84. For example, Gen 18:23–25; Jer 12:1–3; Hab 1:12–17.

85. See, for example, Exod 32:9–14, 30–34; Num 14:11–24.

86. In formulating this issue, I have been aided by comments of Professor Sam A. Meier of the Ohio State University in response to a presentation I gave on March 18, 2014.

TWO
HEART, SOUL, AND MIGHT

1. *m. Avot* 3:7, quoting 1 Chr 29:14.
2. See, for example, Lev 26:3–45 and Deut 28:1–68.
3. All translations from *Siphre Deuteronomy* are taken from *Sifre: A Tannaitic Commentary on the Book of Deuteronomy*, translated, introduced, and annotated by Reuven Hammer (New Haven: Yale University Press, 1986); italics in the original. Pisqah 32 is found on 59–62. Unless otherwise noted, I have replaced Hammer's biblical translations with those of the NJPS. In this instance, I have kept his "fear" and "serve" in Deut 10:20 in place of "revere" and "worship" (NJPS) to facilitate understanding of the rabbinic use of the verse. The chapters and verses refer to Deuteronomy unless otherwise noted.
4. See *Sifre*, 404n3, in which Hammer cites pisqah 354 as support for translating *maṣrikho* (at the very end of the passage) as "needs." The parallel is less than ideal, since in pisqah 354 the word means "make dependent," as Hammer rightly translates it. But the alternative he cites, "when B (the master) forces him to work" seems to make less sense.
5. See 1 Kgs 11:2, in which *davaq* and *'ahav* appear in tandem, and the comment on this in *b. Yevamot* 76b.
6. As suggested in Hammer, *Sifre*, 404n4, where the possibility is mooted that the text "may be a fragment of another homily contrasting the two verses [that is, Deut 10:20 and 11:1] and showing how both motivations are needed and can co-exist."
7. The exact year of Maimonides's birth is not clear.
8. I have changed the NJPS rendering of Deut 6:13 to bring out Maimonides's point about it.
9. The translation, including that of the biblical quote, is taken from Hammer, *Sifre*, 85; italics in the original.
10. I have capitalized "Inclination to Good" and "Inclination to Evil" here because I think they really function as the proper names of the two entities within rabbinic thinking. The exegesis of Deut 6:5 in the Mishnah (*Berakhot* 9:5) closely parallels that in *Siphre Deut* 32. The historical relationship of the two texts is not relevant to our purpose here.
11. See, for example, ibn Ezra to Deut 6:5.
12. Hans Walter Wolff, *Anthropology of the Old Testament* (Philadelphia: Fortress Press, 1974), 20.
13. Jon D. Levenson, *Resurrection and the Restoration of Israel: The Ultimate Victory of the God of Life* (New Haven: Yale University Press,

2006), 111. It should be obvious but needs to be noted that *nepheš* in the Bible has more than one meaning. The point is that "soul" as generally understood in the history of philosophy and common contemporary discourse is not one of them.

14. See, for example, the use of the same word (*'aleykha*) in Sarai's accusation of Abram in Gen 16:5.

15. Ibn Ezra and Ramban (Naḥmanides), among others, say much the same thing in their commentaries. They reflect one of the interpretations of the Mishnah in the passage quoted below (*m. Berakhot* 9:5).

16. The comment clearly reflects the use of *me'od* as a term for "property," a sense that it already had in late Second Temple Judaism. See, for example, the *Damascus Document* 9:11 and 12:10. I thank Professors Diana Lobel and Matthias Henze for bringing these texts to my attention.

17. The word for "wealth" here is the source of the English word "mammon," which comes from the New Testament. See the King James (or Authorized) Version of Matthew 6:24, "No man can serve two masters: for either he will hate the one, and love the other; or else he will hold to the one, and despise the other. Ye cannot serve God and mammon." Luke 16:13 is identical except for reading "no servant" in place of "no man." The saying in these two Gospels (it does not appear in Mark or John) and the midrash in the name of Rabbi Eliezer (who flourished late in the first century CE) come from the same thought-world and may possibly reflect a common origin in homiletical interpretation of the Shema.

18. Note this helpful observation provided by one of the anonymous referees for this book: "The discussion of Hebrew *me'od* as both 'strength' and 'wealth' might include some reference to Greek *dunamis*, which exhibits the same overlap and may well have influenced the evolution of the Hebrew term; with the disappearance of phonemic *aleph*, classical Hebrew *me'od* came to be pronounced *mod* (indeed, Qumranic Hebrew therefore developed a new, adverbial form: *modah*). This pronunciation heightens the connection between *mod, moded* ('measures'), and *modekha* ('thanking You') in the midrash attributed to R. Akiva."

19. The text can be found in Ḥayyim Schirmann, *The Hebrew Poem in Spain and Provence* (Heb.; Jerusalem and Tel Aviv: Mosad Bialik / Devir, 1954), 1:465, where the poem is number 188. It also appears in *Selected Poems of Jehudah Halevi*, ed. Heinrich Brody (Philadelphia: Jewish Publication Society of America, 1924), 105. My renditions in this book of two poems of Halevi, who lived in Spain ca.

1070–1141 and was perhaps the foremost Hebrew poet of medieval Jewry, reflect my use of Brody's translations, though I have made several alterations and modernizations along the way. For an alternate translation, see Raymond P. Scheindlin, *The Gazelle: Medieval Hebrew Poems on God, Israel, and the Soul* (Philadelphia: Jewish Publication Society, 5751/1991), 131, in which I have found the rendering "slip." Scheindlin, borrowing from Franz Rosenzweig and Judah Goldin, reads "O Truth" in line 1, but Schirmann (*The Hebrew Poem*, 1:465), noting the parallel with Jer 32:41, more credibly renders this "in truth" (*be'emet*). I thank Professor Diana Lobel for suggesting the translation "outwardly and inwardly" in line 2 and pointing out that the wording here echoes the terminology of Baḥya ibn Paquda, whose thinking we shall explore in chapter 4 in this volume.

20. Just as David does in Ps 116:3–4, which the text cites just before the verses from Job.

21. *m'd, mdd,* and *ydh*.

22. I am speaking, as is the midrash, of Job as he appears in the prose prologue (chapters 1–2), not as he appears in the poetic disputations (chapters 3–31) of the same book, where he bitterly laments his fate and accuses God of gross injustice.

23. See his response to his wife: "Shall we accept only good from God and not accept evil?" (Job 2:10).

24. I have changed the rendering of *yissurin* as "chastisements" in Hammer, *Sifre Deuteronomy*, in these midrashim to "suffering" in the interest of consistency. I have also changed his "prosperity" to "good fortune" because the Hebrew *ṭovah* encompasses more than a good financial condition.

25. A variant of the same story also appears in the *Mekhilta de-Rabbi Išmael, Baḥodeš* 10.

26. This is number 230 in Schirmann, *The Hebrew Poem* (1:523–24). It appears on p. 17 of *Selected Poems*, ed. Brody.

27. The translation is from the NRSV.

28. See Arthur J. Droge and James D. Tabor, *A Noble Death: Suicide & Martyrdom among Christians and Jews in Antiquity* (San Francisco: HarperSanFrancisco, 1992), especially 17–51; H. A. Fischel, "Martyr and Prophet," *Jewish Quarterly Review*, new series 37 (1947): 265–80, 363–86, especially 267–68; and, more generally, Tessa Rajak, "Dying for the Law: The Martyr's Portrait in Jewish-Greek Literature," in *Portraits: Biographical Representation in the Greek and Latin Literature of the Roman Empire*, ed. M. J. Edwards and Simon Swain (Oxford: Oxford University Press, 1997), 39–67.

29. Cicero, *De Officiis*, trans. Walter Miller (Cambridge, Mass.: Harvard University Press, 1913), 115. See Droge and Tabor, *Noble Death*, 29–39.

30. The translations are from *Plato: Euthyphro, Apology, Crito, and Phaedo, Phaedrus*, trans. Harold North Fowler (Cambridge, Mass.: Harvard University Press, 1914), 223, 225, 229, and 231. See also Droge and Tabor, *Noble Death*, 20–22.

31. Note that in 4 Maccabees, an expansion and philosophical meditation on the martyrdom narrative of 2 Maccabees 6–7, it is immortality to which the martyrs look forward. See, for example, 4 Maccabees 7:3; 9:22; 13:17.

32. The translation is once again from the NRSV.

33. See Levenson, *Resurrection*, 1–22.

34. Various forms of the name of the Roman official appear. I have simply chosen the one most likely ("Tineius Rufus") to be historical. On the text-critical issues, see *The Jerusalem Talmud: First Order; Zeraïm, Tractate Berakhot*, trans. and ed. Heinrich W. Guggenheimer (Berlin: Walter de Gruyter, 2000), 674. The use of the third person ("that man") in a curse is a euphemism. The malediction is aimed at Tineius Rufus himself. On the stories of Rabbi Akiva's death, see Saul Lieberman, "The Persecution of the Jewish Religion," in Saul Lieberman, ed., *Shalom Baron Jubilee Volume* (Heb.; Jerusalem: American Academy of Jewish Research, 5735/1974), 3:222–27; Daniel Boyarin, *Dying for God: Martyrdom and the Making of Judaism and Christianity* (Stanford, Calif.: Stanford University Press, 1999), 102–14; Michael Fishbane, *The Kiss of God: Spiritual and Mystical Death in Judaism* (Seattle: University of Washington, 1994), 66–71; and Rothenberg, *Wisdom of Love*, 115–23. On the connection of love and martyrdom in Tannaitic Judaism more broadly, see S. Safrai, "Martyrdom in the Teaching of the Tannaim" (Heb.), *Zion* 44 (5739): 32–36.

35. Rothenberg (*Wisdom*, 119), commenting on the variant account of Rabbi Akiva's death in *b. Berakhot* 61b, notes another sense in which the sage's gift of his life is absolute and not self-interested: "This amazing discussion between Rabbi Akiva and his students, however, seems to be missing one fundamental element: He chooses not to give the most crucial and obvious answer: life after death."

36. "The Revealed Morality of Judaism and Modern Thought: A Confrontation with Kant," in *Quest for Past and Future: Essays in Jewish Theology* (Boston: Beacon Press, 1968), 223–24; italics in the original.

37. Fischel, "Martyr and Prophet," 268. See also Safrai, "Martyrdom," 36–38. Halakhic limitations on martyrdom can be found in *b. Sanhedrin* 74b.
38. Louis Jacobs, *A Jewish Theology* (New York: Behrman House, 1973), 164–66. The quote is from 165.
39. Boyarin, *Dying*, 107.
40. As documented in the continuation of *y. Berakhot* 9:5 as well as in *b. Menaḥot* 29b.

THREE
THE ONCE AND FUTURE ROMANCE

1. *b. Yoma* 54a.
2. Contrast Rothenberg, *Wisdom of Love*, 5: "All love derives from a single source: love between man and woman."
3. In context, it is unlikely that the prefix conjugation, or imperfect (*tizneh*), is to be translated as a future in v. 2, as in the NJPS ("will stray"). I have thus modified the translation so as to give the verb the sense of a past habitual or the like.
4. Gerlinde Baumann, *Love and Violence: Marriage as Metaphor for the Relationship between YHWH and Israel in the Prophetic Books* (Collegeville, Minn.: Liturgical Press, 2003), 46.
5. See, for example, John Bright, *A History of Israel*, 3rd ed. (Philadelphia: Westminster Press, 1981), 263, though one should note his uncertainty there as well.
6. It is often said that the wife is the husband's property (for example, Baumann, *Love and Violence*, 23), but this is a claim that requires considerable nuancing and qualification. See Roland de Vaux, *Ancient Israel* (New York: McGraw-Hill, 1965), 1:26–27.
7. Here, as often noticed (and decried), biblical law differentiates the genders markedly. A married woman who has sex with a single man commits adultery, but a married man having sex with a single woman does not. This is as one would expect in a society in which a woman becomes a member of her husband's household but a man does not become a member of his wife's, and in which polygyny is legal but polyandry is not. The gender inequality of these provisions is obvious, but it should also be noted that in a society in which the virginity of brides is esteemed (as in Deut 22:13–21), a man who had sex with an unmarried woman and did not consequently wed her would be unlikely to be considered to have acted within the limits of propriety. Of course, if a man had sex with a

married woman, both are guilty of adultery and suffer the death penalty alike (Deut 22:22). In rabbinic law, the standards become more stringent, and norms arise to the effect that a man should never even touch a woman to whom he is not married or be alone with her in a closed room (next of kin excepted).

8. In Hos 2:3, Not-My-People's name similarly becomes "My People" and "Unloved" is renamed "Loved" (*ruḥamah*, which NJPS renders "Lovingly Accepted"). In Hos 2:2, the name Jezreel seems to have been given a positive association, probably on the basis of the etymology "God sows" (see v. 25), in that case now taken to refer to the miraculous increase of his people's numbers. Hos 2:1–3, as an anticipation of the reversals of vv. 16–25, seems to be out of place, and vv. 1–2 show signs of later origin.

9. 1 Kgs 18:1–40.

10. This literal translation is preferable to the NJPS, "between two opinions."

11. See Baumann, *Love and Violence*, 69–76, though, for evidence from elsewhere in the ancient Near East that the wife was to be stripped as part of the ritual of divorce. It is less than clear that Hosea presupposes such a practice when he depicts God as stripping Israel of the clothing made from the wool and linen she falsely attributes to Baal. Just how literally the language of such provisions was understood is also open to debate, and, as Baumann notes, "whether these drastic provisions were ever actually imposed is not clear" (71).

12. Ibid., 12, stating the view of Fokkelien van Dijk-Hemmes, "The Imagination of Power and the Power of Imagination: An Intertextual Analysis of Two Biblical Love Songs: The Song of Songs and Hosea 2," *Journal for the Study of the Old Testament* 44 (1989): 75–88. For a bibliographical survey of feminist critiques of the marriage metaphor, see Baumann, *Love and Violence*, 8–21. To this and to the items in her bibliography on 241–58, a number of other studies can be added. See, for example, the essays in *A Feminist Companion to the Latter Prophets*, ed. Athalya Brenner (Sheffield, England: Sheffield Academic Press, 1995), 39–241. Also relevant is R. Abma, *Bonds of Love: Methodic Studies of Prophetic Texts with Marriage Imagery (Isaiah 50:1–3 and 54:1–10, Hosea 1–3, Jeremiah 2–3)*, Studia Semitica Neerlandica (Assen: Van Gorcum, 1999), especially 25–31.

13. Phyllis Bird, "'To Play the Harlot': An Inquiry into an Old Testament Metaphor," in *Gender and Difference in Ancient Israel*, ed. Peggy L. Day (Minneapolis: Fortress Press, 1989), 75–94, here 89.

14. See n. 7 above. The critique is foundational, for example, to Baumann, *Love and Violence.*

15. Tikva Frymer-Kensky, *In the Wake of the Goddesses: Women, Culture, and the Biblical Transformation of Pagan Myth* (New York: Free Press, 1992), 148. Lest misunderstanding arise from Frymer-Kensky's term "physical," note, as she does on the same page, that biblical law, unlike Middle Assyrian law, says nothing about a man's having the right to beat his wife.

16. But note 2 Sam 11:27–12:12, in which the relationship of a poor man with a ewe serves as a parable for a marriage. We should be careful not to assume that shepherds and slave-masters were devoid of genuine feeling toward their charges.

17. Tikva Frymer-Kensky, *In the Wake,* 147.

18. The larger and much neglected question of whether equality is a useful term outside of formal, abstract contexts like law and mathematics is one we needn't address here.

19. I have retained the translation "plowland of hope" in v. 17, which is based on the verb *pittaḥ,* which can mean "to plow." The alternative "Door of Hope" or "Opening of Hope" is certainly possible as well. The expression, understood in the latter sense, is the origin of the name of Petah Tikva, the early Zionist settlement and now major Israeli town a few miles east of Tel Aviv. "Achor" means "trouble," "hardship." See the parallel oracle in Isa 65:10 and also the narrative in Josh 7, especially its use of "Valley of Achor" in v. 24.

20. For example, Lev 26:25, 37–38; Deut 28:25, 47–48, 49–52.

21. Francis I. Andersen and David Noel Freedman, *Hosea,* Anchor Bible 24 (Garden City, N.Y.: Doubleday, 1980), 282.

22. In v. 21 and v. 22, I have substituted "betroth" for "espouse" (NJPS) partly for stylistic reasons and partly to convey the legal background of the act (compare the use of the verb in Deut 20:7 and 28:30). I have changed "be devoted to" in v. 22 to "know" for reasons that should become clear below.

23. As evidenced in 2 Sam 3:14.

24. As suggested, for example, in the notes to the NJPS.

25. Andersen and Freedman, *Hosea,* 283.

26. Ibid. Note that it also reverses Hos 2:10, "She did not consider this," where "consider" is *yade'ah* (ibid., 284).

27. Herbert B. Huffmon, "The Treaty Background of Hebrew Yāda'," *Bulletin of the American Schools of Oriental Research* 181 (1966): 31–37, here 32 and 33.

28. Ibid., 34–37. Huffmon mentions Hos 2:22 as an example, suggesting that the verb in question be understood to mean "recognize as suzerain" (36).

29. See Huffmon, "Treaty Background," 34–35.

30. It is possible that, as the NJPS suggests, "Judah" should be emended to "Israel," which parallels Ephraim in Hos 5:3 and other verses in the same book, though the implicit claim that the forms of Hosea that predate its Judahite redaction are on principle preferable is not incontestable.

31. *Tirgalti* in v. 3 is obscure and unparalleled. I take it as a tiphʿel of *rgl* and thus translate it as a causative of the word for "foot"—hence, "led." The common translation "taught [him] to walk" seems awkward, since by this point in the story Ephraim is no longer a toddler. Rashi's notion that the verse is a reference to Moses is too specific, but his reading of the word as the equivalent of the hiphʿil *hirgalti* is likely. In any event, the NJPS reading "pampered" seems unwarranted. The NJPS notation that the meaning of the Hebrew of v. 7 is "uncertain" is, however, quite true. For one interesting textual reconstruction (of several that have been offered), see Andersen and Freedman, *Hosea*, 586–87.

32. Deut 24:1–4. The Jeremiah text may be influenced by Hos 2:9, which also spoke of the desire of the wife to return to her first husband.

33. The text can be found in Schirmann, *The Hebrew Poem*, 1:405–6, where it is the third stanza of number 163, and in *Selected Poems of Moses ibn Ezra*, trans. Solomon Solis-Cohen, ed. Heinrich Brody (Philadelphia: Jewish Publication Society, 1934), 101. My translation is indebted to Solis-Cohen's but also departs from it in many places. To render the sense of the citation of Job 13:15 at the beginning of the second stanza, I have used the King James Version.

34. A mystic living in Safed in the Land of Israel in the sixteenth century. This is the seventh stanza of his poem, *Lekha Dodi*, which is sung in synagogues late on Friday afternoon or early Friday evening to welcome the Sabbath.

35. The exodus is not explicit in Jer 2:2, but can reasonably be assumed to be the point of departure into "the wilderness."

36. See Julie Galambush, *Jerusalem in the Book of Ezekiel: The City as [the* LORD*]'s Wife*, Society of Biblical Literature Dissertation Series 130 (Atlanta: Scholars Press, 1992).

37. Jer 2:2.

38. That both the Amorites and Hittites are here taken to be Canaanites is clear from Ezek 16:3.

39. Compare Ruth 3:9.
40. See Moshe Greenberg, *Ezekiel 1–20*, Anchor Bible 22 (Garden City, N.Y.: Doubleday, 1983), 278, and Jacob Milgrom, *Cult and Conscience*, Studies in Judaism in Late Antiquity 18 (Leiden: Brill, 1976), 133–34.
41. Ezek 16:10–13a.
42. See, for example, Ps 48 for the fame and Gen 13:2, 26:12–14, and 30:43 for the wealth.
43. Ezek 16:33–34.
44. In v. 59, I have replaced "pact" (NJPS) with "oath" in order to bring out the resonance with Ezek 16:8, as should become clear. "But" at the beginning of v. 60 better captures the pronominal reinforcement of the person of the verb than does the NJPS "Nevertheless." In v. 63, Greenberg's "absolve" renders the Hebrew *kipper* more accurately and more in keeping with Ezekiel's theology than does the NJPS "forgive." Greenberg, *Ezekiel 1–20*, 273, 291.
45. Ezek 1:3.
46. We should not assume, of course, that the entirety of either passage is the work of the prophet Ezekiel himself.
47. Ezek 8:14–18.
48. See Larry L. Lyke, *I Will Espouse You Forever: The Song of Songs and the Theology of Love in the Hebrew Bible* (Nashville: Abingdon Press, 2007), 31.
49. Unlike the NJPS, I leave v. 24 in place and do not reposition it between v. 21 and v. 22.
50. Lyke, *I Will Espouse*, 30.
51. David M. Carr, "Passion for God: A Center in Biblical Theology," *Horizons in Biblical Theology* 23 (2001): 1–24, here 20.
52. Not counting the superscription (Song 1:1), of course.
53. In v. 2a, I have not used the NJPS translation ("Oh, give me of the kisses of your mouth") but have instead substituted the alternative given in the notes because the third person singular of the Hebrew will be critical to a midrashic interpretation of these words cited later in this chapter.
54. As noted in the NJPS, "garden" and "lover" are plural in form, and the Hebrew of v. 13 is accordingly unclear. Whether *haver* is best rendered as "lover" here is also open to much doubt. Marvin Pope's translation respects the Hebrew forms and renders as "You who dwell in gardens, / Companions are attentive," though what exactly this means remains unclear, if more faithful to the Hebrew of the Masoretic Text. See Marvin Pope, *Song of Songs*, Anchor Bible 7c (Garden City, N.Y.: Doubleday, 1977), 654, 693–95.

55. See Pope, *Song*, 292, 330–32, for the rendering of *'otiyah* as "one who is veiled." There is no need to see here a metathesis of *to'ayah*, "one who strays," the reading of the NJPS.

56. In Song 3:9, I have changed "him" to "himself," which captures the likely meaning better.

57. Francis Landy, "The Song of Songs," in *The Literary Guide to the Bible*, ed. Robert Alter and Frank Kermode (Cambridge, Mass.: Harvard University Press, 1987), 305–19, here 315 and 317–18. On the "three-character scheme" that some have found, see Pope, *Song*, 35–36.

58. Song 1:6 and 5:7.

59. Phyllis Trible, *God and the Rhetoric of Sexuality* (Philadelphia: Fortress Press, 1978), 161.

60. Ibid., 162. The claim that the book has a "message" in the sense of a moral or a social teaching is most doubtful, however.

61. J. Cheryl Exum, *Song of Songs: A Commentary*, Old Testament Library (Louisville, Ky.: Westminster John Knox, 2005), 8.

62. The date of the book is hardly clear, and we cannot assume that all its parts came into being in the same period. A good case for a Hellenistic date can be found in M. H. Segal, "The Song of Songs," *Vetus Testamentum* 12 (1962): 470–90, here 478. Segal rather awkwardly distinguishes the date of composition from the date of writing, viewing the former as Solomonic (481–83). See also the rather agnostic position in Pope, *Song*, 22–33.

63. *Tosephta Sanhedrin* 10:12. See also *b. Sanhedrin* 101a. Note, too, the strictures of Maimonides in his *Commentary on the Mishnah*, *Avot* 1:16 (I thank my editor Neal Kozodoy for drawing my attention to this last passage).

64. A point well established in Jonathan Kaplan, "A Divine Love Song: The Emergence of the Theo-erotic Interpretation of the Song of Songs in Ancient Judaism and Early Christianity" (dissertation in the Department of Near Eastern Languages and Civilizations, Harvard University, 2010).

65. Segal makes a plausible case that in Song 4:8–5:1, "there is a description of the consummation of their love" (*Song*, 470). But even if this is so, the separation of the lovers still dominates afterward.

66. I have changed the "wakeful" (NJPS) in v. 2 to "awake," which seems to me to capture better the immediacy of the situation; "for him" in v. 4 to "within me," in accordance with the manuscripts that read *'alay*; and "had turned and gone" to "had turned, had gone" to capture the suddenness of the asyndetic construction (though the absence of the first verb, *hamaq*, in some versions suggests it may be a gloss).

67. See Exum, *Song*, 73–77.
68. Daniel Boyarin, "Two Introductions to the Midrash on the Song of Songs," Heb., *Tarbiz* 56 (1987): 479–500, here 490. All translations from this essay are my own.
69. Daniel Boyarin, "'This We Know to Be the Carnal Israel': Circumcision and the Erotic Life of God and Israel," *Critical Inquiry* 18 (1992): 474–505, here 496.
70. Boyarin, "Two Introductions," 497.
71. As mentioned earlier in n. 53, the alternative in the NJPS note seems to reflect the way the verse was understood in the midrash with which we are about to deal. It is also grammatically more accurate.
72. *Song of Songs Rabbah* 1:2:1 (that is, the first midrash on Song 1:2).
73. Ibid., 1:2:1–3.
74. The rich vein of interpretation of the Song of Songs in particular and of eros generally in Kabbalistic literature lies outside our purview. On this, see Isaiah Tishby, *Mišnat ha-Zohar* (Heb.; Jerusalem: Mosad Bialik, 5721/1961), 2:297–301, and, more recently, Moshe Idel, *Kabbalah and Eros* (New Haven: Yale University Press, 2005).
75. Pope, *Song*, 17.
76. Singer, *The Nature of Love*, 187.
77. Lewis, *Four Loves*, 111.

FOUR
THE CONSUMMATION OF THE SPIRITUAL LIFE

1. *Mishneh Torah, Hilkhot Tešuvah* 10:3. The translations from *Hilkhot Tešuvah* in this chapter are from a manuscript by Bernard Septimus, to be published in the Yale Judaica Series. I thank Professor Septimus for his great kindness in letting me use it.
2. Most influential has been the ascription of the Pentateuch to Moses, though this was not without dissent, even in the Middle Ages. See Marc B. Shapiro, *The Limits of Orthodox Theology: Maimonides' Thirteen Principles Reappraised* (Portland, Ore.: Littman Library of Jewish Civilization, 2004), 91–121.
3. Pierre Hadot, *Philosophy as a Way of Life: Spiritual Exercises from Socrates to Foucault* (Malden, Mass.: Blackwell, 1995).
4. See Diana Lobel, *A Sufi-Jewish Dialogue: Philosophy and Mysticism in Baḥya ibn Paqūda's "Duties of the Heart"* (Philadelphia: University of Pennsylvania Press, 2007), especially 1–20. My discussion of Baḥya relies heavily on Professor Lobel's superb study, though any errors are very much my own responsibility.

5. *Enneads* 4:8.1, in Plotinus, *Enneads*, trans. A. H. Armstrong, Loeb Classical Library 443 (Cambridge, Mass.: Harvard University Press, 1984), 4:397. My attention was drawn to this passage by Lobel, *A Sufi-Jewish*, 23.

6. These lines appear in Schirmann, *The Hebrew Poem*, 1:258–59, where they begin the second stanza of number 108. They are lines 20–25 of his long philosophical poem, "The Royal Crown" (*Keter Malkut*) and also appear in *Selected Religious Poems of Solomon ibn Gabirol*, ed. Israel Davidson (Philadelphia: Jewish Publication Society of America, 1924), 83–84 (where they are ll. 28–34). My translation makes use of, but also departs from, Davidson's. Ibn Gabirol was a major poet and Neoplatonic Jewish philosopher in eleventh-century Spain. On the connection between these lines and Baḥya ibn Paquda, see Lobel, *Sufi-Jewish*, 89–91. Professor Lobel's translation of these lines on p. 89 has been helpful to me here.

7. Lobel, *A Sufi-Jewish*, 22. Lobel is here paraphrasing David Blumenthal, "Maimonides' Intellectualist Mysticism and the Superiority of the Prophecy of Moses," in *Approaches to Judaism in Medieval Times*, Brown Judaic Studies 54 (Chico, Calif.: Scholars Press, 1984), 28, whose claim, she notes, some scholars dispute.

8. Of course, pagan Neoplatonism had vanished long before, and the Neoplatonic tradition lived on solely in Muslim, Jewish, and Christian philosophy.

9. Lobel, *A Sufi-Jewish*, 23–24.

10. Ibid., 9. On the love of God in Baḥya, see Georges Vajda, *La théologie ascétique de Baḥya ibn Paquda*, Cahiers de la Société Asiatique 7 (Paris: Imprimerie Nationale, 1948), 123–37, and *L'amour de Dieu dans la théologie juive du moyen age*, Études de philosophie médiévale 46 (Paris: Librairie Philosophique J. Vrin, 1957), 92–98.

11. My own Arabic having become defunct long ago, I have been instructed by the following translations in an attempt to produce the most fluent English reading: *The Book of Direction to the Duties of the Heart*, introduction, translation, and notes by Menahem Mansoor with Sara Arenson and Shoshana Dannhauser (London: Routledge and Kegan Paul, 1973); *Duties of the Heart* by R. Bachya ben Joseph ibn Paquda, translated from the Arabic into Hebrew by R. Yehuda ibn Tibbon, with an English translation by Daniel Haberman (New York: Feldheim, 1996), two volumes (with continuous pagination; henceforth, referred to as "Haberman"); Joseph Kafaḥ, *Duties of the Heart* (Heb.; Jerusalem: Feldheim, 1984). Professor Diana Lobel has generously reviewed my translations and

suggested many changes based on her extraordinary command of the Arabic of medieval Jewish and Muslim philosophical and mystical sources. Any errors that remain are, of course, owing to my own limitations.

12. See Levenson, *Resurrection*, especially 1–22.

13. See Gershom Scholem, *"Devekut*, or Communion with God," in *The Messianic Idea in Judaism and Other Essays on Jewish Spirituality* (New York: Schocken, 1971), 203–27. The essay appeared originally in *Review of Religion* 4 (1949–50): 115–39. See also Tishby, *Mišnat ha-Zohar*, 2:289–93; 301–6, for a different view of the Zoharic material.

14. In Baḥya's case, the influence of the Sufi notion of union with the divine (*ittiṣāl*) is very much in evidence as well. See Diana Lobel, *Between Mysticism and Philosophy: Sufi Language of Religious Experience in Judah Ha-Levi's Kuzari* (Albany: State University of New York Press, 2000), 22–25.

15. Vajda is careful to note that Baḥya does not speak of an actual union of the soul with God. Vajda, *La théologie ascétique*, 136–37.

16. Lobel, *A Sufi-Jewish*, 9–10.

17. *Duties* 4:7.

18. Ibid., 3:3. The translation is from Haberman, 1:249, with a small adjustment.

19. Lobel, *A Sufi-Jewish*, 181. More than a thousand years earlier, another Jewish Platonist, Philo of Alexandria, took essentially the same position. See Levenson, *Inheriting Abraham*, 144–45.

20. Lobel, *A Sufi-Jewish*, 182.

21. See chapter 1, n. 52, in this volume.

22. *Duties* 10:3.

23. Ibid., introduction to the Tenth Gate.

24. Ibid.

25. The reference is to the Evil Inclination; see chapter 2 in this volume. In general, when the rabbis use the word *yeṣer* without an adjective, it is the Evil Inclination they have in mind.

26. The chain of transmission of this hadith appears to be weak. On this, see David Cook, *Understanding Jihad* (Berkeley: University of California Press, 2005), 35–36, where the tradition is dated to the first half of the ninth century CE. See also G. F. Haddad, "Documentation of 'Great Jihad' Hadith" (http://www.livingislam.org/n/dgjh_e.html). I thank Professor Diana Lobel for drawing these sources to my attention.

27. See Lobel, *A Sufi-Jewish*, ix. She points out that the story moves much later from the *Duties* into Hasidic literature.

28. *Duties* 10:3.
29. Ibid. 10:4.
30. Unless otherwise noted, the quotations from the *Duties* in this section are taken from 10:6.
31. See n. 10 above.
32. See chapter 2 in this volume.
33. Haberman, 2:871.
34. Ibid., with some adjustments.
35. 1 Kgs 8:46.
36. *Duties* 10:7.
37. The first stanza of a poem by Rabbi Elazar Azikri, a mystic living in Safed in the Land of Israel in the sixteenth century, that is often sung at the beginning of the Sabbath and at the end of the third Sabbath meal.
38. The exact year of his birth is unclear.
39. On the love of God in Maimonides, see Vajda, *L'amour*, 118–40.
40. All translations from this book are taken from Moses Maimonides, *The Guide of the Perplexed*, 2 vols. with continuously numbered pages, trans. Shlomo Pines (Chicago: University of Chicago Press, 1963), here 2:512–13. (References to the Pines translation in these notes are to the volume and page number, not to the book and chapter in the *Guide* itself.)
41. Warren Zev Harvey, "Notions of Divine and Human Love in Jewish Thought: An Interview with Warren Zev Harvey," *Journal of Jewish Thought* 3 (2012): 1–11, here 7.
42. Pines, *Guide*, 2:619.
43. Ibid., 2:629.
44. Ibid., 2:630.
45. Ibid., 1:89.
46. I have changed "is devoted" and "keep him safe" (NJPS) to "passionately love" and "set him on high" to accord better with Maimonides's likely understanding of the verse.
47. Pines, *Guide*, 2:627. I have adjusted Pines's transliterations to fit the system I have been using.
48. Harvey, "Notions," 2.
49. The translation accepts the alternate ending of v. 6 proposed in the note in the NJPS (and paralleled in Pss 42:12 and 43:5), which connects the first Hebrew word of v. 7 with v. 6.
50. I have very slightly changed the wording of the quotation from Deut 6:5 and the abbreviation for the Song of Songs in Bernard Septimus's translation. I have kept his wording "sick with love" in

Song 2:5, which strikes me as more in keeping with Maimonides's point than "faint with love" (NJPS).

51. Pines, *Guide*, 2:621, 623. This *ideal* is exactly that. Maimonides goes on to say that it has been reached only by Moses and the patriarchs (623–24).

52. Ibid., 2:497.

53. The translation of the biblical verse departs from the NJPS to bring out the understanding of it in the Talmud and Maimonides.

54. See Vajda, *L'amour*, 140: "la dilection portée par Dieu au people élu n'est suggérée, très rarement, que de façon rapide et discrète."

55. Harvey, "Notions," 2.

56. Ibid., 2–3.

57. Ibid., 3. See also Warren Zev Harvey, *Physics and Metaphysics in Ḥasdai Crescas* (Amsterdam: J. C. Gieben, 1998), 101–2.

58. See *b. Soṭah* 14a.

59. See n. 1 above.

60. Aristotle, *Metaphysics*, vol. 18, Loeb Classical Library 287 (Cambridge, Mass.: Harvard University Press, 1935), 149–53, here 151 and 153 (from *Metaphysics* 12:7).

61. Wilhelm Windelband, *A History of Philosophy* (New York: Harper & Row, 1958), 1:145–46. (The German original dates to 1898. I have omitted Windelband's Greek terms.) Note, however, that some later Jewish Aristotelians did affirm that God experiences love and joy. On this, see Harvey, *Physics*, 100–105.

62. Windelband, *History of Philosophy*, 1:146.

63. See, for example, Charles Hartshorne, *The Divine Relativity: A Social Conception of God* (New Haven: Yale University Press, 1948) and *The Logic of Perfection and Other Essays in Neoclassical Metaphysics* (Lasalle, Ill.: Open Court, 1962). We shall examine Buber at some length in chapter 5.

64. See Harvey, "Notions," 3–4.

65. See Vajda, *L'amour*, 261–67.

66. Harvey, *Physics*, 111–12. Harvey is translating from Crescas's *Light of the Lord*, book 2, section 6.

67. See Vajda, *L'amour*, 267–74.

68. See above on *Guide* 3:51.

69. The translation is taken from Joseph Albo, *Sefer Ha-ʿIkkarim: Book of Principles*, ed. and trans. Isaac Husik (Philadelphia: Jewish Publication Society of America, 1930), 3:346–47. (All quotations from Albo are from bk. 3, chap. 37.) Here and again below, I have made a few inconsequential changes in Husik's text to accord with the

style of this book. The possible implication that a man might reasonably love a woman for her beauty alone, however regrettable, does not affect Albo's point about the reality of "a free love, due to the will of the lover alone and without any reason."

70. I have again rendered *'ahavat* (v. 8) as "loved" rather than "favored" (NJPS) for reasons of context.

71. Albo, *Sefer Ha-'Ikkarim*, 3:347–48.

FIVE
"BECAUSE HE HAS SOLD HIMSELF TO US WITH THE TORAH"

1. Franz Rosenzweig, *Der Stern der Erlösung* (Frankfurt am Main: Suhrkamp Verlag, 1988), 174. I have been greatly aided in my translations from *The Star of Redemption* by those of William W. Hallo (New York: Holt, Rinehart and Winston, 1970), here 156, and Barbara E. Galli (Madison: University of Wisconsin Press, 2005), here 169. Rosenzweig is also the source of the title of this chapter. See below, n. 24.

2. See chapter 1 in this volume.

3. On this, see Leora Batnitzky, *How Judaism Became a Religion: An Introduction to Modern Jewish Thought* (Princeton: Princeton University Press, 2011), especially 13–28. Necessarily, the characterization I give here is brief and does not reckon with the highly uneven and varying social reality of Jewish experience even in the lands in which emancipation progressed most dramatically, nor does it reckon with the self-enclosed communities that have continued the premodern mode of life to a significant degree.

4. Martin Buber, *I and Thou*, trans. Walter Kaufmann (New York: Touchstone, 1970). The German original was first published in 1923.

5. Ibid., 54.

6. Ibid., 62. I have changed Kaufmann's "actual" to "real," which I think captures Buber's sense better. The German is "Alles wirkliche Leben ist Begegnung." Martin Buber, *Ich und Du* (Stuttgart: Philip Reclam jun. & Co., 1995), 12.

7. Ibid., 55.

8. Ibid., 123.

9. Buber, *I and Thou*, 66.

10. Franz Rosenzweig, *On Jewish Learning*, with an exchange of letters between Martin Buber and Franz Rosenzweig, ed. N. N. Glatzer (New York: Schocken, 1955), 111. The context is Buber's letter to Rosenzweig of June 24, 1924.

11. But note that in Buber's analysis of biblical texts, one readily receives the impression that there is an unbridgeable divide from the literature of the rest of the ancient Near East and that the Israelite literature could not have come into being through the dynamics of cultural change alone but must instead have been the result of some transcendent causation. On this, see Mara Benjamin, "The Tacit Agenda of a Literary Approach to the Bible," *Prooftexts* 27 (2007): 254–74, especially 261. Note, for example, that in a later book, *Moses: The Revelation and the Covenant* (New York: Harper & Row, 1958; originally published in 1946), Buber seems to back off a bit from the antinomian spirituality of his earlier works, highly praising elements of biblical law and sharply contrasting the biblical texts with their parallels in the ancient Near East, again as if to imply that they have a suprahistorical origin. But, on the question of Jewish observance as a living—and obligatory—reality, neither in theory nor in practice does he ever move away from the position he takes in the passage above.

12. Note his insistence that the I-It mode is not "changed by adding 'inner' experiences to the 'external' ones." "Inner things like external things," he laments, "things among things!" Buber, *I and Thou*, 56.

13. Rosenzweig, *On Jewish Learning*, 114, in a letter to Rosenzweig of July 5, 1924.

14. On this, the classic work is Charles Taylor, *Sources of the Self: The Making of the Modern Identity* (Cambridge, Mass.: Harvard University Press, 1989).

15. On the connections of Buber's and Rosenzweig's respective philosophical commitments to their thinking about the Torah and its commandments, see Leora Batnitzky, "Revelation and *Neues Denken*—Rethinking Buber and Rosenzweig on the Law," in *New Perspectives on Martin Buber*, ed. Michael Zank, Religion in Philosophy and Theology 22 (Tübingen: Mohr Siebeck, 2006), 149–64.

16. Franz Rosenzweig, *Stern*, 196 (Hallo, 176; Galli, 190).

17. Ibid., 196–97 (Hallo, 176–77; Galli, 190–91).

18. Rosenzweig, *On Jewish Learning*, 114.

19. Stéphane Mosès, *System and Revelation: The Philosophy of Franz Rosenzweig* (Detroit, Mich.: Wayne State University Press, 1992), 99. On the technical philosophical background of this, see also Benjamin Pollock, *Franz Rosenzweig and the Systematic Task of Philosophy* (New York: Cambridge University Press, 2009), 204–25.

20. Mosès, *System*, 102–3 (emphasis in the original).

21. Rosenzweig, *Stern*, 197–98 (Hallo, 177; Galli, 191–92).

22. Rosenzweig, *On Jewish Learning*, 116, from his letter to Buber of July 16, 1924. Glatzer's rendering "with fear and trembling" is an error in the translation of the words that actually appear in the letter. What Rosenzweig wrote, in Hebrew characters, was *ḥilu urḥimu*, which could be translated as "trembling and love/compassion" but seems instead to be an error for the Aramaic expression *rḥimu ud-ḥilu*, "love and fear," which occurs several times in medieval mystical literature. The text can be found in Franz Rosenzweig, *Briefe*, ed. Edith Rosenzweig with the assistance of Ernst Simon (Berlin: Schocken, 1935), 505, where, oddly, the expression is glossed in the notes, presumably by Simon, with "fear and trembling" (*Furcht und Zittern*). This may be what Rosenzweig meant, but it is not what he wrote.

23. Fackenheim, "The Revealed," 225. The three terms of the relationship in question are God, the individual, and the neighbor.

24. Ibid., 117. I have changed Glatzer's "with his Torah" to "with the Torah" to correspond with the underlying German (*Denn er hat sich uns mit der Tora verkauft*). Rosenzweig, *Briefe*, 505.

25. Franz Rosenzweig, "The Builders: Concerning the Law," in *On Jewish Learning*, 72–92, here 85. Glatzer glosses some words with the German originals. I have left this out.

26. Franz Rosenzweig, "The Commandments: Divine or Human?" in *On Jewish Learning*, 119–24, here 121. Glatzer provides a title for this letter to four friends that it does not have and makes the actual title into a subtitle, which he translates "Divine or Human," though the German (*Göttlich und menschlich*) means "Divine and Human." See Rosenzweig, *Briefe*, 518. The two Hebrew "benedictions" cited by Rosenzweig thank God for the gift of the Torah; to this, the first adds an expression of gratitude for "choosing us from among all the nations," and the second for "planting within us eternal life."

27. See Pollock, *Franz Rosenzweig*.

28. Rosenzweig, *Stern*, 472 (Hallo, 424, and Galli, 447).

29. Rosenzweig, "The Commandments: Divine or Human?," in *On Jewish Learning*, 121–22. I have inserted the ellipsis to indicate a place in which Glatzer leaves out some of the German.

30. See the text referred to in n. 17 above.

31. Wilfred Cantwell Smith, "Transcendence," *Harvard Divinity Bulletin* 18:3 (Fall 1988): 10–15, here 12. The article was Smith's Ingersoll Lecture at Harvard Divinity School on March 10, 1988.

2015.10.28   29.95 (22.00)